Governing Technology for Sustainability

Governing Technology for Sustainability

Edited by Joseph Murphy

earthscan
from Routledge

First published by Earthscan in the UK and USA in 2007

For a full list of publications please contact:
Earthscan
2 Park Square, Milton Park, Abingdon, Oxfordshire OX14 4RN
711 Third Avenue, New York, NY 10017

First issued in paperback 2014

Earthscan is an imprint of the Taylor & Francis Group, an informa business

ISBN 13: 978-1-84407-345-0 (hbk)
ISBN 13: 978-1-138-00198-5 (pbk)

Typesetting by MapSet Ltd, Gateshead, UK
Cover design by Yvonne Booth

A catalogue record for this book is available from the British Library

Library of Congress Cataloging-in-Publication Data

Governing technology for sustainability / edited by Joseph Murphy.
    p. cm.
  ISBN-13: 978-1-84407-345-0 (pbk.)
  ISBN-10: 1-84407-345-9 (pbk.)
  1. Technological innovations–Environmental aspects. 2. Green technology–Political aspects. 3. Sustainable development. 4. Technology and state–Environmental aspects.
I. Murphy, Joseph.
  T173.8.G69 2006
  338.9'27–dc22

200621886

Contents

Section I Introduction

Section II People and Sustainability: Appreciating Multiple Identities

Section III Technology and Sustainability: Contextualized Accounts

Section IV Governance and Sustainability: Consensus and Conflict

Section V Conclusion

List of Figures and Tables

Figures

Tables

List of Contributors

Panayiota Alevizou is a PhD student in the Management School at the University of Sheffield, UK.

Sally Caird is a Research Fellow in the Design Innovation Group of the Department of Design and Innovation at the Open University, UK.

Patrick Devine-Wright is a Senior Lecturer in the School of Environment and Development at the University of Manchester, UK

Tim Foxon is a Research Associate in the Cambridge Centre for Climate Change Mitigation Research (4CMR) at the University of Cambridge, UK.

Kumju Hwang is a Research Fellow in the Sustainability Research Institute at the University of Leeds, UK.

Seonaidh McDonald is a Senior Lecturer in Aberdeen Business School at the Robert Gordon University, UK.

Joseph Murphy is RCUK Academic Fellow in the Sustainability Research Institute at the University of Leeds, UK.

Caroline Oates is a Lecturer in the Management School at the University of Sheffield, UK.

Stephen Potter is Professor of Transport Strategy in the Department of Design and Innovation at the Open University, UK.

Robin Roy is Professor of Design and Environment in the Department of Design and Innovation at the Open University, UK.

Raphael Sauter is a Research Fellow in the Science and Technology Policy Research Unit (SPRU) at the University of Sussex, UK.

Rachel Slater is a Research Fellow in the Integrated Waste Systems Group at the Open University, UK.

Adrian Smith is a Research Fellow in SPRU at the University of Sussex, UK.

Dave Toke is a Senior Lecturer in environmental policy in the Department of Sociology at the University of Birmingham, UK.

Jim Watson is a Senior Fellow in SPRU at the University of Sussex, UK.

Mark Winskel is a Research Associate in the Institute for Energy Systems at the University of Edinburgh, UK.

William Young is a Senior Lecturer in the Sustainability Research Institute at the University of Leeds, UK.

Acknowledgements

The Governance of Sustainable Technologies Network met three times between September 2004 and January 2006. Members explored ways of linking people, technology and governance in the context of sustainable development. The network was funded by the Economic and Social Research Council's (ESRC) Sustainable Technologies Programme and 15 scholars, with projects funded under the programme, took part. Meetings were held at the Open University, Edinburgh University and Sussex University, leading to the publication of this book.

As organizer of the network I accumulated many debts of gratitude along the way. David Wield helped to launch the network and provided invaluable support throughout. I am very grateful for his help on this and other projects. Frans Berkhout and Fred Steward, as Directors of the ESRC Sustainable Technologies Programme, engaged with the network enthusiastically, and without their support it would not have happened.

In many practical ways I was supported by Mansfield College, University of Oxford, where I was a Senior Research Fellow for most of the period. I am particularly grateful to the Principal of the College, Diana Walford, and to the Fellows. My position at Mansfield College was funded by the UK's Landfill Tax Credit Scheme. I would also like to thank Robin Williams for providing me with a convivial and stimulating berth at Edinburgh University's Research Centre for the Social Sciences.

Obviously, I am particularly indebted to members of the network. A large number of obstacles are being placed in the way of collaborative and speculative efforts like this one. In this case, however, a group of enthusiastic scholars responded to my invitation to take part in a series of discussions. All the meetings were very enjoyable and constructive. I hope they feel that this book is a faithful and worthwhile outcome. In addition to the contributors I would like to thank Adrian Monaghan for his contribution.

Finally, I would like to thank Marlene Gordon for administrative support. This was offered with enthusiasm and understanding, even when I scheduled a meeting of the network in Brighton that clashed with the Labour Party conference.

Projects

Results from the following projects, funded by the Economic and Social Research Council under its Sustainable Technologies Programme, are given in this book:

- 'Trade-offs in decision-making for sustainable technologies', November 2003 until March 2006, grant number RES-338-25-0001 – see Chapter 2.
- 'Supporting and harnessing diversity? Experiments in appropriate technology', January 2003 until June 2005, grant number RES-332-25-0005 – see Chapter 5.
- 'Integrating micro-generation into energy networks and buildings', October 2004 until September 2006, grant number RES-338-25-0003 – see Chapter 6.
- 'Policy drivers and barriers for sustainable innovation', October 2002 until December 2004, grant number RES-332-25-0009 – see Chapter 7.
- 'Delivering sustainable technologies for waste: improving uptake through partnership', January 2004 until December 2005, grant number RES-338-25-0002 – see Chapter 8.
- 'Accounting for the outcomes of windfarm planning applications', October 2002 until December 2005, grant number RES-332-25-0001 – see Chapter 9.
- 'Building renewable energy innovation systems', February 2004 until January 2006, grant number RES-338-25-0011 – see Chapter 10.

In addition, results from the following project, funded by the Engineering and Physical Sciences Research Council in partnership with others, are given:

- 'SUPERGEN Consortium for Future Network Technologies', October 2003 until September 2006, grant number GR/S28082/01 – see Chapter 4.

List of Acronyms and Abbreviations

AAT	Awel Aman Tawe
ACE	Association for the Conservation of Energy
AT	alternative or appropriate technology
BedZED	Beddington Zero Energy Development
BETTA	British Electricity Trading and Transmission Arrangements
BWEA	British Wind Energy Association
CCC	Climate Change Capital
CD	compact disc
CFL	compact fluorescent lamp
CGG	Commission on Global Governance
CHP	combined heat and power
COI	Central Office of Information
CRI	Community Renewables Initiative
CSR	corporate social responsibility
CWS	community waste sector
DARE	Devon Association for Renewable Energy
DEFRA	Department of the Environment, Food and Rural Affairs
DETR	Department for Environment, Transport and the Regions
DH	district heating
DNOs	Distribution Network Operators
DTI	Department of Trade and Industry
EC	European Commission
ECI	Environmental Change Institute
ECT	Ealing Community Transport
EEACs	Energy Efficiency Advice Centres
EMEC	European Marine Energy Centre
ENDS	Environmental Data Services
ELCRP	East London Community Recycling Partnership
ESCO	energy service company
ESI	electricity supply industry
ESRC	Economic and Social Research Council
EU	European Union
FES	Future Energy Solutions
FMCG	fast-moving consumer goods
FREDS	Forum for Renewable Energy Development in Scotland

FSC	Forest Stewardship Council
GM	genetically modified
HCEAC	House of Commons Environmental Audit Committee
HCSTC	House of Commons Science and Technology Committee
HLSTC	House of Lords Science and Technology Committee
HWP	Hackney Waste Partnership
ICEPT	Imperial College Centre for Energy Policy and Technology
IEA	International Energy Agency
IP	intellectual property
ITI Energy	Intermediary Technology Institute for Energy
KWe	kilowatt electricity
KWh	kilowatt hour
LA21	Local Agenda 21
LED	light emitting diode
LTS	large technical system
LZC	low and zero carbon
MLG	multi-level governance
MW	megawatt
MWe	megawatt electricity
NETA	New Electricity Trading Arrangements
NEPI	new environmental policy instrument
NFFO	Non-Fossil Fuel Obligation
NGO	non-governmental organization
NIMBY	not in my back yard
ODPM	Office of the Deputy Prime Minister
OECD	Organisation for Economic Co-operation and Development
OES	Ocean Energy Systems
Ofgem	Office of Gas and Electricity Markets
ONS	Office of National Statistics
OST	Office of Science and Technology
OVE	Organisation for Renewable Energy
PFI	Private Finance Initiative
PIU	Performance and Innovation Unit
PPG	Planning Policy Guidance
PV	photovoltaic
R&D	research and development
RCEP	Royal Commission on Environmental Pollution
RIR	Renewables Innovation Review
RO	Renewables Obligation
ROC	Renewable Obligation Certificate
SBGI	Society of British Gas Industries
SCR	Sustainable Consumption Roundtable
SIAM	System Impacts of Additional Micro-generation
SNM	strategic niche management
SP	Scottish Power
SPECC	Scottish Parliament Enterprise and Culture Committee

SPRU	Science and Technology Policy Research Unit
SRF	Scottish Renewables Forum
SSE	Scottish and Southern Energy
STA	Solar Trade Association
STP	Sustainable Technologies Programme
SWP	Somerset Waste Partnership
TIC	Techno-Institutional Complex
TRV	thermostatic radiator valve
UCCCRJ	United Church of Christ Commission for Racial Justice
VAT	value added tax
WET	Waste and Emissions Trading
WTO	World Trade Organization

Section I
INTRODUCTION

Chapter 1

Sustainability: Understanding People, Technology and Governance

Joseph Murphy

Introduction

In April 2006 the New Economics Foundation released a report on UK 'interdependence'. It attracted media attention because it identified a date when the average UK citizen begins to live off the rest of the world.

> *The moment we begin living beyond our natural means is what we call our ecological debt day. At current levels of natural resource use in the UK, the average person goes into ecological debt on 16 April. As our total consumption grows, it moves ever earlier in the year. In 1961 it was 9 July, advancing to 14 May in 1981.* (Simms et al, 2006, p2)

Using reports like this one, non-governmental organizations (NGOs) and others are increasingly trying to make consumption and lifestyles in the richest countries a core concern for sustainable development.

There can be little doubt that lifestyles in the richest countries represent a profound challenge for sustainability, but after making this observation we encounter different ways of defining the problem. For example, are we consuming too much or just producing it in a wasteful and inefficient way? If the answer is 'both', what is the relative importance of each problem? Questions like this are important because different ways of defining problems imply different solutions and ways of allocating scarce resources in an effort to bring about change. Winners and losers will also emerge in relation to different strategies and policy agendas.

The environmental social sciences can make two valuable contributions to the sustainable development debate in this context. Scholars can help society to understand and define problems and, in doing so, influence what constitutes solutions. They can also critique the ways in which other stakeholders, such as NGOs, businesses and governments, seek to do the same, perhaps to support policy agendas other than (or in addition to) sustainable development. The accounts that will emerge from the social sciences are likely to be more complex and nuanced but this should be understood as their strength and not as a weakness.

This book makes a contribution along these lines by focusing on people, technology and governance in the richest countries. It is important to focus on these aspects because they are regularly simplified and caricatured in sustainable development debates, often in a way that co-opts them to other policy agendas. For example, people are regularly reduced to being only self-centred consumers, and technology is cast simplistically as a solution to environmental and social problems. Governance is naively portrayed as multi-stakeholder cooperation to solve problems based on an unlikely consensus over how they should be understood and addressed.

In this chapter I explore more complex and accurate accounts and map out the terrain for the following chapters. The first section draws on sustainable consumption, environmental justice and environmental decision-making research to understand people in relation to sustainable development. The second section focuses on technology and draws on ideas from the alternative technology movement, social shaping of technology and socio-technical transitions. The third section explores governance through research on environmental governance, ecological modernization and new environmental policy instruments. I conclude by outlining the book's aim and the chapters that follow.

People and sustainability:
Motivation, justice and participation

Policy documents and public debates regularly simplify and caricature people in relation to sustainable development. They are often, for example, cast as heavy consumers of unsustainable products, or as a barrier that needs to be overcome so that technology can run efficiently. It is widely accepted that such representations reflect the power and application of the economic/market and technological/engineering perspectives on society (Murphy and Cohen, 2001; Shove, 2004a). This means that specific assumptions are in widespread use – for example, people can act only as egoistic self-centred welfare maximizers – and these assumptions underpin sustainable development policies (Murphy and Cohen, 2001; Paavola, 2001). In this section I discuss different ways of thinking about people and sustainability, beginning with refinements to the conventional consumer perspective.

Sustainable consumption: Motivation and identity

Sustainable consumption researchers have taken up the challenge of contributing a more nuanced understanding of people and consumption to sustainable development debates, particularly compared with the conventional consumer/market perspective (Cohen and Murphy, 2001; Princen et al, 2002; Jackson, 2006). This work has involved close examination and questioning of widely accepted ideas, such as:

- people are self-centred and motivated only by increases in personal welfare;
- increases in consumption lead to increases in happiness;
- people have their own preferences and they are unaffected by what others consume.

Research in areas as diverse as ethics, psychology, anthropology, sociology and cultural studies has been drawn together to produce alternative or additional insights.

The values and motivations that underpin consumption in practice are a useful starting point. The standard model of the consumer is based on a view of people that has been described as 'self-centred welfarism'. This suggests that consumers are rational actors interested only in maximizing personal welfare within the constraints of a fixed budget. However, as Paavola (2001) argues, consumption in practice involves other value positions as well. People may indeed be concerned about the future implications of consumption but not necessarily in relation to their own welfare. Outcomes other than improvements in personal welfare may be important. In addition, consumers can put personal welfare and other future consequences to one side, to some extent, in order to consume in a way that is consistent with their beliefs.

Psychologists and social psychologists have contributed to this debate by exploring identity and lifestyle choices. In research on the voluntary simplicity movement, Zavestoski (2001) makes an important distinction between environmental and quality of life motivations behind changing consumption. Although it is sometimes the case that voluntary simplicity is motivated by a desire to 'save the planet', this research shows that the majority of people are actually motivated by a desire to improve their quality of life. The choice to adopt a simpler lifestyle, and to consume less, happens as people begin to question the positive relationship between consumption and happiness, and in fact begin to see a negative one. This might be linked to the overburdening of the individual by modern lifestyles and existential crisis.[1]

Disciplines like anthropology, sociology and cultural studies emphasize that material goods are important in all societies because of the role they play in identity and communication. Perhaps the most famous phrase to capture this is 'conspicuous consumption' (Veblen, 1899) – consumption that confirms and communicates status. Such research reaches beyond the welfare aspects of consumption, with important implications. It suggests, for example, that environmental policy proposals that ignore the role of material goods in satisfying non-material human needs, such as status and group membership, should be viewed with at least as much scepticism as those policies that assume that consumers are only self-centred welfare maximizers.

The sustainable consumption debate, therefore, has done a great deal to refine the understanding of the relationship between consumption and sustainable development. Perhaps the most significant problem, however, is that it continues to engage with people primarily as consumers, although in more sophisticated ways. If it is a problem that people are only understood as consumers, as is the case in a consumer society, a limited amount is achieved by trying to inform debates with a better understanding of this aspect. To avoid this trap I will discuss other perspectives on the relationship between people and sustainability – people as sufferers of injustice and bearers of useful knowledge.

Environmental justice and intergenerational equity

The environmental justice debate takes us beyond consumption and offers an alternative way of linking people and sustainability. In doing so it draws attention to issues that are often marginalized or lost entirely. The origins of environmental justice research are found in the backlash against landfill sites and polluting industries in the US in the 1980s. In 1987 the landmark report *Toxic Wastes and Race in the United States* (United Church of Christ Commission for Racial Justice, (UCCCRJ) 1987) drew attention to the fact that many sources of pollution tend to be located in poor black neighbourhoods. This led some to raise the spectre of 'environmental racism' and a public and political debate followed.

In the 1990s the environmental justice agenda spread beyond the US. Social scientists and policy actors in the UK, amongst others, contributed to the debate. This wider adoption was accompanied by more critical reflection on causal claims. Been (1994), for example, suggested that in the US poorer people migrate to areas where land and property prices are depressed by industrial and waste facilities. This argument challenges the view that city planners and others impose polluting facilities on poor communities. Weinberg (1998) acknowledged the value of documenting injustice whilst arguing that if researchers want to make causal claims they must study social processes and not outcomes.

What are the links between environmental justice and sustainability? Agyeman et al (2002) argues that there are at least two. First, justice is a desirable characteristic of any future society, particularly a developed and sustainable one. Second, and more practically, environmental injustice is often associated with environmental degradation. As Agyeman et al state:

> Our interpretation of ... [sustainable development] places great emphasis upon the need to ensure a better quality of life for all, in a just and equitable manner, whilst living within the limits of supporting ecosystems. Sustainability, we argue, cannot be simply a 'green' or 'environmental' concern, important though 'environmental' aspects of sustainability are. (Agyeman et al, 2002, p1)

This research, therefore, makes justice and equity, at individual and community levels, a central concern for how people and sustainable development are linked.

Environmental decision making: Knowledge, participation and power

A third perspective on the relationship between people and sustainability is provided by environmental decision-making research. Much of the work in this area has been done in the UK, where at least two developments in the 1990s drew attention to processes of inclusion and exclusion in policy making. The first was the implementation of Local Agenda 21 (LA21) with LA21 plans being seen as an opportunity to include people in planning for sustainability at the local level. The second was conflict and protest around various infrastructure projects, particularly roads, which highlighted tensions between national policy-making processes and local or alternative perspectives.

At the centre of much environmental decision-making research is the problem of knowledge and participation in decision-making processes (Evans, 2004). This concern has led researchers to draw on a wide range of social theorists, particularly Jurgen Habermas and his work on deliberative democracy (Doganay, 2004). Implicitly and explicitly, scholars have explored participation in politics as a way of extending the public sphere, and deliberation as the desirable normative basis of democracy. There is critical reflection on the practical and theoretical problems associated with the ideal of deliberative democracy, but there is also a broad consensus that democracy can be renewed by transforming existing institutions along more deliberative lines (e.g. Barrett and Usui, 2002).

Perhaps the most difficult challenge that scholars have taken up in this area is analysing and critiquing decision making that is based on scientific (and other technical) knowledge. Researchers have identified a process they refer to as the 'scientization of politics', which involves political choices being represented as scientific and technical ones. As Bäckstrand (2004, p4) has argued, it 'implies that political and social issues are better resolved through technical expertise than democratic deliberation'. As Beck (1992, p159) has argued, when politicians effectively evade responsibility in this way, experts 'maintain their monopoly claim to rationality against the non-specialised public sphere'.

Strategies of this kind, which lead away from democracy and deliberation to technocracy, can and do have unforeseen consequences. Not least of these is public protest that targets new technologies and infrastructure developments, including those that might increasingly be justified in relation to the policy agenda of sustainable development. But as Nelkin (1979, p11) argued in the 1970s, in a technological controversy protest may be aimed 'less against specific technological decisions than against the declining capacity of citizens to shape policies that affect their interests; less against science than against the use of scientific rationality to mask political choices'.

Environmental decision-making research, therefore, gives us a third perspective on people and sustainability. It suggests that sustainability in practice is intimately associated with processes of decision making and how such processes treat knowledge of different kinds. At the practical level this research reveals just how difficult it is to achieve widespread participation in decision making and this raises questions about the 'renewal of democracy' agenda. More generally this research sensitizes us to the way in which the imperative of sustainable development might be exploited in various ways, particularly using scientific and technical data to justify decisions, thereby masking the political choices involved.

Technology and sustainability: Alternatives, shaping and transitions

The relationship between technology and sustainability attracts great deal of attention. In most debates technology is understood to mediate between resources and our goals and objectives. This leads us to a focus on energy and material efficiency. The concept of 'eco-efficiency' is a good example (Schmidheiny, 1992; De Simone and Popoff, 1997).[2] There is no doubt that more efficient technology will make an important contribution to sustainable development, but this perspective has many limitations. The emphasis on efficiency, for example, prevents questions being raised about goals and objectives and aggregate impacts. The replacement of old and inefficient technologies can also be presented as an apolitical process that leaves society largely untouched. This is attractive but not realistic. In this section I outline more accurate and subtle accounts of technology and sustainability.

The alternative technology movement

The idea of alternative or appropriate technology (AT) is a useful starting point. It was popularized by Ernst Schumacher in *Small is Beautiful* and it remains central to environment and development debates. Indeed, the tension between mega-technologies and appropriate technologies is one of the most profound in research and practice. In his classic book Schumacher argues that AT is something that fits the context. In a developing country it is labour intensive, small scale, context specific and affordable. It is also developed, to a significant extent, bottom-up. This can be contrasted with what Schumacher refers to as 'grandiose projects' and 'large scale projects on the level of the most modern technology' (see particularly Schumacher, 1974, pp143–159).

The AT tradition has also influenced debates in developed countries. Smith (2003, p129) outlines some of its focus and history:

> The AT movement supports a system of needs provision tailored to local circumstances, and which fulfils social and environmental dimensions as well as purely economic ones ... in this respect, the AT movement has been concerned with sustainable technologies for nearly 30 years and provides a rich seam of empirical mate-

> *rial... An orientation to meeting needs through local production, using low inputs and local resources, in closed cycles, and with high social inclusion ... positions AT at the 'local stewardship' ... or 'deep green' end of sustainable development...*

As a social movement and as a research area AT has experienced a renaissance in recent years. This is associated with the backlash against globalization, amongst other things, and the search for radical socio-technical solutions to sustainability problems.

From this discussion it is clear that the vision and practice of AT challenge mainstream technologies in different ways. There is an emphasis on local and decentralized approaches, rather than centralized and hierarchical ones. One of the intended outcomes of this is that technological change becomes a more participatory and democratic process, rather than one imposed from above with the help of experts. There is also an emphasis on consciously linking progressive social and environmental agendas. This contrasts with conventional eco-efficient technological interventions, which can carry a model of society with them but leave it implicit.

Sustainability and the social shaping of technology

Scholars in sociology have been examining the social construction and shaping of technology since the 1970s (see Bijker and Law, 1992; MacKenzie and Wajcman, 1999).[3] The fight against technological determinism underpins this research effort. According to Mackenzie and Wajcman (1999, p3) this is the view that 'Technologies change, either because of scientific advance or following a logic of their own; and they then have effects on society'.[4] Scholars in technology studies are interested instead in the relationship between technology and society and how these shape each other.

By focusing on the adoption of technology we begin to see the contribution that this research effort can make. Studies of adoption confirm that this is a political process. It is not explained by the technology being 'better' or 'cheaper' in a simple sense, although retrospectively it is often explained in this way. In practice, new technologies have an 'interpretive flexibility', which allows them to mean different things to different social groups (Kline and Pinch, 1999, p113). Adoption, therefore, involves the framing of a technology as a solution.

In the context of environment and sustainability, interpretive flexibility is clear in the case of genetically modified (GM) crops. Some claim this technology is a threat to sustainable agriculture, and others argue it is a route to it. Researchers in technology studies have identified a process of 'closure' through which the meaning and role of a technology becomes stable and widely accepted. When closure occurs the technology is taken for granted and its contested origin is forgotten. That said, interpretive flexibility can return. Nuclear power technology, for example, shows how some technologies fail to reach the point of 'closure', or become contentious once again if they do.

Moving beyond adoption, the work of Shove (1997, 2004a and b) shows how sociological research on the use of technology informs the sustainability debate. Shove's work has focused mainly on technologies in the domestic setting and particularly on the way that social norms and technologies shape each other. She shows how assumptions about warmth and cleanliness, for example, are shaped by interactions between people and technology. In the case of room heating, although physiologists use the idea of an 'optimum' temperature, in practice room temperature is determined by social norms and interactions between technology and people. An important feature of this research is that social practices, such as clothes washing, are the link between norms and technology.[5]

Innovation and the transition to sustainability

In the 1990s, innovation studies informed a great deal of research on environment and sustainability. Much of this examined the regulation-innovation-competitiveness nexus at micro- and macro-economic levels (see, for example, Porter and van der Linde, 1995; Wallace, 1995; Kemp, 1997; Gouldson and Murphy, 1998; Murphy and Gouldson, 2000). This research informed the argument that environmental regulation could be used to shape and drive industrial innovation to the benefit of the environment and competitiveness. More recently, perhaps because of the realization that product and process innovations alone will not deliver environmental sustainability, the research effort has moved on to innovations in whole socio-technical systems.

In their introduction to *System Innovation and the Transition to Sustainability: Theory, Evidence and Policy* (Elzen et al, 2004) the editors argue that optimizing an existing socio-technical system might produce a factor 2 improvement in the efficiency with which resources are used. Environmental sustainability, however, implies much greater improvements, and this underpins the interest in system innovation (also known as transitions) (Geels, 2004, 2005a, b):

> ... *transitions to sustainability require changes from, for example, one transport system to another and from one energy system to another. Such system innovations not only involve new technological artefacts, but also new markets, user practices, regulations, infrastructures and cultural meanings.* (Geels et al, 2004, p1)

The socio-technical system as a unit of analysis is central to the sustainable transitions debate for a number of reasons. From a theoretical standpoint it is useful because it can accommodate and integrate research that is focused in other ways, and often at the micro level. Industrial ecology research, for example, tends to focus at the material level and only on production. Sustainable consumption, on the other hand, tries to link material and cultural dimensions but it focuses on 'the demand side'. The focus on socio-technical systems is a way of overcoming such divisions and making use of the insights that the research provides. One risk, however, is that the origins of the transitions concept mean that it will tend to privilege some perspectives over others, for example, production or the development of technologies over consumption and the meaning of artefacts (Shove, 2004b).

More practically, the focus on socio-technical systems helps to explain why superior technologies with better environmental performance are not being adopted. In broad terms this is explained by a wide range of factors, usually operating together – regulatory frameworks, cultural values, market imperatives, infrastructural constraints and so on. This implies that a systemic view is important but, as Geels et al (2004, p8) point out: 'Although the importance of system innovation is increasingly emphasized in sustainability debates, little is known about how system innovations occur and how policy makers can influence them.' The more fundamental question, however, is not 'how' policy makers can influence system innovation but 'if' it is possible for any group to steer a system in a specific direction.

Much of the practical work associated with the transition to sustainability debate revolves around the idea of 'transition management'. Kemp and Rotmans (2004), for example, emphasize the need for policy interventions that try to shape beliefs and expectations as well as industrial production and market activity – production being the traditional focus for policy. They argue that the transition to sustainability will be an iterative process – 'goal oriented incrementalism' – involving the articulation of visions and 'learning-by-doing', amongst other things. Not surprisingly, Teisman and Edelenbos (2004) argue that this requires a new form of politics because existing ways of governing are not well placed to manage the process of transition.

Governance and sustainability: Framing, institutions and instruments

In recent years governance has emerged as one of the most important concepts in international relations, political science and policy studies.[6] Hajer and Wagenaar (2003, p1) argue that this reflects actual changes in politics and policy making from the late 1980s onwards. As part of this trend, environmental governance and governance for sustainability are increasingly being discussed (e.g. Adger et al, 2003; Davidson and Frickel, 2004; Evans, 2004; Jasanoff and Martello, 2004). Indeed, Hajer and Wagenaar (2003, p3) go on to argue that environment and sustainability have played a role in the emergence of governance more generally by raising questions about the relationship between the state and society. In this section I discuss environmental governance and explore issue framing, institutional change and new environmental policy instruments.

Environmental governance: Functionalist and critical perspectives

Many scholars agree that politics has been transformed since the late 1980s by a shift from government to governance. Or, more modestly, that governance has emerged as a more important feature of government over this period. In these debates government is understood as centralized, hierarchical and perhaps technocratic, whereas governance involves power moving away from the centre, and policy making through complex networks. Bache and Flinders (2004) suggest that governance refers to the increased role of NGOs in public policy making and delivery. It captures a more complex relationship between state and society where the state's role is coordination rather than control.

Governance is particularly clear in the area of environment and sustainability. From a functionalist perspective this can be explained as the state's response to the complexity of problems and its own limited resources (Raman, 2003). A related view suggests that the driving force behind environmental governance is the poor performance of public policy in this area. Functionalist accounts suggest that environmental governance draws more actors into the policy process because their knowledge and commitment is likely to produce more successful policies. These accounts tend to assume a consensus on problems and how they can be solved and it is this that underpins cooperation between stakeholders.

There are, of course, more critical accounts. These take the legitimacy problems that governments are experiencing in relation to environment and sustainability as their starting point and they focus on efforts to manage these. In some cases they highlight tensions across policy agendas being pursued by governments, such as conflict between economic growth and environmental protection (Jonas and Gibbs, 2003; Murphy and Levidow, 2006). Evidence of legitimacy problems is found in new social movements at the global level, such as those that are labelled anti-capitalist or anti-globalization, as well as in more local protests against controversial developments and technologies.

From a critical perspective, environmental governance can be understood as a way of managing legitimacy problems by drawing some critics into a relationship with the state whilst at the same time marginalizing others. This is achieved through 'participation' and 'partnership'. Arguments along these lines raise doubts about the existence of a convenient consensus regarding environmental problems and how they might be solved. They examine instead how problems are defined or framed, and solutions identified, in ways that include some policy actors in a hegemonic policy coalition whilst at the same time excluding others (Murphy and Levidow, 2006).

The environmental transformation of institutions

Ecological modernization research has examined the institutional changes that accompany a shift from government to environmental governance. In an early contribution Weale (1992) referred to 'the new politics of pollution', and subsequent work has explored the transformation of a wide range of institutions in the face of environmental challenges. Formal and informal institutions associated with regulation, production and consumption have been examined, particularly to see what happens as the environment moves from being a peripheral to a core concern.

For the purposes of this discussion it is useful to focus on government and regulation from the ecological modernization perspective. Discussions concerning the role of governments in the process of ecological modernization have been profoundly influenced by political modernization debates (see Jänicke, 1990). Drawing on these influences, Mol (1995, pp46–47) identified two strategies that might be used to overcome the deficiencies of the traditional bureaucratic state in environmental policy making:

> *First, a transformation of state environmental policy is necessary: from curative and reactive to preventive, from exclusive to participatory policy-making, from centralized to decentralized wherever possible, and from domineering, over-regulated environmental policy to policy which creates favourable conditions and contexts for environmentally sound practices and behaviour on the part of producers and consumers. The state will have to ... focus more on steering via economic mechanisms and change its management strategy by introducing collective self-obligations for economic sectors via discursive interest mediation. The second, related, option includes a transfer of responsibilities, incentives and tasks from the state to the market. This will advance and accelerate the ecological transformation process, mainly because the market is considered to be a more efficient and effective mechanism for coordinating and tackling environmental problems than the state ... the central idea is not a withering away of the state in environmental management, but rather a transformation of the relation between state and society and different accents on the steering role of the state. The state provides the conditions and stimulates social 'self-regulation', either via economic mechanisms and dynamics or via the public sphere of citizen groups, environmental NGOs and consumer organizations.*

This view of the changing role of the state resonates with recent work on metagovernance. Jessop (1998, 2002, 2004) has used this concept to explore how central governments might operate in complex multi-actor and multi-level contexts. It is 'the organization of the conditions for governance in its broadest sense' (Jessop, 2004, p240). This involves efforts to manage complexity and interactions, possibly by creating visions and agreeing targets in more deliberative ways, whilst at the same time choosing when implementation should be pursued through mandatory, market or more participatory mechanisms.

The concept of metagovernance implies that subtle steering mechanisms will become increasingly important. If this is the case then in the future we are likely to see institutional innovations of various kinds. In the case of GM crops in the UK we recently had the 'GM nation' debate, although it is unclear what role this experiment was supposed to play. In a paper on risk and new technologies, Walls et al (2005) argued that rather than witnessing a shift from government to governance, we might be witnessing a shift to governance and the state's response to this, the governance of governance – metagovernance.

New environmental policy instruments: From technical reason to political reason?

We can usefully explore the design and implementation of specific policies in this context. The transition from government to (meta)governance has been accompanied by the emergence of a wide range of new environmental policy instruments (NEPIs) and practices. Examples include eco-taxes, eco-labels, voluntary agreements (covenants) between government and business, environmental management systems, public information/education campaigns and citizens' juries. A great deal of research has examined how these are justified, used and linked.

The use of command and control regulatory instruments is closely associated with government in its traditional form (Pierre, 2000). As Jordan et al (2005, pp478–479) argue, however, new policy instruments '... are assumed to allow social actors freedom to coordinate amongst themselves in pursuit of societal goals, with far less (or even no) central government involvement'. These authors argue that environmental policy is a particularly interesting test case for the broader shift to new policy instruments because the strong legacy of command and control environmental regulation from the late 1960s would suggest that such a shift is unlikely (see also Jordan et al, 2003).

After examining the use of NEPIs in eight countries in the European Union (EU) the authors draw out a number of interesting conclusions. Overall they find plenty of evidence of NEPIs being used but this varies a lot across jurisdictions, sectors and instrument types. In many cases the new instruments are being used to plug gaps or to deal with new problems, rather than replace traditional approaches. Significantly, many of the new policy instruments also require state involvement. The authors argue that 'Far from eclipsing government, governance therefore often complements and, on some occasions, even competes with it...' (Jordan et al, 2005, p477).

Other work has drawn the same conclusion regarding the use of traditional approaches alongside newer ones. In a study of environmental regulation and industrial innovation in the UK and The Netherlands, Gouldson and Murphy (1998) explored the relationship between command and control approaches (statutory environmental targets or technology standards) and more novel voluntary ones (covenants and environmental management systems). These authors emphasize the role of traditional instruments in establishing environmental imperatives, and their use alongside newer instruments that try to build the capacity of business to respond.

The research discussed here indicates that there is need for caution regarding the shift from government to governance in the area of environment and sustainability in general and specifically regarding NEPIs. The cautious approach is clear when Jordan et al (2005, p492) say:

> *Broadly speaking, our nine jurisdictions have, on balance, shifted from a position of 'government' to one of 'governance' with respect to their use of (environmental) policy instruments. However, the total distance travelled along the continuum by the nine jurisdictions has been surprisingly modest... [also] in spite of the rhetorical commitment to find less direct and hierarchical forms of state involvement (that is, more governance), governments (and the EU) find themselves inexorably drawn into the detailed process of designing, adopting and overseeing the implementation of all (environmental) policy instruments... (emphasis original)*

To conclude, it is worth reflecting more broadly on the environmental policy process in the context of government and governance. Raman (2003) has explored this by distinguishing between technical and political reason. If environmental problems are understood to speak for themselves at the empirical level, and the policy process is understood as a series of more or less logical stages, then technical reason will tend to hold sway. This might take the form of foregrounding the evidence of problems using scientific models, followed by the use of expert methodologies (e.g. cost–benefit analysis) to identify actions. Alternatively, if environmental problems are understood as emerging in relation to the way they are framed, and who participates in that process, and the policy process itself is understood as one involving argument, deliberation and power, then political reason becomes more important. Policy making in this context would place more emphasis on critical reflection on the way problems are being understood, and institutional opportunities to debate and argue about them.

Purpose and outline of the book

I have discussed people, technology and governance in relation to environment and sustainability. The accounts I have given are more complex and subtle than those that dominate popular and policy debates. I have introduced concepts and arguments from a wide range of social sciences but I have not tried to link them. The main purpose of this book is to do this, and I argue in the final chapter that there is a people-technology-governance nexus that is profoundly important to environment and sustainability. If this is true then it should become a focus for multidisciplinary research and policy making. The chapters that follow contribute a great deal to our understanding of this nexus and to the process of linking social science perspectives. They are organized into the same three sections as this chapter – people, technology and governance – but in practice they overlap.

Section II focuses on people and sustainability. In Chapter 2 Seonaidh McDonald and her colleagues use the 'circuit of culture' theoretical framework from cultural studies. Through this they examine how consumers 'decode' the governance aspects of sustainable technology products, after their 'encoding' by public, private and civil society organizations. The chapter focuses on actual purchases of products, such as energy-efficient fridges, water-conserving washing machines and low-energy light bulbs. It also compares purchases of such technologies with more everyday purchases like food and household cleaning products. The chapter draws on data from around 80 semi-structured interviews with people who have consciously tried to buy more sustainable technologies, and it includes fascinating extracts from them.

In Chapter 3 Robin Roy and his colleagues explore the adoption and use of low and zero carbon technologies. These technologies, such as solar water heaters and micro combined heat and power systems, have an important role to play in UK and EU climate change strategies. That said, consumer adoption is slow and, even when they are adopted, such technologies are not always used effectively. This chapter examines the factors that influence consumer adoption and use, drawing on existing literature and an exploratory empirical survey. It introduces a model of the adoption process which shows that these technologies are often designed without taking sufficient account of consumer requirements. This leads the authors to argue for a people-centred approach to eco-design and they identify 'hotspots' that might be used to encourage adoption and effective use.

In Chapter 4 Patrick Devine-Wright presents a social-psychological analysis of energy technologies and systems and how they change over time. Different ways of understanding energy are identified and linked to different ways of understanding and representing people as users of energy. Devine-Wright argues that representations of people that circulate in policy play an important role in determining how energy technologies and systems evolve. Despite playing this role, however, such representations are left implicit in energy policy and they are rarely reflected upon or exposed to critical debate. Towards the end of the chapter it is argued that 'energy citizenship', in contrast to the currently dominant 'consumer/deficit' view of people, offers a more suitable basis for the development and widespread adoption of sustainable energy technologies.

Section III focuses on technology and sustainability. In Chapter 5 Adrian Smith examines the alternative technology movement and eco-housing in the UK since the early 1970s. He describes how this socio-technical context produced a range of technologies that are getting more attention now in relation to sustainable housing and communities. Smith argues that the eco-housing movement can be understood as a 'green niche' and he examines 'intermediary developments', such as Beddington Zero Emission Development (BedZED), as places where technologies and practices are translated from niche to mainstream. Towards the end of the chapter he explores the governance of a sustainable technology across this divide and he outlines two possibilities: adapting lessons and practices from the niche so that they can be adopted by the mainstream; and altering the socio-technical context of the mainstream so that it is more receptive to niche ideas and practices.

In Chapter 6 Raphael Sauter and Jim Watson examine the possible impact of domestic micro-generation technologies on the electricity supply system. Domestic micro-generation is often described as radical or disruptive because it blurs the boundary between energy supply and demand and could change consumer-provider relationships, leading to fundamental changes in electricity system architecture, operation and governance. Sauter and Watson examine the case using the large technical systems (LTS) framework. This allows them to consider the electricity system as a whole, including its technologies, institutions, regulations and actors. The authors argue that micro-generation is not inherently disruptive. Its impact will depend on the model of deployment and related ownership, financing, operating and technology arrangements, producing different 'patterns of disruptiveness'.

In Chapter 7 Tim Foxon discusses innovation systems research and the concept of 'systems failure'. He argues that this concept might underpin policy interventions that aim to encourage the development of more sustainable technologies. The concept of 'systems failure' encompasses, and goes beyond, the traditional idea of 'market failure'. This latter concept is based on mainstream neoclassical economic thinking and it is widely used (implicitly and in some cases explicitly) by policy makers. The chapter draws mainly on innovation studies literature but it also explores ideas from governance and social shaping of technology research. Towards the end of the chapter Foxon discusses lessons that can be drawn from the transition approach to innovation that is being applied by the Dutch government.

Section IV focuses on governance and sustainability. In Chapter 8 Rachel Slater examines the role of partnerships in the delivery of local government waste management services in the UK. Sustainable waste management in practice will require a shift away from waste disposal at landfill to waste minimization, re-use and recycling. Bringing about this change is one of the UK's most pressing environmental challenges, but achieving it has been complicated by the shift from government to governance in the planning and delivery of public services at the local level. The UK government is increasingly calling for local services that respond to local needs, with more power being passed to local communities and non-state actors, and emphasis is being placed on service delivery through partnerships. This chapter analyses the Somerset Waste Partnership (SWP) and Hackney Waste Partnership (HWP) and uses them to draw out wider implications for the relationship between local governance and technologies of waste management.

In Chapter 9 David Toke examines the governance of wind power in the EU. To explain the installation of generating capacity, the existing debate focuses on financial procurement mechanisms and/or land planning. Although adequate financial support and planning consent are necessary for wind power, arguments over the relative merits of different financial mechanisms and barriers associated with planning process can be misleading. Chapter 9 takes a broader view of wind power by exploring related networks of policy actors and their ontological and epistemological aspects. Toke uses the idea of ontology to discuss the structure and relationships of wind power networks, and epistemology is used to explore the role of knowledge within them. The chapter discusses and compares five European countries – the UK, The Netherlands, Germany, Spain and Denmark – and it provides a rich account of wind power in these contexts.

In Chapter 10 Mark Winskel examines multi-level governance (MLG) and innovation in marine energy technology – wave and tidal flow devices. Scottish devolution in the late-1990s resulted in energy policy in Scotland being shared between the Scottish and UK executives. Devolution also coincided with a number of significant changes in the UK energy system, including an extensive policy review, and the growing importance of European and international level decision making on climate change. A distinctive energy policy arena has emerged in Scotland and differences of emphasis and intent compared with the UK level have become clearer. Winskel argues that while MLG is a challenge from the perspective of policy integration, it opens up new possibilities for reform and experimentation that might benefit the marine energy technology sector in Scotland.

Section V is the Conclusion. In Chapter 11 I explore ways of linking people, technology and governance in relation to the imperative and challenge of sustainable development. I begin by exploring the challenge of sustainable development by linking its ecological/material and social/cultural aspects. I move on to draw out initial key insights that should underpin discussion of people, technology and governance in relation to technology – the multiple identities of people, contextualized accounts of technology, critical and functionalist accounts of governance. The rest of the chapter explores sustainability and the people-technology-governance nexus and illustrates how insights from different social sciences can be combined to produce new insights.

Notes

1   The importance of research like this becomes clear as evidence of the psychological cost of modern life grows. Towards the end of April 2006 Richard Layard, emeritus professor at the Centre for Economic Performance of the London School of Economics, argued that depression, anxiety and other forms of mental illness have overtaken unemployment as the greatest social problem in the UK (*The Guardian*, Friday 28 April, p9).

2   In relation to production there are close links to policy concepts like 'waste minimization', 'clean technologies' and 'clean production'. In relation to society more broadly, similar ideas have been pursued in the so-called 'Factor 4' and 'Factor 10' debates (von Weizsäcker et al, 1997) – these phrases indicate the improvement in resource efficiency that is needed to achieve environmental sustainability.

3   Defining technology has been a challenge for scholars in Technology Studies. Consumers and people in industry might hold the view that technology is a 'gadget' or bit of 'kit', but for scholars this is a fragile perspective; the knowledge of how to use the 'gadget' must be part of the technology because otherwise it is useless. Proceeding along these lines Bijker (1995, p231) identifies the following as aspects of technology:

> *... physical artifacts (such as dikes), human activities (such as making dikes), and knowledge (such as the know-how to build dikes and the fluid dynamics used to model them in the laboratory). Additionally, I will consider the word technology to apply not only to hardware technology (such as fascine mattresses) but also to 'social' technology (such as the traditional dike-management system used in the Netherlands).*

Bijker acknowledges that this is a broad definition, and that it cuts across some existing distinctions, but it is defended on the grounds that such distinctions are fragile anyway.

4   Bijker (1995, p238) argues slightly differently. The argument that technology determines society is a theory of society and as a result it should be referred to as technological determinism. The argument that technology is autonomous, however, is a theory of technology and not of society, and consequently this should not be labelled technological determinism.

5   Chappells et al (2001) have extended this approach to examine how technology constructs not only social norms but also the meaning of 'natural resources'. These authors point out that technical and policy debates assume that water is homogenous or something that can be described adequately using a small number of categories defined in physical terms – for example, grey water or clean water. From a consumer perspective, however, it has multiple identities that are constructed in relation to three genres of technology – barriers, containers and purifiers.

6   The discussion here focuses on governance in relation to policy and its implementation. The concept is used in other ways. The most common is 'good governance' in business, particularly following the collapse of ENRON. In this context it usually refers to financial control. Good governance is also used in relation to developing countries and financial assistance from the World Bank and similar institutions. In this context it also refers to financial control, but it can be extended to cover democracy and human rights.

References

Adger, N., Brown, K., Fairbrass, J., Jordan, A., Paavola, J., Rosendo, S. and Seyfang, G. (2003) 'Governance for sustainability: Towards a "thick" analysis of environmental decisionmaking', *Environment and Planning A*, vol 35, pp1095–1110

Agyeman, J., Bullard, R. and Evans, B. (2002) 'Exploring the nexus: Bringing together sustainability, environmental justice and equity', *Space & Polity*, vol 6, no 1, pp77–90

Bache, I. and Flinders, M. (2004) 'Multi-level governance and British politics', in Bache, I. and Flinders, M. (eds) *Multi-level Governance*, Oxford University Press, Oxford, pp93–106

Bäckstrand, K. (2004) 'Civic science for sustainability', *Global Environmental Politics*, vol 3, no 4, pp24–41

Barrett, B. and Usui, M. (2002) 'Local agenda 21 in Japan: Transforming local environmental governance', *Local Environment*, vol 7, no 1, pp49–67

Beck, U. (1992) *Risk Society: Towards a New Modernity*, Sage, London

Been, V. (1994) 'Locally undesirable land uses in minority neighbourhoods', *Yale Law Review*, vol 103, p1383

Bijker, W. (1995) 'Sociohistorical technology studies', in Jasanoff, S., Markle, G., Petersen, J. and Pinch, T. (eds) *Handbook of Science and Technology Studies*, Sage, London, pp229–256

Bijker, W. and Law, J. (eds) (1992) *Shaping Technology/Building Society: Studies in Sociotechnical Change*, MIT Press, London

Chappells, H., Selby, J. and Shove, E. (2001) 'Control and flow: Rethinking the sociology, technology and politics of water consumption', in Cohen, M. and Murphy, J. (eds) *Exploring Sustainable Consumption: Environmental Policy and the Social Sciences*, Elsevier, Oxford, pp157–170

Cohen, M. and Murphy, J. (eds) (2001) *Exploring Sustainable Consumption: Environmental Policy and the Social Sciences*, Elsevier, Oxford

Davidson, D. and Frickel, S. (2004) 'Building environmental states: Legitimacy and rationalization in sustainability governance', *International Sociology*, vol 19, no 1, pp89–110

De Simone, L. and Popoff, F. (1997) *Eco-Efficiency: The Business of Sustainable Development*, MIT Press, Cambridge, MA

Doganay, U. (2004) 'Rethinking democratic procedures: Democracy and deliberative experiences in Turkey's LA21 process', *Political Studies*, vol 52, pp728–744

Elzen, B., Geels, F. and Green, K. (2004) *System Innovation and the Transition to Sustainability: Theory, Evidence and Policy*, Edward Elgar, Cheltenham

Evans, J. (2004) 'What is local about local environmental governance? Observations from the local biodiversity action planning process', *Area*, vol 36, no 3, pp270–279

Geels, F. (2004) 'From sectoral systems of innovation to socio-technical systems: Insights about dynamics and change from sociology and institutional theory', *Research Policy*, vol 33, pp897–920

Geels, F. (2005a) 'The dynamics of transitions in socio-technical systems: A multi-level analysis of the transition pathway from horse-drawn carriages to automobiles (1860–1930)', *Technology Analysis and Strategic Management*, vol 17, no 4, pp445–476

Geels, F. (2005b) *Technological Transitions and System Innovation: A Co-Evolutionary and Socio-Technical Analysis*, Edward Elgar, Cheltenham

Geels, F., Elzen, B. and Green, K. (2004) 'General introduction: System innovation and transitions to sustainability', in Elzen, B., Geels, F. and Green, K. (eds) *System Innovation and the Transition to Sustainability: Theory, Evidence and Policy*, Edward Elgar, Cheltenham, pp1–16

Gouldson, A. and Murphy, J. (1998) *Regulatory Realities: The Implementation and Impact of Industrial Environmental Regulation*, Earthscan, London

Hajer, M. and Wagenaar, H. (2003) *Deliberative Policy Analysis: Understanding Governance in the Network Society*, Cambridge University Press, Cambridge

Jackson, T. (2006) *Reader in Sustainable Consumption*, Earthscan, London

Jänicke, M. (1990) *State Failure: The Impotence of Politics in Industrial Society*, Polity Press, Cambridge

Jasanoff, S. and Martello, M. (2004) *Earthly Politics: Local and Global in Environmental Governance*, MIT Press, Cambridge, Massachusetts

Jessop, B. (1998) 'The rise of governance and the risk of failure', *International Social Science Journal*, vol 50, issue 155, pp29–45

Jessop, B. (2002) *The Future of the Capitalist State*, Polity Press, Cambridge

Jessop, B. (2004) 'Multi-level governance and multi-level meta-governance', in Bache, I. and Flinders, M. (eds) *Multi-level Governance*, Oxford University Press, Oxford, pp49–74

Jonas, A. and Gibbs, D. (2003) 'Changing local modes of economic and environmental governance in England: A tale of two areas', *Social Science Quarterly*, vol 84, no 4, pp1018–1036

Jordan, A., Wurzel, R. and Zito, A. (2003) '"New" instruments of environmental governance: Patterns and pathways of change', *Environmental Politics*, vol 12, no 1, pp3–25

Jordan, A., Wurzel, R. and Zito, A. (2005) 'The rise of "new" policy instruments in comparative perspective: Has governance eclipsed government?', *Political Studies*, vol 53, pp477–496

Kemp, R. (1997) *Environmental Policy and Technical Change: A Comparison of the Technological Impact of Policy Instruments*, Edward Elgar, Cheltenham

Kemp, R. and Rotmans, J. (2004) 'Managing the transition to sustainable mobility', in Elzen, B., Geels, F. and Green, K. (eds) *System Innovation and the Transition to Sustainability: Theory, Evidence and Policy*, Edward Elgar, Cheltenham, pp19–47

Kline, R. and Pinch, T. (1999) 'The social construction of technology', in MacKenzie, D. and Wajcman, J. (eds) *The Social Shaping of Technology* (2nd Edition), Open University Press, Maidenhead, pp113–115

MacKenzie, D. and Wajcman, J. (eds) (1999) *The Social Shaping of Technology* (2nd Edition), Open University Press, Maidenhead

Mol, A. (1995) *The Refinement of Production: Ecological Modernization Theory and the Chemicals Industry*, CIP-Data Koninklijke Bibliotheek, The Haag

Murphy, J. and Gouldson, A. (2000) 'Environmental policy and industrial innovation: Integrating environment and economy through ecological modernisation', *Geoforum*, vol 31, no 1, pp33–44

Murphy, J. and Cohen, M. (2001) 'Consumption, environment and public policy', in Cohen, M. and Murphy, J. (eds) *Exploring Sustainable Consumption: Environmental Policy and the Social Sciences*, Elsevier, Oxford, pp3–20

Murphy, J. and Levidow, L. (2006) *Governing the Transatlantic Conflict over Agricultural Biotechnology*, Routledge, London

Nelkin, D. (1979) 'Science, technology and political conflict', in Nelkin, D. (ed) *Controversy: Politics of Technical Decisions*, Sage, London, pp9–24

Paavola, J. (2001) 'Economics, ethics and green consumerism', in Cohen, M. and Murphy, J. (eds) *Exploring Sustainable Consumption: Environmental Policy and the Social Sciences*, Elsevier, Oxford, pp79–94

Pierre, J. (2000) 'Conclusions: Governance beyond state strength', in Pierre, J. (ed) *Debating Governance*, Oxford University Press, Oxford, pp241–246

Porter, M. and van der Linde, C. (1995) 'Green and competitive: Ending the stalemate', *Harvard Business Review*, vol 73, no 5, pp120–133

Princen, T., Maniates, M. and Conca, K. (eds) (2002) *Confronting Consumption*, MIT Press, Cambridge, MA

Raman, S. (2003) 'The significance of political rationality in governance: Assessing the energizing of UK building regulation 1990–2002', PhD thesis, University of Pittsburgh

Schmidheiny, S. (1992) *Changing Course: A Global Business Perspective on Environment and Development*, MIT Press, Cambridge, MA

Schumacher, E. (1974) *Small is Beautiful: A Study of Economics as if People Mattered*, Abacus, London

Shove, E. (1997) 'Revealing the invisible: Sociology, energy and the environment', in Redclift, M. and Woodgate, G. (eds) *The International Handbook of Environmental Sociology*, Edward Elgar, Cheltenham, pp261–273

Shove, E. (2004a) 'Efficiency and consumption: Technology and practice', *Energy and Environment*, vol 15, no 6, pp1053–1065

Shove, E. (2004b) 'Sustainability, system innovation and the laundry', in Elzen, B.,
    Geels, F. and Green, K. (eds) *System Innovation and the Transition to Sustainability:*
    Theory, Evidence and Policy, Edward Elgar, Cheltenham, pp76–94
Simms, A., Moran, D. and Chowla, P. (2006) *The UK Interdependence Report: How*
    the World Sustains the Nation's Lifestyles and the Price it Pays, The New Economics
    Foundation with The Open University, London
Smith, A. (2003) 'Transforming technological regimes for sustainable development:
    A role for Appropriate Technology niches?', *Science and Public Policy*, vol 30, no 2,
    pp127–135
Teisman, G. and Edelenbos, J. (2004) 'Getting through the "twilight zone": Managing
    transitions through process-based, horizontal and interactive governance', in Elzen,
    B., Geels, F. and Green, K. (eds) *System Innovation and the Transition to*
    Sustainability: Theory, Evidence and Policy, Edward Elgar, Cheltenham, pp19–47
United Church of Christ Commission for Racial Justice (1987) *Toxic Wastes and Race*
    in the United States, UCCCRJ, New York
Veblen, T. (1899) *The Theory of the Leisure Class: An Economic Study of Institutions*,
    Macmillan, London
Wallace, D. (1995) *Environmental Policy and Industrial Innovation: Strategies in*
    Europe, the US and Japan, Earthscan, London
Walls, J., O'Riordan, T., Horlick-Jones, T. and Niewöhner, J. (2005) 'The meta-gover-
    nance of risk and new technologies: GM crops and mobile telephones', *Journal of*
    Risk Research, vol 8, pp635–661
Weale, A. (1992) *New Politics of Pollution*, Manchester University Press, Manchester
von Weizsäcker, E., Lovins, A. and Lovins, H (1997) *Factor Four: Doubling Wealth,*
    Halving Resource Use, Earthscan, London
Weinberg, A. (1998) 'The environmental justice debate: A commentary on methodolog-
    ical issues and practical concerns', *Sociological Forum*, vol 13, no 1, pp25–32
Zavestoski, S. (2001) 'Environmental concern and anti-consumerism in the self-
    concept: Do they share the same basis?' in Cohen, M. and Murphy, J. (eds)
    Exploring Sustainable Consumption: Environmental Policy and the Social Sciences,
    Elsevier, Oxford pp173–190

Section II
PEOPLE AND SUSTAINABILITY: APPRECIATING MULTIPLE IDENTITIES

Chapter 2

Decoding Governance: A Study of Purchase Processes for Sustainable Technologies

*Seonaidh McDonald, Panayiota Alevizou,
Caroline Oates, Kumju Hwang and William Young*

Introduction: The individual and sustainable technologies

In this chapter we will examine the relationships between sustainable technologies and the governance structures in which they are embedded. These structures and relationships involve government, business and civil society groups. We present data gathered through 81 semi-structured interviews with a wide range of green consumers about their purchase processes for technology-based products, such as fridges, washing machines and light bulbs. We will examine the data in order to uncover to what extent the governance practices of public institutions, private companies and civil society groups are evident in the purchase (or non-purchase) process. In other words we aim to discover how governance is being decoded by the end user (Du Gay et al, 1997).

Like the consumers cast as obstacles in energy efficiency research (Shove, 1997), consumers are often drawn in the governance debate as invisible, automatic in their responses, or passive in their acceptance of information and products. Our work seeks to question this view of the consumer by problematizing the relationship between production and consumption and examining the purchase process in minute detail. In this study we will therefore focus on individual members of the public. We do not, however, view the public as a homogenous mass, or as a group of 'market segments' that are more or less disposed to 'green products' such as might be presented in traditional marketing (e.g. Solomon, 2002). Rather we follow Peattie (1999) and view each individual as the author of a range of separate purchase decisions. These will add up to a portfolio of purchase verdicts which characterize that individual's consumption patterns. Within that portfolio there will be decisions that seem to be incompatible with other purchases or lifestyle choices. There could also be a heterogeneity of purchase processes and influences within the set of choices made by any one individual.

From this perspective, the link between sustainable technologies and sustainable consumption is a series of individual purchases. If people do not purchase products that incorporate sustainable technologies, then any reduced environmental impact or other innovation that designers and manufacturers intended can never be achieved. Individual purchases lie at the heart of the problem of sustainable development because they are at the crossover point between production and consumption practices. That is not to say that we view this relationship as a simple one. We see purchase processes as complex, socially embedded, situated acts. We believe that they are informed by (competing and/or paradoxical) lifestyle values, which an individual develops (implicitly and explicitly) and lives out (implicitly and explicitly) over time.

The individual and governance structures

From our individual-centric point of view, governance (and technology) can be seen as part of the social infrastructure and context of purchasing. As such, it impacts on individual purchases through a wide range of factors such as availability, variety and price. Private and public institutions and civil society groups all influence, directly and indirectly, the types, specifications and numbers of products that are manufactured and therefore available on the high street. If innovations are not subsidized (in the widest sense of the term) by government or championed by companies, then they will not be part of the spectrum of products that individuals can choose between. In this way, governance structures (private, public and societal) act as a sort of filter, which pre-selects a range of products that the consumer can then consider.

Furthermore, governance structures and relationships clearly have a significant impact on the ways in which social, ethical or environmental problems are framed, and therefore on the ways that they are understood by individual consumers. However, the multilayered and interdependent effects of governance also have a profound and implicit effect on the ways that consumers 'read' and understand technology products. That is not to say that we would regard the public as a group of individuals who are the passive recipients of government policy, corporate advertising or civil society group lobbying. The ways in which individuals engage with, and make sense of, the potential relationship between technology-based products, the purchase processes they might take part in and the global issues that concern them will be endlessly complex, changing and essentially unpredictable.

Individuals do have a degree of power within these governance structures. For example, their voting and purchasing acts may effect gradual changes in the operation of public and private institutions over time. Equally, they can use their membership of civil society groups to signal their views to public and private sector bodies in order to hasten change. This is not a uniform process, as green consumers may use their consumer power to back fair trade, or any number of other issues, whilst grey consumers are simultaneously trying to use theirs to influence price, for example. However, our units of analysis are real purchase processes that are located in the near past, and so this incremental process of change lies outside the scope of our problematic.

In terms of the perspectives on sustainability outlined at the start of this book (Murphy, this volume), our approach clearly fits within the environmental decision-making approach. However, our concern is not with inclusivity or participation in the explicit democratic processes of government, but with the implicit democratic processes of governance through consumption. Ours is a practical focus, which deals with the sub-structure, or wide end of democracy.

Method

This study is part of a wider project that aims to uncover a detailed picture of the consumer decision-making processes involved in the purchase of sustainable technologies. The work has taken a grounded approach to researching actual purchases of a wide range of products with a technological component, such as domestic white goods, energy tariffs, cars and light bulbs. For this study we conducted 81 semi-structured interviews with individuals who had recently purchased these products. Most of our sample were green consumers, although we also interviewed a number of grey consumers in order to compare and contrast the purchase experiences of these groups. Interviewees were recruited through a process of snowball sampling. This process was initiated by interviewing individuals contacted through a wide range of publications and organizations, including the *Ethical Consumer*, wholefood shops, Friends of the Earth, UK Quakers sustainability self-help group, Buddhist centres, organic vegetable box schemes and *Pure* magazine. The final sample contained a balanced mix of age, gender and socio-economic groups. In order to help consumers to articulate the relevant level of detail, laddering techniques were used (Gutman, 1982, 1987; Reynolds and Gutman, 1988). Each interview lasted around an hour and covered the purchase of two or more products, as well as a commentary on the individual's more routine weekly shopping habits.

There are two features of this micro focus that we view as particularly important for our research. The first is the level of detail that we elicit about the purchase process itself as well as its social context. This means that we do not view the purchase at the moment of sale, but see it as an indefinite process that may begin with the explicit search for information or the implicit echoing of family values, political views or advertising claims. We see the purchase act itself as socially situated and part of a developing lifestyle.

The other strength of this micro approach is that it deals with specific purchases. Hence we are not interested in asking participants to talk about future, hypothetical purchases, but rather about actual purchases they have been involved in. Thus we would like to signal the contrast between the sometimes conceptual and abstract view of 'technology' and 'sustainability' with our research into concrete and specific purchase decisions about those technologies, which play out as more or less sustainable patterns of consumption.

Based on the data, a number of different, inter-related analyses have been undertaken. For example, we have looked at how decision criteria are involved and evolved in the purchase process (Young et al, 2005), and how different kinds of information sources are used by consumers (Oates et al, 2005). In this chapter we present the results of an analysis of how different aspects of governance are manifest in the consumer practices and conceptualizations of purchases processes.

In line with our grounded approach we have examined the purchase narratives for evidence of governance concepts. Examples of this would include, for instance, where people discuss the effects of regulation (such as the European Union (EU) Energy Label), or aspects of corporate social responsibility (such as good or bad working conditions), or the influence of consumer groups (such as Soil Association labels). We have not asked our interviewees to reflect on governance issues, but simply asked them to tell us in detail about their (non)purchase processes. Therefore, if issues relating to significant governance debates are not present in the data, we might assume that either these notions are too deeply implicit to articulate, or that the artefacts discussed are silent on such matters. In this way, the research can be seen to be taking a grounded approach to the problem of whether or not governance is being decoded by green consumers. The outcome of this process is presented below.

Theoretical framework: Circuit of culture

The circuit of culture model has its roots in the work of Stuart Hall (1980) and his colleagues at the Centre for Contemporary Cultural Studies (Johnson, 1986). His encoding/decoding model was part of a movement towards poststructuralism in cultural studies. Hall used this model to conceptualize the processes that were encapsulated by watching television. The model is based on his insight that meaning is jointly socially constructed by both the 'author' and the 'reader' in a continuous circuit of moments of production, distribution and consumption of cultural objects (Du Gay et al, 1997). What this means is that an unread 'text' or object does not have a complete meaning until it has been consumed; that its meaning cannot be determined by its author alone. Meaning is not fixed in the sense that it remains the same over time, nor will it necessarily be understood in similar ways by different readers.

This approach has resonance with the notion of 'interpretive flexibility' that has been developed in the Technology Studies literature (Kline and Pinch, 1999). This raises the idea that an artefact can be 'read' differently by different social groups. However, a cultural analysis would extend this insight and contend that, due to the context dependent nature of the purchase process, the same artefact can be 'read' in different ways by the same consumer at different times. In fact, a green consumer may read an artefact in different ways at the same time as they struggle to make sense of competing cultural frames such as fair trade, resource use and anti-consumption values. That is not to say that no cultural consensus is ever reached about the meaning of an artefact, just that this process is never viewed as complete, apolitical or unproblematic. As Baudrillard (1998, p27) states: 'Few objects today are offered *alone*, without a context of objects which "speaks" them' [emphasis in original]. What we are investigating then is not a single, fixed or uncontested 'meaning' of governance activities. Rather, we hope to uncover some of the layers of interdependent influences that are gathered in the 'symbolism' (Murphy and Cohen, 2001) of technology products and the purchase processes that consumers engage with.

The circuit of culture model is interesting for our analysis of governance in the discourse of green consumers about their purchase of sustainable technologies. It allows us to separate the notion of the production (both physically and, more significantly, culturally) of an object (like a low-energy light bulb) in a cultural sense from the 'moment' of consumption of the meaning of that object (Burgess, 1990). In the analysis that follows, we will focus on the process of decoding and 'allow ourselves to be practically preoccupied with one moment' in the circuit of culture (Johnson, 1986, p284). We will analyse the detailed accounts of purchasing sustainable technologies that have surfaced in our work with green consumers in order to discover how (and whether) they are decoding the information relating to the governance for sustainability that is encoded in their (non)purchases.

In this analysis we are going to highlight the formal institutions (Neale, 1987), such as governments, companies and civil society groups. Elsewhere we consider more informal institutions (Oates et al, 2005) such as kinship groups, habits, routines, cultural values and social norms (Parto, 2005). Our analysis seeks evidence of several different scales of governance in the data and considers different levels of interrelation (Parto, 2005). In particular, we look for data that help us understand the decoding of:

- Business – Examples of corporate-level governance activities might include corporate social responsibility (CSR) initiatives like greener production, including energy and waste reduction or use of recycled materials, ethical labour conditions and other forms of social justice. These issues could be linked to the company as a whole, or to an individual product. As well as focusing on the production of the product, information may be decoded about the way that the product can be used (e.g. the Wash Right campaign) or disposed of (e.g. design for recyclability). There may also be evidence of industry-level governance initiatives that are being implemented across whole sectors like Fairtrade or Soil Association accreditation.
- Government – Here we may uncover local government actions such as waste systems or community education programmes. This category would also

include all the national government and EU policies, guidelines and regulations that target sustainability in some way. In the case of sustainable technologies, the EU Energy Label is a good example.
- Civil Society Groups – This might include evidence of ways in which different groups are trying to frame environmental or social issues and/or link them with the use of specific technologies (e.g. carbon emissions and car usage). Equally interesting is the information that civil society groups provide in the hope of mediating the relationship between the consumer and the marketplace (such as *Which?* magazine and the *Ethical Consumer* magazine).

There are a number of issues which cut across these three. For example, the EU Energy Label is at the same time a regulation that is imposed by supra-national government, an industry-wide scheme for white goods, a measure that the company uses to communicate the energy usage of a particular product and a measure advocated by *Which?* magazine for determining running costs. What we are trying to discover is whether there is any evidence of governance activities having an impact on the consumers' decision-making processes. Every product purchased (or not) can be viewed as the culmination of a variety of different governance processes. When people engage with the end products, do they 'read' the evidence of any of the governance processes, or do these remain invisible to the consumer?

Findings

In the following sections we shall consider how governance concepts are being decoded by consumers in relation to the three main stakeholder groups: Business, Civil Society and Government.

Business and governance

Perhaps the most interesting pattern that has surfaced in our data is the very different ways that consumers treat the purchase of technology-based products compared with their approach to weekly shopping. This is perhaps not surprising in itself: the marketing literature would characterize these as high- and low-involvement purchases, respectively (Hansen, 2005). However, what is very interesting for our research is that while consumers are quite discerning about the companies that they buy coffee or chocolate from, they do not take the same approach to decoding meanings about either the companies or the retailers that they purchase technology-based products from.

This is articulated in several ways. First, there is a group of individuals who treat these products groups in different ways but who do not see their behaviour as inconsistent, or in fact see it at all. For example, there are a number of consumers who are very concerned about the use of supermarkets because of the effect that they are having on supply chains and local producers. These concerns have led them to boycott supermarkets in favour of other outlets such as wholefood shops or local independent stores for their weekly food shopping. However, the same consumers make use of the large white-goods supermarket chains such as Comet and Curry's and do not apply the same level of social or ethical critique to these retail outlets when they are making purchases of technology-based products.

There is, however, a second group who treat the two product groups as 'legitimately' different. This group see, for example, that all white goods are produced overseas, by large multinationals in unknown but probably poor working conditions, and therefore any product and/or company is as bad as the next. Once they have made the decision to purchase a fridge they see themselves as helplessly bound to making an unethical purchase and simply make a decision based on another criterion, such as energy efficiency, instead.

> *...most cookers are made out of metal and glass so there is not a huge choice of materials...* (Interview 22)

> *...but from what I understand most electronic equipment is as bad as each other anyway...* (Interview 4)

> *I assumed, probably wrongly, that all manufacturers of consumer electrical goods are probably as bad as one another...* (Interview 64)

> *I don't think any of these electrical firms are ethical...* (Interview 80)

> *Electronic and electrical goods, very difficult I think partly because there is not a huge amount to choose between different manufactures...* (Interview 74)

> *...there seems to be so little ethical difference in a way between the suppliers ... that's why I made the decision on reliability and facilities...* (Interview 65)

These views are consistent with current thinking in the sustainable development literature, where people judge themselves, not on individual acts, but on a holistic picture of their lifestyle. Thus they do not worry about individual unsustainable products, as long as, on the whole, they are following the principles of sustainability in most aspects of their lives (Gilg et al, 2005). This also has resonance with Peattie's (1999) understanding of consumers as making a portfolio of purchase decisions that are highly context dependent and not necessarily consistent with each other.

The final group try to implement the green or ethical approaches that they take in buying fast-moving consumer goods (FMCG), such as foodstuffs, household cleaning products or toiletries, in their purchase processes for technology products. This group encounter enormous difficulties and are forced to make compromises due to the huge amount of research time, the availability of products, the cost of products or the non-existence of what they see as reliable information. For example, some of these consumers wish to buy second-hand appliances but then do not have information about the energy efficiency of the appliance and cannot select from a full range of brands, limiting their ability to select a more ethical manufacturer. This sort of compromise often sits heavily with the consumers, who are 'troubled' by the purchase process.

> *Well I am ashamed, I am a bit ashamed to say I bought a Creda so that didn't rate highest in* Ethical Consumer's *environmental list but the Consumer Association recommended it for various reasons in terms of efficiency and so on...* (Interview 69)

> *...although it is very difficult because you know every day you hear some bad news about some firms that you previously thought was ok and people who you shopped with for years or bought from and thought were alright and suddenly it seems they are the baddies and I think it is hard. Some firms seem to be good in one area and bad in another and I think if you are trying to do the right thing it is very confusing and takes up an awful lot of time and at the end of it you think well I am just one small person but I do think about it, well yes definitely...* (Interview 71)

> *Yes to an extent I suppose there are loads of different filters I would apply to purchasing and if I apply them all too strictly then I am not going to find anything at all.* (Interview 74)

> *Most of the bicycles are made in far eastern sweatshops and it's very hard to find a bicycle that's got any recycled parts to it. The only thing I have found so far is second hand again, and that's probably what I'll do, but I was trying to buy a new bicycle. It seemed impossible to find an environmentally and socially acceptable bicycle. Which is quite odd because it's a 'green, cycling to work' thing.* (Interview 4)

Corporate social responsibility initiatives

In the purchase processes of the consumers we interviewed some brands were seen as safeguards against unethical practices and were used as shortcuts to dealing with complex global issues. The most frequent example of this in our data is the Co-operative Bank. In sustainable technologies there were perceptions of some German brands as environmentally superior. Sometimes this decoding was done on the basis of a national stereotype without any specific information about the company or whether the product was actually made in Germany.

> *I would imagine a German company would be as good as any because I know that the legal system in Germany is much tougher than ours on pollution...* (Interview 64)

> *Bosch probably have a better and more developed environmental policy as do most of the German manufacturers as compared to the American ones or the Italian ones...* (Interview 74)

These sorts of associations with country-of-origin are not uncommon and have been discussed in the marketing literature (Liefield, 2004).

Lack of corporate social responsibility

Where concrete ideas about CSR were being decoded, we found that these were, more often than not, negative messages. Often the company name was used as a 'brand' to dismiss products. For example,

> *...if someone is in a car and I'm in the car with them I won't let them fill up in 'Esso'...* (Interview 6)

> *I don't buy named brands like I would never buy Nike or anything; I would kill myself first...* (Interview 72)

However, sometimes consumers had decoded specific meanings from brands:

> *...Coca-cola particularly recently hearing about their issues like water use in India and also links to death squads in Columbia so I have recently you know I have more recently found out about that we avoid Coca-cola products...* (Interview 70)

> *...avoid Marks & Spencers because at the moment they are it is not because they are...it is not that they are bad alone but that they support the Israeli invasion of Palestine so until that ends even though I actually really like Marks & Spencers products and things I won't shop there just from a personal and political perspective...* (Interview 72)

Still other consumers identify an issue and then evaluate all brands on a single criterion. For example,

> *I would certainly boycott companies or corporations which I know for example might fund animal experimentation...* (Interview 78)

> *...but I try to avoid companies that I know have supported President Bush and I try to avoid things that I know come from Israel...* (Interview 80)

Where we did find evidence that CSR activities were being decoded in the purchase process for technology products or FMCGs, we found that it was the company that was being judged to be 'good' or 'bad' and not the individual products. This has interesting implications for companies who seek to launch 'green' products alongside their more established 'grey' counterparts (e.g. Nestlé's launch of a Fairtrade coffee).

Lack of information on CSR activity

The most common response in our data pertaining to CSR was about how little information is available on the firms involved in producing technology products. Several of our respondents described looking for this kind of information but not being able to find any, or not knowing how to go about finding it.

> ...*for example with cleaning products it's very easy to find environmental alternatives to the main brands that aren't environmental. But obviously with technological products it's not so easy to find...* (Interview 14)

> ...*[I] would like to do things like get a green or environmentally friendly energy and perhaps furniture that used you know that were good green companies as well. I don't know how I would find those or source those kind of companies...* (Interview 77)

> ...*bigger purchases like for the house as well such as furniture, kitchens, bathrooms things like that there is very little information you can make a judgement on the ethics of the company that supply those things...* (Interview 73)

> ...*so we asked the staff and they weren't aware in B&Q whether it was FSC (Forest Stewardship Council) or not and in the end we didn't buy anything...* (Interview 41)

> *I have been interested in ethical consumerism for as long as I can remember really but I wasn't aware that there were any ethical ratings for things like that for appliances.* (Interview 23)

Civil society groups and governance

For many consumers, the most reliable guide to help them make sense of which companies are 'good' is the *Ethical Consumer*, which is a magazine produced by the consumer group the Ethical Consumer Research Association. Another trusted source of reference for consumers is *Which?* magazine, published by the Consumers' Association, which is an independent charity. A number of consumers reported using either or both of these sources:

> ...*according to the* Ethical Consumer *magazine Nokia have a better ethical record than others and I bought a Nokia mobile phone.* (Interview 79)

> ...*and we actually went for a Bosch which was one of the less bad choices from* Ethical Consumer... (Interview 74)

...but it was Ethical Consumer *that I would rely on in making my decisions...* (Interview 45)

One of the starting points was that we have the Which? *magazine and my wife likes to read that so we use that as a sort of the starting point.* (Interview 12)

Just because I trust them [referring to the Which? *Magazine] to be independent and to look at various aspects of for example with the washing machine, the noise level, the durability, the energy usage and the performance. If they've tested it against other machine they will give an impartial view, which is the best...* (Interview 14)

I think largely...it is hard to remember I think largely based on the Which? *magazine report which narrowed it down to only a couple of models and then I was looking at the price on those models and the factors we talked about before their reliability and efficiency and everything...* (Interview 75)

Well we started basically from an Ethical Consumer *point of view and we had gone around to a few shops like the big superstores and asked questions and then we kind of checked online at a few sites, we did look at* Which? *magazine kind of to see comments from them as well so we kind of got going from that and kind of went from there so it was kind of accumulating a lot of things...* (Interview 72)

Although both of these associations have made many of their reports available online, the consumers that we interviewed still seemed to be using the physical versions of these publications available through friends, family or local libraries. This reliance on print-based media is perhaps surprising in this electronic age.

A number of other civil society groups also represent a trustworthy source of information for green consumers:

I think it may well have been Friends of the Earth, who provided the information, probably set out a schedule of the companies and which were the best and which were the most satisfactory and I probably just went ahead from there. In fact I'm pretty sure that's what happened... (Interview 35)

Well again we get The Ecologist, *we get* The Green Party's *information, we get newsletters from Greenpeace and Friends of the Earth and you know yeah just and talking to friends, yeah...* (Interview 49)

I suppose Friends of the Earth is a source of information that I would well recommend I think it would be quite trustworthy... (Interview 48)

> *I did consult Friends of the Earth to ask them if I should consider diesel and they told me that as far as second-hand cars went it wasn't really going to make much difference to the environment...* (Interview 55)

> *I would normally go to Friends of the Earth or Greenpeace. I go to the website usually and if I couldn't find what I was after I would ring them up...* (Interview 55)

Government and governance

The only really visible element of this stakeholder group is at EU level. The EU Energy Label indicates the power consumption of an appliance (in kilowatt hours) under standard running conditions. The EU Energy Label rates appliances from A (most efficient) to G (least efficient) and provides additional appliance-performance information. The energy efficiency label must, by law, be shown on all fridges, freezers, fridge freezers, washer driers and dishwashers, and on light-bulb packaging.

> *I suppose with a washing machine you do look at the star rating don't you, you do look at the efficiency rating...* (Interview 16)

> *Looking at a fridge for example I would first eliminate anything that was not an A rated...* (Interview 74)

> *So I used the EU rating [for buying a washing machine]. Yes so I just went looking at all the panels stuck to the front and that was part of my basis for a decision. It was a big part of my basis for a decision...* (Interview 32)

Of all the information about sustainability, the EU Energy Label was the most consistently and universally decoded. This rating scheme is unquestioned by even the most cynical of our respondents. It is widely noticed, and it is 'understood' as apolitical and unproblematic. It has made a significant impact on the purchase of technology-based products for a wide range of different kinds of green consumers. The success of this scheme can be likened to the levels of trust that people equate with the Fairtrade and Soil Association labels on foodstuffs. In contrast, schemes such as the EU Eco-label (which often appears within the EU Energy Label) go completely undecoded by consumers.

On the other hand, the success of the EU Energy Label, and the way in which it is decoded, could be argued to lead to an overly simplistic framing of energy use as an issue. Since most consumers seem to get no further in their decoding of the label than 'A=good', it could be seen as obscuring the complexity (and politics) of measuring energy use for appliances. So although consumers using the label to guide their choices will select appliances that consume less energy in their day-to-day use, they do not know how much energy the appliance uses, how much was used in its manufacture or how much was used in its distribution, or even which of these aspects the A rating actually refers to.

Further, it is interesting to note that although the use of the EU Energy Label is enshrined in law, it is not being decoded by consumers as an EU regulation. Instead, it is being read in terms of CSR as either the result of the manufacturer's efforts to produce a better, more efficient product, or as an information source that has been provided by the retailer.

Discussion and conclusions

Shortcuts to making sense of sustainability

What our research shows is that sustainable technologies are products that are embedded in multilevel, inter-related, and sometimes paradoxical, social complexities. Consumers appear to deal with this by tackling the decoding through a number of different strategies.

Many of the individuals in our study sought to simplify the problem by relying on a *third party* that they trust to unpick the issues on their behalf. In this case, the most common third parties were the *Ethical Consumer* or *Which?* magazines. Others approached the task of simplification by privileging particular *brands* (such as Bosch or Míele) or groups of brands (such as German manufacturers). A third strategy was to identify the most important sustainability issue for them personally and then make their choices based on a *single criterion*. As discussed above, a common choice is energy efficiency, based on the very successful EU Energy Label. A slightly more sophisticated version of this response was where consumers did not confine their searches to one issue but explicitly *prioritized one aspect* of sustainability. We also found that some consumers employ a mixture of these approaches.

What is interesting here is that, on the whole, the consumer reaction to the complexity of the problem of sustainable consumption is to try one or more methods of (conceptual) simplification. This is a natural response, but a cultural analysis highlights the fact that these solutions are themselves framed by governance activities. Some of the examples discussed above show consumers trying to extend the familiar recipes for short cuts developed by the grey consumer (e.g. brand) to a more complex, important and dynamic problem. Of course brand (as a concept) can be understood to be a culturally constructed designator in itself. What is missing here is an appreciation of the relationship between the ways in which governance structures and relationships have influenced the framing of the 'problems' and 'issues' that the consumers see in the first place. The EU Energy Label, for example, is a product of inter-related and media-brokered governance activities which have, over time, identified domestic energy use as: a) problematic; b) addressable; c) the responsibility of the individual household. The governance structures are doing more than generating policy to address issues. Here we can see how they are influencing the issues, the terminology, the tools and approaches as well as the possibilities of how, why and by whom they might be solved. Our research shows that the consumers who grapple with this level of governance influence are few and far between.

Contrast with FMCG behaviour

By far the most common response to the difficulty of making sense of sustainability, even amongst consumers who were actively engaging with the problems of sustainability in other product groups, such as FMCG, was to apply different criteria to the purchase of sustainable technologies. These findings confirm Peattie's (1999) conception of green purchase processes as inconsistent and context specific. Our research certainly suggests that consumers' approaches to purchase processes vary significantly according to product type. This kind of behaviour has also been observed in studies of tourism consumption, where green consumers do not necessarily become green travellers (Watkins, 1994; Wearing et al, 2002). As indicated above, sometimes a different approach is taken knowingly by green consumers, but it was equally likely that consumers subconsciously chose different purchase criteria.

This curious situation can in part be explained by the lack of information that can be readily decoded that is perceived to be available to consumers. The decoding process has broken down because of two competing information problems. The first decoding problem is that in fact there is an endless amount of information about a huge range of competing or even conflicting sustainability issues. However, the second problem is that consumers do not know how to begin to decode this information for technology-based products. In other words, even if consumers do know how and where to obtain information on all the aspects of sustainability that they feel are pertinent, they do not know how to go about evaluating this information.

The success of the EU Energy Label is particularly interesting. This is information which is presented as 'fact' in a 'standardized' format and reduced to a single scale that is displayed on every product. This information has been decoded in very similar ways by all our interviewees. Further, it remains unquestioned even by the most cynical green consumers. As such, it has been decoded in a way that is similar to the decoding of the Fairtrade or the Soil Association symbols for FMCG. More research is needed to understand whether the success of the EU Energy Label is due to its simplicity, its authoritativeness or just the fact that it is ubiquitous for white goods.

Implications for governance

On the whole, we have found that the governance activities of public and private sector institutions are not really having an impact on the purchase of sustainable technologies. Representations of civil society groups such as the *Ethical Consumer* magazine seem to be better trusted by the public than either of these two groups. However, the same consumers who regularly seek out information about working conditions for the production of the food and clothing products that they buy are apt to ignore the production processes, distribution networks and retailers of their white good purchases. The ways in which other goods and services are 'read' by green consumers, and the success of the EU Energy Label, both suggest that consumers are willing and able to tackle the complex problems of sustainability as part of their purchasing decisions. This points to the relative invisibility of governance issues uncovered here being the result of a lack of encoding by the formal institutions rather than a lack of decoding by individuals.

Whilst some positive messages about CSR are being decoded during the purchase process, much of what we have found is about bad practices, actual or political. Even less represented in the discourses of green consumers about their technology purchases are the governance activities of local authorities, national government or retailers.

What we can see, however, is that governance structures are certainly having an effect on how sustainability is being framed by members of the public. The problems that are being privileged by many of our respondents are concerned with energy consumption. For white goods, this means an A rating on the EU Energy Label is preferred, and for cars this translates into fuel efficiency. This is interesting as this is a measure that for some equates to reduced financial running costs rather than increased environmental benefits per se. In our interviews we also found discourse about the ethical and social elements of sustainability, although this was mostly in the context of FMCGs rather than sustainable technologies. On the other hand, we found hardly any mention of production waste, distribution resources or disposal practices for any product type. It seems that the issues that the public are attracted to for sustainable technologies are the ones that are a matter of individual (rather than corporate) responsibility: they can be reduced to an 'objective' measure and addressed through technological solutions.

References

Baudrillard, J. (1998) *The Consumer Society: Myths and Structures*, Sage, London

Burgess, J. (1990) 'The production and consumption of environmental meanings in the mass media: A research agenda for the 1990s', *Transactions of the Institute of British Geographers*, vol 15, pp139–161

Du Gay, P., Hall, S., Janes, L., Mackay, H. and Negus, K. (1997) *Doing Cultural Studies: The Story of the Sony Walkman*, Sage, London

Gilg, A., Barr, S. and Ford, N. (2005) 'Green consumption or sustainable lifestyle? Identifying the sustainable consumer', *Futures*, vol 37, pp481–504

Gutman, J. (1982) 'A means-end chain model based on consumer categorization processes', *Journal of Marketing*, vol 46, pp60–72

Gutman, J. (1987) 'Means-end chains as goal hierarchies', *Psychology and Marketing*, vol 14, no 6, pp545–560

Hall, S. (1980) 'Encoding/decoding', in Hall, S., Hobson, D., Lowe, A. and Willis, P. (eds) *Culture, Media, Language*, Hutchison, London

Hansen, T. (2005) 'Perspectives on consumer decision making: An integrated approach', *Journal of Consumer Behaviour*, vol 4, no 6, pp420–437

Johnson, R. (1986) 'The story so far: And further transformations?' in Punter, D. (ed) *Introduction to Contemporary Cultural Studies*, Longman, London, pp277–313

Kline, R. and Pinch, T. (1999) 'The social construction of technology', in MacKenzie, D. and Wajcman, J. (eds) *The Social Shaping of Technology*, Open University Press, Maidenhead, pp113–115

Liefield, J. P. (2004) 'Consumer knowledge and use of country-of-origin information at the point of purchase', *Journal of Consumer Behaviour*, vol 4, no 2, pp85–96

Murphy, J. and Cohen, M. (2001) 'Sustainable consumption: Environmental policy and the social sciences', in Cohen, M. and Murphy, J. (eds) *Exploring Sustainable Consumption: Environmental Policy and the Social Sciences*, Elsevier, London, pp225–240

Neale, W. C. (1987) 'Institutions', *Journal of Economic Issues*, vol 21, no 3, pp1177–1206

Oates, C. J., McDonald, S., Young, C. W. and Hwang, K. (2005) 'Marketing sustainability: Use of information sources and degrees of voluntary simplicity', Proceedings of the Academy of Marketing, 5–7 July, Dublin Institute of Technology

Parto, S. (2005) 'Economic activity and institutions: Taking stock', *Journal of Economic Issues*, vol 39, no 1, pp21–52

Peattie K. (1999) 'Trappings versus substance in the greening of marketing planning', *Journal of Strategic Marketing*, vol 7, pp131–148

Reynolds, T. J. and Gutman, J. (1988) 'Laddering theory, methods, analysis and interpretation', *Journal of Advertising Research*, vol 28, no 1, pp11–31

Shove, E. (1997) 'Revealing the invisible: Sociology, energy and the environment', in Redclift, M. and Woodgate, G. (eds) *The International Handbook of Environmental Sociology*, Edward Elgar, Cheltenham, pp261–273

Solomon, M. R. (2002) *Consumer Behaviour: Buying, Having and Being*, Prentice Hall, New Jersey

Watkins, E. (1994) 'Do guests want green hotels?', *Lodging Hospitality*, vol 50, no 4, pp70–72

Wearing, S., Cynn, S., Ponting, J. and McDonald, M. (2002) 'Converting environmental concern into ecotourism purchases: A qualitative evaluation of international backpackers in Australia', *Journal of Ecotourism*, vol 1, no 2/3, pp133–148

Young, C. W., Hwang, K., McDonald, S. and Oates, C. J. (2005) 'Decision making for sustainable consumption', Proceedings of the International Sustainable Development Conference, 6–8 June, Finlandia Hall, Helsinki

Chapter 3

People Centred Eco-Design: Consumer Adoption and Use of Low and Zero Carbon Products and Systems

Robin Roy, Sally Caird and Stephen Potter

Background

In order to address the problem of climate change, and meet its sustainable development objectives, the UK government set a challenging long-term target of reducing the UK's carbon emissions by 60 per cent from their 1990 levels by 2050 (Royal Commision on Environmental Pollution (RCEP), 2000; Department of Trade and Industry (DTI), 2003). Although the government is struggling to meet its interim target of a 20 per cent reduction in emissions by 2010, it is committed at least to satisfy its obligations under the Kyoto Protocol of a 12.5 per cent reduction in greenhouse gas emissions between 2008 and 2012.

The development and rapid adoption of 'low and zero carbon' (LZC) consumer products and systems, together with improving the energy efficiency of the existing housing stock and the construction of energy-efficient new homes, including those with household-level micro energy-generation technologies, are key elements of the government's carbon reduction strategy. Given that homes account for 30 per cent of the energy consumption and 28 per cent of total UK carbon dioxide emissions, a focus on the domestic sector is hardly surprising (DTI, 2004).

Many energy-efficient, low-carbon and some renewable energy zero-carbon products and systems are available for domestic use. They range from products based on established technologies, such as cavity wall insulation, compact fluorescent lamps (CFLs), condensing boilers and solar water heating, to more innovative technologies such as light-emitting-diode (LED) lamps, micro combined heat and power (CHP), micro wind turbines and domestic photovoltaic (PV) systems. However, consumer adoption of most LZC products/systems has been slow. The improvements in the energy efficiency of products, buildings and systems that have taken place during the past decade have been driven mainly by regulation, such as EU energy labelling of domestic appliances and tightening UK building regulations. The design and construction of LZC eco-housing, such as the Beddington Zero Energy Development (BedZED) scheme in South London and the Hockerton Housing Project in Nottinghamshire, while showing what can be achieved, remain as largely experimental 'green niches' created by highly committed individuals and organizations (see Smith in this volume).

One factor in the slow take-up of LZC products/systems by mainstream consumers is that often they have been designed without taking sufficient account of user requirements – that is without a people-centred approach to design. They tend to be viewed by designers and policy makers as purely functional, technical devices, without sufficient regard for their aesthetic and ergonomic design and brand image, which can have a crucial role in adoption and effective use. More generally, as Jackson (2005, p6) says, '... material goods are important to us, not just for their functional uses, but because they play vital symbolic roles in our lives'.

This narrow view of LZC products/systems is partially explained by the dominance of a techno-centric model of innovation that assumes that consumers are rational decision makers who will adopt these goods once they become aware of their environmental and money-saving benefits. For example, replacing a 100-watt light bulb with a 20-watt CFL costing £6 should save over £40 in electricity bills and replacement light bulbs over its life, as well as offering environmental benefits. Rational consumers would therefore be expected to adopt CFLs in large numbers. Nevertheless, CFLs have taken many years to achieve only limited penetration into UK homes, even when subsidized to reduce their purchase price. This appears to be because of issues such as their size and shape, incompatibility with existing light fittings, warm-up time and the quality of their light compared to incandescent light bulbs. Even though manufacturers have addressed some of these issues by introducing smaller, conventionally shaped electronically controlled CFLs, consumers are taking a long time to become aware of the new designs, partly because of poor communications and retail availability (Environmental Change Institute (ECI), 2001).

Factors influencing adoption of LZC products and systems

In-depth studies of purchase decisions reveal that green consumers attempt to consider a web of technical, financial, practical, environmental and, occasionally, ethical criteria when deciding to buy an energy consuming product, such as a refrigerator or washing machine. However, because of the difficulty of balancing and trading off the criteria, such consumers are often forced to decide on the basis of their own functional and symbolic requirements, aided by the most easily understood indicator of environmental performance – the EU Energy Label (see McDonald et al in this volume). Likewise, green pioneers apply a combination of practical requirements and environmental criteria when deciding whether to adopt innovative low-carbon products or systems. A German study of early adopters of fuel-cell micro CHP systems for home heating and electricity generation found that although motivated by technical interest, some environmental consciousness (though not in any radical sense) and the pioneering aspect of testing a new technology, they were also concerned with cost-effectiveness, reliability and user friendliness (Fischer, 2004, p13). On the other hand, surveys of consumers who had adopted simple energy-saving measures such as loft and cavity wall insulation gave the main reason as saving money, with only 3 per cent citing the environment as their main motivation (Central Office of Information (COI), 2001, p7).

The factors influencing adoption thus differ for different LZC products and systems. Cavity wall insulation, for instance, is a purely functional product for reducing heat loss and thus saving money, whereas double glazing fulfils several other functions such as adding comfort and improving the visual appearance and value of a home. For yet other products (e.g. refrigerators or cars), energy efficiency is one of a variety of features that different people may value. Designers and manufacturers of such products fully recognize that environmental factors generally only enter consumer purchasing decisions after product performance, quality, reliability and value for money criteria are satisfied (Roy et al 1998, pp268–269). As Volvo's environmental advisor pithily observed, customers for its cars 'tend to rate environmental impact one below the CD player' (Stathers, 2004, p49).

The income and socio-economic status of potential adopters are also important factors. For example, the study of fuel-cell micro CHP adoption found that the pioneer adopters of this experimental technology were mainly older, technically educated males with their own homes, from middle class populations and with a good income. Likewise, most German adopters of solar water heating and domestic photovoltaic (PV) systems were well-educated professionals interested in technology (Fischer, 2004, p7). Adopters of loft or cavity wall insulation, on the other hand, include families or pensioners on low incomes, benefiting from a subsidized energy-saving scheme.

A third factor influencing adoption is the communication sources people are exposed to. The UK has a network of Energy Efficiency Advice Centres (EEACs) that provide official information and advice to the public on home insulation, and energy-efficient heating and lighting. Surveys show that people who have contacted the EEACs install nearly double the number of energy-saving measures as the general UK population (COI, 2001, pp7, 21). People who contacted the Building Research Establishment for information on, and grants for, solar water heating under the government's 'Clear Skies' renewable energy support programme were likely to proceed to installation (Solar Trade

Association (STA), 2005). Interpersonal communications are also important. For example, adopters of solar water heating in the US are often found in clusters, since neighbours observe and discuss the costs and benefits of installing this technology (Rogers, 2003, p16).

What all this indicates is that consumer adoption of LZC products/systems is not a straightforward, rational matter of saving money or the environment, but is influenced by a complex network of factors that vary for different product types, socio-economic groups and communication sources.

Factors influencing use of LZC products and systems

However, even if people are persuaded to adopt LZC products/systems, this is not enough. To actually reduce carbon emissions, consumers have both to *choose* products that use less energy than the ones they replace and *use* them effectively. There are three aspects of consumer behaviour that can reduce the energy- and carbon-saving potential of LZC products.

First, it is recognized that for many products, people are continually trading up. The savings from greater energy efficiency are partly or fully cancelled out by consumers buying more goods (e.g. several television sets per household) and choosing larger, more powerful, more feature-laden models. Thus, Boardman (2004, p14) makes the following comment on the outcome of several years experience of energy labelling and minimum efficiency standards for refrigerators and freezers:

> *The substantial improvements in energy efficiency have been absorbed into more and larger products. At some stage, society needs to recognise that ever-higher standards of living are threatening our ability to limit climate change and, therefore, reducing our future quality of life.*

So, while regulations such as the EU's energy labelling of domestic appliances have stimulated manufacturers to produce, and consumers to buy, energy-efficient models, they fail to address the 'rebound' or 'take-back' effect from the increased consumption of such goods.

Second, even if adopted, these supposedly LZC products/systems may not be used as intended. For example, many people fail to understand, or could not be bothered with, controls such as thermostatic radiator valves (TRVs) or central heating programmers. This is estimated to forego large amounts of energy savings per year (Market Transformation Programme, 2005, p36). In the case of gas-powered micro CHP, although laboratory tests indicate that the units should reduce carbon emissions compared to a condensing boiler and grid-supplied electricity, a programme of field trials is underway to see if the efficiencies are realized in actual domestic use. Early results from 31 households indicate micro CHP performance is not as encouraging as had been hoped. About a third of the installations appear to reduce emissions and about a third increase them, with the remainder showing no discernable difference. It seems likely that this is due to the intermittent heat demand of real households, which reduces efficiency of the units (Carbon Trust, 2005, pp1, 6). And even if low-carbon products are used correctly there may be further rebound effects, such as people leaving energy-efficient heating and lighting on for longer, because running costs are lower.

Third, some consumers may reject LZC products or systems after trying them out. Rejection is more likely if LZC products or systems are imposed rather than actively chosen by the householders concerned (Chappells et al, 2000), or if items are low-cost, such as CFLs.

Rebound effects, inappropriate or sub-optimal use, and rejection of energy-efficient products/systems means that merely getting people initially to adopt LZC products or systems does not guarantee a reduction in energy use or carbon emissions. Boardman (2004, p3) comments:

> *In reality, many consumers choose ... a mixture of a higher stan-dard of living and energy conservation. That is why the level of energy that will be conserved as a result of an energy efficiency improvement requires careful analysis if it is to be successfully predicted.*

Such predictions, however, are very difficult to make given that, as Boardman admits, little is known about how people actually use low-carbon products after they have adopted them.

Those who have investigated consumer behaviour towards the environment generally do not view people's actions as deliberately obstructive of attempts to save energy. Indeed, the behaviour often arises for quite practical reasons; for example, tenants of passive solar housing schemes closing curtains over their large south-facing windows to prevent their carpets fading or the neighbours looking in, and people leaving lights on for safety or security. More fundamen-tally, sociologists have pointed out that the behaviour is often the result of practices that have become 'normal' or embedded for particular social groups given prevailing values, available technology and institutional arrangements. For example, Hand et al (2003, pp13, 17) discuss the emergence in Britain of the habitual practice of daily, or twice daily, (power) showering, using more energy and water than the traditional once or twice weekly bath, as the result of a mix of technical change, practical, social, cultural and psychological factors. People may also be 'locked' into particular patterns of consumption because of the demands of, for example, family or job (Jackson, 2005, p6). The desire for, and expectation of, ever improving comfort and convenience, coupled with demands of an increasing pace of life, are very powerful drivers of increas-ing energy use (Shove, 2003).

Within this social context of rising demands and 'lock-in' are the practical attempts to understand and change energy consumption behaviour. The Association for the Conservation of Energy (ACE), for instance, studied tenant behaviour in housing association homes that had recently been subject to energy efficiency improvements. A quarter of the households used their heating system in an optimally efficient manner, a half used their systems reasonably efficiently given their household circumstances, while another quarter, especially the unemployed and those suffering from ill-health, used their heating inefficiently. An indicator of energy-efficient behaviour was general energy awareness, such as knowing whether their appliances had energy labels, while a specific influence was the location of thermostat, which was more likely to result in energy-efficient behaviour when positioned in the living room rather than elsewhere (ACE, 2004, pp38–40). A major survey for the UK network of EEACs showed that giving consumers energy-saving advice changed behaviour in over 40 per cent of households, resulting in reduced energy consumption and carbon emissions. This was mainly because, when given advice, many consumers use heating and lighting more economically to save money. The amounts of energy and carbon saved, however, were only small (COI, 2001, pp33–35).

The often relatively limited effect of energy saving programmes is at least partly due to their dependence on the rational techno-economic model of consumer behaviour mentioned above. Some qualitative research for the Sustainable Development Commission and the National Consumer Council with several groups of consumers reveals a potentially more promising approach in which the symbolic role of the LZC experience is recognized. This found that actively adopting - or as a housing association tenant being provided with – well-designed, innovative LZC technologies, such as solar water heating, mini wind turbines and heat pumps helped to positively change attitudes and behaviour towards the use of energy.

> *It seems that micro-generation provides a tangible hook to engage householders emotionally with the issue of energy use... Householders described the sheer pleasure of creation and self-sufficiency: 'It's like growing your own vegetables' was one of the often cited parallels.* (Sustainable Consumption Roundtable (SCR), 2005, p7)

People's behaviour in choosing and using LZC products/systems thus depends on a complex set of factors, including their circumstances and constraints, embedded habits, desire for increasing levels of comfort and convenience, awareness of information about saving energy, and the design of the products and systems themselves.

Demand- or supply-led policies?

It is clear that persuading consumers to adopt LZC products/systems and use them in a manner that saves energy faces considerable difficulties. UK (and EU) household carbon reduction policy is therefore mainly *supply* led, with the problem framed as one of technological change rather than that of reducing consumption. This is seen as posing far fewer governance problems than trying to change consumer behaviour. Such supply-led policies focus on energy technology research and development (R&D) support, regulation (e.g. tighter building regulations), energy policies on fuel switching (e.g. to renewable energy or nuclear power), and encouraging manufacturers and suppliers to develop technical solutions.

On the *demand* side the main strategy is to provide consumers with information and advice about LZC products and systems, via the UK network of EEACs, for example, supported by targeted grants and subsidies for measures like loft and cavity wall insulation and domestic PV systems, and better training (e.g. of heating engineers). However, there is an institutional reluctance to go any further by investigating, let alone attempting to influence, how different people's needs, desires and wishes and lifestyles affect the adoption and use of LZC products/systems, or to involve users in their design.

The people-centred eco-design research project

Research by the Open University Design Innovation Group aims to fill some of the gaps by providing information that could help manufacturers design more user-friendly and attractive LZC products/systems by identifying what people want from these goods and how they choose and experience them, and to help governments to develop more effective policies for household carbon reduction. Drawing on our strengths in design and innovation, the research investigates key influencing factors on the total process of adoption and subsequent experience of using LZC products/systems. This includes established products, such as home insulation, which the UK government's 2003 Energy White Paper identifies as having a significant role in reducing carbon emissions up to 2010, and new technologies that are likely to have a significant role up to 2020, such as solar water heating (DTI, 2003, p33).

In attempting to achieve actual reductions in carbon emissions, it is important not to fall into the trap of viewing the task simply as one of stimulating 'drivers' and reducing 'barriers' to the widespread adoption and effective use of LZC products/systems. Guy and Shove (2000, p64) regard a focus on drivers and barriers as far too simplistic. As we have seen, the adoption and use of LZC products does not just involve the autonomous decisions of individuals and households, but is influenced by the social contexts of those decisions.

Nevertheless, in our research we are not attempting to identify LZC products or policies that depend on major changes in people's lifestyles. While it is recognized that such changes are needed in the longer term to move towards environmental sustainability (Jackson and Michaelis, 2003, p4), in the short to medium term more widespread adoption of LZC products/systems, and any behavioural changes needed to choose and use them effectively, is a more realistic aim. As Harper (2000, p2) says:

> the deep green perspective is so much at variance with the main thrust of modern culture that it would take rather a long time for it to make a serious difference... We need technology as a short-term holding operation to allow the more fundamental cultural changes to take root and become effective.

While it may be argued that a focus on technical solutions may delay or undermine attempts to address the more difficult issue of unsustainable consumption, the two are related. The SCR research mentioned above showed that by adopting innovative technologies, such as solar water heating and micro wind power, people's general awareness of energy consumption improved and some behavioural changes followed. This does not mean that technical solutions are sufficient, but combined with regulation and other measures they can provide a politically realistic bridge to more fundamental change.

Models of product adoption and diffusion

We have seen that in order to identify key factors influencing the adoption and use of LZC products/systems it is necessary to consider the total decision-making process, together with the social, economic and technical context in which the process takes place. Rogers (2003) provides a useful model of the total process of an individual's or social group's decisions to adopt, use, confirm or reject an innovation. Figure 3.1 shows a modified version of the model.

In this project, we aim to identify and compare the key influencing factors on the adoption and effective use of LZC products by grouping the products and users according to their position along the stages of the innovation-decision process. Our categories (and their relation to Rogers' model) are as follows:

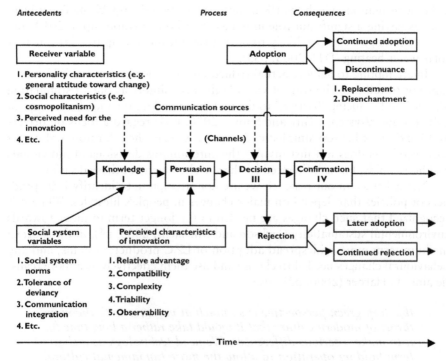

Source: University of Twente, based on Rogers (2003, p170)

Figure 3.1 *Rogers' model of the innovation-decision process*

- *Potential adopters*: people who are seriously considering purchasing or adopting a LZC product or system (Knowledge/Persuasion).
- *Non-adopters*: people who have seriously considered purchasing or adopting a LZC product or system, but have decided against (Decision/Rejection).
- *Adopter-users*: people who have purchased or acquired and continue to use a LZC product or system (Decision/Adoption). Adopter-users can be subdivided into *engaged-users*, who realize most or all of the environmental benefits (not covered in Rogers' model, but is related to Confirmation), and *non-engaged-users*, who continue to be users but their behaviour reduces or eliminates the environmental benefits. (Rebound effects are not covered in Rogers' model.)
- *Reject-users*: people who have purchased or acquired, but subsequently stopped using a LZC product or system (Adoption/Discontinuance).

Rogers (2003, pp15–16) identifies five perceived characteristics of an innovation that affects its rate of adoption:

1 *Relative advantage* (over existing products, in terms of perceived economic benefit, convenience, satisfaction and/or status giving).
2 *Compatibility* (with potential adopters' values and needs and with existing ideas and products).
3 *Complexity* (how difficult the innovation is to understand and use).
4 *Trialability* (whether the innovation can be tried out on a limited basis).
5 *Observability* (how visible adopting the innovation is to others).

We could have used Rogers' innovation characteristics to model the product-related factors influencing the adoption and use of LZC products/systems. However, Rogers' model was developed largely to explain the rate of adoption of agricultural and other innovations rather than consumer adoption of ecological products. Also, Rogers mixes technical, economic, sociological and psychological factors in his list of innovation characteristics that we wished to disentangle.

Hence, we decided to use the properties of objects identified by Murphy and Cohen (2001, pp230–231) to help explain consumer behaviour in relation to the consumption of sustainable goods and services. Murphy and Cohen's properties of objects are: *usefulness* (assuming that in purchase decisions the consumer will focus on utility factors such as performance, ease of use, safety, reliability and energy efficiency of the object, relative to other products within a given price bracket); *interconnectedness* (recognizing that in practice objects are purchased and used in relation to a wide variety of other products and services); and *symbolism* (including factors such as the image, brand, appearance and novelty of the object, in turn dependent on peer group influences and the goals, attitudes and values of individuals).

Both Rogers and Murphy and Cohen include a number of 'non-price' factors that affect adoption, but do not separate them from price factors. Since much attention has been given to price in discussing the adoption of ecological products, Murphy and Cohen (2001) deliberately highlighted the non-price factors. However, in economics a product's purchase price and running costs relative to competing products are considered as distinct from non-price factors and of crucial significance for a product's adoption and use. The degree of investment involved is also a key factor in adoption decisions. The investments involved in purchasing LZC products and systems range from a few pounds for a CFL, to several hundreds of pounds for an A+ rated fridge-freezer, to tens of thousands of pounds for a PV roof. In general, the larger the investment, the less willing people are to take risks with innovative, untested goods and the more people may be concerned with payback – the length of time it takes to recover the initial outlay. The availability of grants and subsidies, as well as guarantees and trusted brands, are often essential to reduce risk in major purchase decisions. So, financial issues including price, running costs, payback and the level of investment involved are likely to be key variables in any study of the adoption and use of LZC products/systems.

Methodology

The Design Innovation Group's research project is being conducted in two phases: an exploratory phase, the method and some results of which are outlined below, and a main phase, the aims of which are outlined towards the end of the chapter and whose results will be discussed in further publications.

Exploratory phase studies

The exploratory phase involved three studies:

1   Semi-structured, face-to-face interviews with a small number of volunteer consumers to develop the methodology for the main phase and to gain some insights into the factors influencing the adoption and use of LZC products/systems.
2   A literature review and discussions with professionals in the field of energy efficiency and renewable energy, to identify which LZC products/systems to focus on, issues affecting consumer adoption and use, plus ideas for improving those products/systems.
3   An internet survey of energy professionals to evaluate the improvement ideas and generate further ideas that would facilitate consumer adoption and effective use of LZC products/systems.

The research model

The exploratory study guided the development of a model of an individual consumer's or household's decision to adopt and use ecological products and systems. It builds on Rogers' model of the innovation-decision process and employs Murphy and Cohen's classification of product properties. Our model presents the process that people go through when deciding to adopt, use or reject LZC products/systems and includes four sets of variables that influence the process – namely, the socio-economic context, communication sources, consumer variables and product/system properties (Figure 3.2).

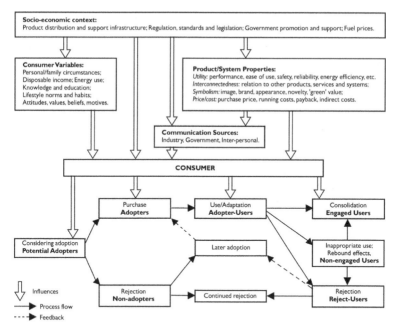

Figure 3.2 *Research model of adoption and use of ecological products and systems*

Exploratory interviews with consumers

In the exploratory study fourteen people who volunteered in response to internal intranet advertisements at the Open University were interviewed about a range of ecological products they had adopted, were seriously considering, or had rejected. Most of the volunteers had a professional or personal interest in the environment and so were 'greener' than the general population. The interviews concerned the following LZC products/systems, involving different levels of investment:

- *Potential adopters* of a condensing boiler, cavity wall insulation, green tariff electricity.
- *Non-adopters* of solar water heating, a PV roof.
- *Adopter-users* (both *engaged* and *non-engaged*) of CFLs, energy-efficient appliances, condensing and condensing/combination boilers, a hybrid petrol-electric car, central heating controls and solar water heating.
- *Reject-users* of CFLs and rechargeable batteries.

Our preliminary findings suggest there could be 'hotspots', by which we mean common factors that could affect many people and LZC product/system types at different stages of the adoption-use-consolidation or rejection process, and that may be amenable to change by introducing technical/design improvements, regulation, consumer information or financial measures. So while many influencing factors may be resistant to change, these hotspots might provide points of leverage for the achievement of carbon reduction targets.

Russell and Williams (2002, pp145–146) make a similar general point about the need to identify points and means of leverage in any transition to sustainability:

> *The major weakness of many calls for sustainability, however, is in failing to ... identify means of intervening in current patterns and institutions, and to diagnose possible obstacles and sources of resistance. There is a much greater chance of producing the desired outcomes if we take as a starting point the dynamics of current development, select points and means of leverage carefully, and are prepared for continuing and flexible intervention as the changes unfold.*

Examples of hotspot influences

Below are some candidate examples of hotspot influences on the different adopter categories from the exploratory study. They are classified according to Murphy and Cohen's (2001) product/system properties of utility, interconnectedness and symbolism, plus a separate category of price factors. This proved to be a useful lens through which to view the other factors in the research model: socio-economic context, consumer variables and communication sources.

INFLUENCES ON POTENTIAL ADOPTERS

Utility. People are more likely to adopt and use products designed for ease and convenience of use. For example, products currently using removable rechargeable batteries would be more acceptable if redesigned with a built-in rechargeable battery/charger, like mobile phones.

Interconnectedness. Integration of related products/systems into packaged systems should reduce costs, purchasing effort and complexity, and so encourage adoption. For example, if a condensing central heating boiler and solar water heating system were provided as an integrated technical, financing and installation package, adoption of the latter would be more likely. Sometimes the desire to address an unrelated household problem can trigger interest in adopting LZC technologies. For example, one potential adopter became interested in solar water heating as a result of a concern that her roof could do with a reinforcing layer (of panels) to protect it from wind. This suggests that solar water heating might be best promoted and installed as part of other changes to the house.

Symbolism. Product aesthetics varies in importance for different consumers and products. For example, one interviewee's partner wanted the fashionable colours and styling of some refrigerator models, while highly efficient refrigerators were generally just a 'white box'. Some people like to display their green credentials by installing an observable eco-innovation. For example, one house-holder seriously considered solar water heating as one way of demonstrating their 'greenness' and encouraging discourse with neighbours about environmental issues. Another potential adopter of solar water heating described it as offering a 'spiritually pure' experience of bathing unmediated by geopolitics, adding that it was the green status symbol equivalent of a 4x4 car.

Utility/symbolism. The poor reputation and image of some eco-products and systems often deters adoption even if their performance and/or technology have been improved in subsequent generations. For example, some interviewees mentioned bad experience with products such as unreliable early condensing boilers or large, slow to warm-up early CFLs, and the hazardous reputation of initial types of foam cavity wall insulation, even though the latter two problems have been dealt with (Guy and Shove, 2000).

Interconnectedness. Lack of systems integration often deters or prevents adoption of LZC products and systems. For example, a crucial factor in the decision of one household not to adopt solar water heating was because they discovered it was incompatible with a combination ('combi') boiler they had installed, partly to avoid the need for a hot water tank.

Utility/cost. Perception of complexity, poor durability and value for money often acts as a deterrent to adoption. For example, one interviewee decided against adopting a condensing boiler (before the 2005 building regulations that require new boilers to be energy-efficient) because the installation is complex, requiring a fanned flue and electrical wiring. He felt that the costs to maintain it would outweigh the savings and expected it would last only 10–15 years.

Price/cost. Initial purchase price, and often anticipated payback, is a dominant issue for many medium to high LZC investments. For example, several interviewees mentioned that, despite the availability of government grants, the installation cost of solar water heating was prohibitive and the payback period was too long. Nor did solar water heating add significantly to the value or saleability of a dwelling. Price/cost influences are particularly significant for tenants living in rented accommodation. One non-adopter, greatly interested in LZC technologies, mentioned (unaware that tax concessions for landlords were introduced in the 2004 budget) that there needs to be more incentives for landlords because tenants will only invest in low-cost energy-efficient measures.

Utility/interconnectedness. A key issue for technologies that require installation such as condensing boilers and solar water heating is the effectiveness of the installation process and follow-up service if any problems arise. One house-holder had a bad experience following the installation of a condensing boiler, resulting in every spare part needing replacement. Though continuing to use the system, this person lost faith in the reliability of condensing boilers. Another issue is the requirement to interconnect new installations with existing household systems. For example, one solar water heating system adopter was disappointed that her plumber had not connected the heater to the dishwasher, reducing the utility of the solar energy system.

Symbolism. This aspect can work in complex ways. For example, the adopter of a hybrid petrol-electric car, although he wanted the vehicle to demonstrate his green credentials to himself and his peers, chose a model that was not too conspicuous or unusual in design.

Price/cost. The availability of grants and subsidies can encourage purchase of LZC products/systems, especially those involving high investment. For example, an Energy Saving Trust grant was an important factor in the decision to buy the hybrid petrol-electric car.

Communications. The provision of comprehensive product information, including energy consumption data and easy-to-understand summaries, encourages adoption. For example, the colour-coded energy label and good internet information assisted purchasers of white goods in assessing best buys, prices, running costs and payback. Interviewees also cited the importance of a trusted brand and retailer when buying energy-efficient white goods. (This supports the findings of McDonald et al in this volume.)

INFLUENCES ON ENGAGED ADOPTER-USERS

Utility/symbolism. Feedback to the user on the energy consumption and/or cost-saving of a product or system can encourage energy-saving behaviour. For example, the adopter of the hybrid petrol-electric car appreciated the feedback on fuel consumption and costs provided by the vehicle's electronic displays. This encouraged fuel-efficient driving and also provided a 'feel-good' factor. Nevertheless, he admitted that higher fuel economy made him less concerned about driving long distances.

Interconnectedness. An infrastructure for servicing and maintenance is important for the adoption of innovative LZC products/systems. For example, the purchaser of the hybrid car observed he had to locate convenient, and not too costly, trained servicing facilities, before deciding to buy the vehicle.

INFLUENCES ON NON-ENGAGED ADOPTER-USERS

Price/cost. Reduced running costs can lead to greater product use, thus reducing environmental benefits through rebound effects. For example, one interviewee admitted that his family left low-energy lamps switched on longer, thereby reducing the amount of energy saved. The rebound effect of the high fuel economy of the hybrid car was noted above.

Consumer variables/communications. Householders may have inefficient energy-consumption practices due to poor understanding. For example, one interviewee believed that it is better to leave heating on permanently during the heating season because of the inconvenience of adjusting timer and thermostat settings and the erroneous belief that it would be more costly to turn up the heating to achieve the required temperature.

INFLUENCES ON REJECT-USERS

Utility. Dissatisfaction with adopted products/systems sometimes leads to non-engagement or product rejection. Several users mentioned dissatisfaction with CFL's in terms of their size, appearance, and quality of light produced. Some users who had decided against bulky early CFL's were unaware of subsequent technical and design improvements. One reject-user mentioned that the expensive CFL she bought failed after a year, when a 12-year life was promised; she would not buy CFLs again.

Utility/symbolism. Inconvenience can lead to rejection of eco-products by people with busy lives. For example, several users rejected the use of rechargeable batteries and battery chargers because the batteries had to be charged in advance and the life of the recharged batteries was not consistently reliable. A comment regarding rechargeable batteries was, 'life's too short'.

Exploratory survey of energy professionals

The exploratory interviews, although conducted with a relatively small number of 'greener' consumers, suggested some important influences on the adoption and use of LZC products and systems. The interviews, along with the literature and our discussions with energy professionals, helped choose which LZC products/systems to focus on, and suggested some ideas for improving them to facilitate their adoption and effective use. To assess the improvement ideas and to generate further ones, as well as to obtain more information on the factors influencing consumers, we conducted an online survey of subscribers to a newsletter for energy efficiency professionals, including home-energy advisers, architects and energy consultants.

Fifty responses were obtained concerning the energy professionals' views on the significant influences on the adoption and use of the following LZC products/systems: loft insulation of up to 250mm depth; CFLs; LED lighting; heating controls; condensing central heating boilers; micro CHP units; and solar water heating systems. They also responded with their views on technical, design and other improvement ideas that could facilitate consumer adoption and effective use.

What clearly emerged from the responses was that the influences on the adoption and use of each of the LZC technologies were different, but all could be classified within our research model (shown in Figure 3.2), thus giving us confidence in its validity.

The following is a selection from the findings of this survey.

Loft insulation

Interconnectedness was identified as the most significant influence on installing loft insulation of up to 250mm thickness because installation often requires clearing of cluttered lofts and/or removal of boarding and is likely to mean a loss of storage space and/or the potential for a loft conversion.

Consumer variables are significant, as some consumers believe that (extra) loft insulation is not worthwhile, especially since it is not 'observable' and if the loft already has some insulation.

Improvement ideas (to utility/interconnectedness): these included low-cost materials to give equivalent of 250mm mineral fibre insulation with thinner/less bulky material; and new methods, other than raising the joists and boarding, to create loft storage space above the insulation.

Compact fluorescent lamps

Utility. Some CFLs do not reach full brightness instantly or provide a sufficiently bright or pleasant light, which deters some consumers.

Interconnectedness. CFLs often do not fit existing lamp shades and are incompatible with dimmers.

Symbolism. CFLs are considered too large and/or ugly when not hidden from view.

Price/cost. CFLs are still expensive compared to incandescent lamps.

Improvement ideas (to utility/interconnectedness/socio-economic context). These were that CFLs should be designed to be the same sizes and shapes as incandescent lamps and provide a similar quality of light; and that incandescent lamps could be taxed, thereby providing an incentive to buy energy-efficient light-bulbs.

Light-Emitting-Diode Lighting

Utility. Although highly energy-efficient and long-lasting, LEDs are not bright enough for general lighting and the quality or colour of light is not yet suitable, except for decorative applications.

Communications. A key influence on the adoption of LED lighting is the lack of consumer awareness of their potential for lighting.

Improvement ideas (to utility/communications). These were that technical improvements are needed to LED light quality and colour rendering, and to fittings to distribute light adequately. An educational campaign is needed to demonstrate the different ways this technology can be used.

Heating controls

Utility. Controls, which are often non-standard and over-complex, are difficult to understand and operate, which acts against adoption and efficient use.

Interconnectedness. Controls are often used ineffectively as users do not understand how programmer, thermostats and controlled radiators contribute to the efficient operation of a heating system. Poor location for controls inhibits effective use; for example, programmers are often hidden in airing cupboards.

Improvement ideas (to utility/communications). Suggested improvements included ergonomic/inclusive designs of controls that provide feedback to the user on energy consumed and money saved; better instructions on effective use; and location in prominent positions such as the kitchen.

Condensing central heating boilers

Utility/socio-economic context. The reputation of condensing boilers for unreliability is exacerbated by poor installation by untrained installers, many of whom are negative in their attitudes to this technology. The 2005 Building Regulations requiring new or replacement boilers to be energy-efficient should enforce changes in attitudes and practices.

Consumer variables. Consumers do not understand how condensing boilers work.

Improvement ideas (to utility). These included a boiler that displays its working efficiency; and an easier to service condensing boiler.

Solar water heating

Price/cost. The high initial cost and a long payback time was the main deterrent to installing solar water heating.

Utility. Inadequate reliability and durability, given the long payback time, added to the deterrent effect.

Interconnectedness. Lack of compatibility between solar water heating and systems without a hot water tank (e.g. combination central heating boiler). No suitable site for the solar panels.

Socio-economic context. Inadequate control of 'cowboy' installers, which gives solar water heating a reputation similar to that of double glazing in the past. Also, some local authorities require planning permission for installations, which acts as a constraint.

Improvement ideas (to interconnectedness/socio-economic context). These were to design solar panels for integration with the roof or for installation from inside the house; and to establish standards and publish performance data for solar water heating systems.

Micro combined heat and power

Utility/consumer variables. Micro CHP is a new technology with uncertain performance, reliability and carbon savings, which acts as a deterrent to installation.

Interconnectedness. Difficulty in finding a suitable location for the unit so that it readily connects with household electrical and plumbing systems.

Price/cost. A costly new technology with unknown payback, partly dependent on the price obtained for surplus electricity sold to the national grid.

Socio-economic context. The difficulty in finding a trained installer and servicing.

Main phase consumer surveys

The exploratory studies provided the conceptual framework and enabled the development of a set of semi-structured questionnaires for the main phase consumer surveys to be carried out via telephone interviews and online questionnaires.

The main phase surveys aim to:

- Identify the influencing factors at each phase of consumers' experience of adopting and using a range of LZC products/systems, namely consideration, adoption (or early rejection), use and consolidation (or later rejection).
- Identify hotspot influences, both generic and specific, on the widespread adoption and effective use of these LZC products/systems that may be amenable to change by technical or design improvements, regulatory and fiscal measures, consumer information and education.
- Provide information to designers and manufacturers on how LZC products/systems might be (re)designed to be more user-friendly and attractive to consumers.

The LZC products/systems chosen for investigation represent a range of technologies and levels of investment and include: products costing up to £50, such as CFLs and LED lighting; products costing from £50 to £500, such as loft insulation and heating controls; products/systems costing from £500 to £5000, such as condensing boilers, solar water heating, and micro CHP units.

The consumers surveyed are members of the general public selected from databases of enquirers about insulation and condensing boilers to local EEACs, and enquiries concerning solar water heating to an organization that promotes and provides information about alternative and renewable energy technologies. This information is supplemented by a large-scale online survey of people accessing a website linked to a BBC/Open University television series on climate change, broadcast in mid 2006.

Preliminary conclusions

There exists much research on UK household energy consumption, with policy initiatives and practical action given impetus by the urgent need to reduce carbon emissions. Until some recent official publications (e.g. HM Treasury, 2005; Oxera, 2006), much of this research, policy and practice has been based on a techno-economic model of rational consumer decision making, which does not fully recognize that consumer goods have both a functional and a symbolic role, and assumes that people will readily adopt LZC products/systems when their financial and environmental benefits are communicated. In practice, numerous other factors often enter the adoption decision, including the socio-economic context, the circumstances, disposable income, attitudes and values of the adopters, and how well the products and systems are designed to meet their functional and symbolic needs and wants. These needs and wants differ depending on the properties of the LZC product or system, ranging from a simple energy-saving measure like cavity wall insulation to products with several functions and interactions, like energy-efficient lighting or appliances. To ensure rapid adoption of LZC products/systems, it is therefore necessary to consider all the influences on consumer decision making, including appropriate governance measures for technically sophisticated 'pioneer' adopters, main-stream consumers and reluctant adopters; and to ensure that each product or system is designed from a people-centred perspective.

Much existing research, policy and practice also assumes that getting people to adopt LZC products is sufficient. However, merely persuading people to adopt LZC products/systems does not guarantee reduced carbon emissions. This is because of rebound or take-back effects in which consumers may reduce or cancel out the environmental benefits by trading up or by increasing consumption of the product. They may also bypass the energy-saving features or even reject the LZC product or system they adopted. It is therefore necessary to ensure the consumers not only adopt LZC products/systems, but also choose appropriate ones and use them effectively.

It is clear from the above that persuading consumers to adopt LZC products/systems and use them in a manner that saves energy and reduces emissions is a complex matter that faces considerable difficulties. UK (and EU) household carbon reduction policy is therefore framed as a technological rather than a consumption problem, which is seen as posing far fewer difficulties in governance than trying to change consumers' behaviour. Such supply-led policies focus on R&D support, regulation, fuel switching, and encouraging manufacturers to develop technical solutions. On the consumption side the main policies involve providing consumers with information and advice about LZC products/systems, supported by targeted grants and subsidies.

To increase the effectiveness of both policy options, our exploratory studies confirm the importance of examining the total process of consideration, adoption, use, consolidation or rejection to identify the factors that may encourage people first to adopt, and then use LZC products/systems effectively. This has led to the development of a model of consumer decision making for LZC products/systems and the key factors that influence it – product/system properties, socio-economic context, consumer variables and communication sources.

Our exploratory studies suggest there could be hotspots, or points of leverage, both generic and specific to each product or system, which if tackled should facilitate consumer adoption and effective use. We found that hotspots could usefully be categorized according to Murphy and Cohen's (2001) product/system properties of utility, interconnectedness and symbolism, together with price/cost factors and the other key influencing factors.

If we take solar water heating, examples of hotspots that should facilitate *adoption* include:

- The high initial cost and long payback time of solar water heating could be tackled by designing systems that integrate with roofing and/or by extending available grants and subsides.
- Combination of related products/systems into packaged systems should encourage adoption. For example, if a condensing central heating boiler and solar water heating system were provided by energy suppliers as an integrated package, with financing service support included, adoption of the latter would be more likely.
- Since some people like to display their environmental credentials, solar water heating might best be promoted as the 'green' equivalent of a desirable car.
- The urgent need to control 'cowboy' installers, through a system of performance standards and/or energy labelling similar to that on appliances.

If we consider heating controls, examples of hotspots that should promote more effective use include:

- Better ergonomic designs of heating controls, which are often difficult for users to understand and to operate easily and conveniently.
- Standards and training for installers on designing for users, to ensure, for example, that they locate programmers in a prominent position rather than hiding them in airing cupboards.
- Controls that provide feedback to users on energy consumption, and money spent or saved, to encourage energy-saving behaviour and user satisfaction.
- The need for better consumer information on the use of controls, since many users do not understand how different controls function together to operate a heating system effectively.

From the viewpoint of governance, it is notable that these hotspot influences and suggested changes are a mixture of new or improved regulations and standards, financial measures, information for suppliers and consumers, effective marketing, and technical and design improvements. In other words, to promote the adoption and effective use of LZC products/systems it is necessary to combine sustainable production and consumption strategies with a new emphasis on improving the design of the products and systems themselves from a user viewpoint.

References

Association for the Conservation of Energy (2004) *User Behaviour in Energy Efficient Homes*, ACE, London

Boardman, B. (2004) 'Achieving energy efficiency through product policy: The UK experience', *Environmental Science and Policy*, vol 7, issue 3, pp165–176

Carbon Trust (2005) 'The Carbon Trust's small-scale CHP field trial update', The Carbon Trust, London, www.thecarbontrust.co.uk/ accessed in December 2005

Chappells, H., Klintman, M., Linden, A. L., Shove, E., Spaargaren, G. and van Vliet, B. (2000) *Domestic Consumption, Utility Services and the Environment*, Final report of the Domus Project, funded by the European Commission DG XII, University of Lancaster, UK

Central Office of Information (2001) *The 2000/2001 Energy Efficiency Advice Survey*, NFO/BJM, London

Department of Trade and Industry (2003) *Energy White Paper. Our Energy Future: Creating a Low Carbon Economy*, The Stationery Office, London

Department of Trade and Industry (2004, updated from 2002) *Energy Consumption in the UK*, DTI, London, www.dti.gov.uk/energy/inform/energy_consumption/index.shtml/ accessed in November 2004

Environmental Change Institute (2001) 'Retail therapy: Increasing the sales of CFLs', ECI, Oxford

Fischer, C. (2004) 'Who uses innovative energy technologies, when, and why? The case of fuel cell micro-CHP', Transformation and Innovation in Power Systems programme (TIPS), Forschungsstelle für Umweltpolitik, Freie Universität Berlin, Germany, August, www.tips-project.de/ accessed in December 2005

Guy, S. and Shove, E. (2000) *A Sociology of Energy, Buildings and the Environment: Constructing Knowledge, Designing Practice*, Routledge, London

Hand, M., Southerton, D. and Shove, E. (2003) 'Explaining daily showering: A discussion of policy and practice', ESRC Sustainable Technologies Programme Working Paper, no 2003/4, Economic and Social Research Council, Swindon

Harper, P. (2000) 'The lifestyle lab', *Schumacher Lecture 2000*, Centre for Alternative Technology, Machynlleth

HM Treasury (2005) *Energy Efficiency Innovation Review: Summary Report*, HMSO, London, December, www.hm-treasury.gov.uk/ accessed in January 2006

Jackson, T. (2005) 'Motivating sustainable consumption: A review of the evidence on consumer behaviour and behavioural change', Report to the Sustainable Development Research Network, January, www.sd-research.org.uk/ accessed in December 2005

Jackson, T. and Michaelis, L. (2003) 'Policies for sustainable consumption: A report to the Sustainable Development Commission', UK Sustainable Development Commission, September, www.sd-commission.gov.uk/ accessed in March 2005

Market Transformation Programme (2005) 'Sustainable products 2005: Policy analysis and projections, future energy solutions', Didcot, www.mtprog.com/ accessed in January 2006

Murphy, J. and Cohen, M. J. (2001) 'Sustainable consumption: Environmental policy and the social sciences', in Cohen, M. J. and Murphy, J. (eds) *Exploring Sustainable Consumption: Environmental Policy and the Social Sciences*, Elsevier Science Ltd, Oxford, pp225–240

Oxera (2006) 'Policies for energy efficiency in the UK household sector', a report prepared for DEFRA, Oxera Consulting Ltd., Oxford, January

Rogers, E. M. (2003) *The Diffusion of Innovations* (5th Edition), The Free Press, New York

Roy, R., Smith, M. T. and Potter, S. (1998) 'Green product development – factors in competition', in Barker, T. and Köhler, J (eds) *International Competitiveness and Environmental Policies*, Edward Elgar, Cheltenham, pp265–275

Royal Commission on Environmental Pollution (2000) 'Energy – The changing climate', RCEP 22nd Report, The Stationery Office, London

Russell, S. and Williams, R. (2002) 'Concepts, spaces and tools for action: Exploring the policy potential of the social shaping perspective', in Williams, R. and Sørensen, K. H. (eds) (2002) *Shaping Technology, Guiding Policy: Concepts, Spaces and Tools*, Edward Elgar, Cheltenham, pp133–154

Shove, E. (2003) *Comfort, Cleanliness and Convenience: The Social Organisation of Normality*, Berg Publishers, Oxford

Solar Trade Association (2005) 'The Solar Trade Association's response to the micro-generation and low carbon buildings strategy', STA, Milton Keynes, September

Stathers, K. (2004) 'Volvo's lonely green book', *Green Futures*, March/April 2004, pp49–50

Sustainable Consumption Roundtable (2005) *Seeing the Light: The Impact of Micro-Generation on the Way we Use Energy*, The Hub Research Consultants, London

Chapter 4

Energy Citizenship: Psychological Aspects of Evolution in Sustainable Energy Technologies

Patrick Devine-Wright

Introduction

The perspective on energy system evolution taken in this chapter involves two interdependent levels of analysis: the socio-cultural level, where the main concern is how issues are socially constructed (cf. Berger and Luckman, 1967), and the psychological level, detailing the cognitive and affective processes involved in shaping behaviour. Whilst there is an extant literature on energy at each level (e.g. Guy and Shove (2000) at the socio-cultural level, embedded within a wider literature on the sociology of technology; and Black et al (1985) at the individual level, embedded within applied social and environmental psychology), these are rarely integrated into a single perspective that situates individual human experience and action within processes of socio-cultural communication and contestation.

Social and psychological aspects of energy are typically neglected in analyses that prioritize technical and economic issues (Lutzenhiser, 1993). Yet they are important in discussing how an evolving technological system might contribute to economic, environmental and social policy goals, that is to represent a 'sustainable' energy system (Tleubayeva and Devine-Wright, 2006). This chapter will draw attention to multiple and conflicting social representations of the public, currently embedded within different facets of UK energy policy and practice, which suggest quite different pathways for the governance of system evolution, and will situate such representations in the context of specific psychological processes that are implicated in shaping behaviours.

Social and psychological perspectives on technological change

Stern (2000) describes three spheres in which environmentally significant behaviour takes place: in private (e.g. at home), in public (e.g. activist political behaviour) and in the corporate/institutional context (e.g. decisions made by professionals about new technologies or policies). Whilst the private sphere is most commonly researched in environmental psychology (e.g. determinants of home recycling or energy conservation), the others are equally if not more significant contexts to understand environmentally significant behaviour. Technologies are normally viewed by environmental psychologists as aspects of the context or situation that shapes human behaviour, borrowing from the social psychologist Kurt Lewin the basic understanding that behaviour is a function of context by personal characteristics ($B = P \times C$). Whilst environmental psychologists typically presume the context as a 'given' in their study of human behaviour, it is also useful to research how changes in the context take place, for example, examining the psychological processes involved in the emergence and development of new energy technologies, which in turn open up, or close down, opportunities for behaviour. Such an agenda for research would extend the remit of energy-focused psychological research to encompass not only the private sphere (e.g. public beliefs or attitudes about new energy technologies; behavioural adoption of energy technologies), but also the public sphere (e.g. citizenship actions to influence technology policies) and corporate/institutional sphere psychological processes (e.g. what kinds of beliefs are held by technical designers and policy makers about the users of new energy technologies).

Social representations theory (Moscovici, 1984) is a useful framework to apply to the study of 'common sense' beliefs about energy users since it is a social-psychological theory of knowledge that aims to identify and account for shared ways of thinking that are regarded as obvious or self-evident by individuals within a particular social context. Social representations differ from the more conventional concept of 'attitudes' in being more evidently shared within groups or across society, influenced by socio-cultural communication (for example the mass media), dynamic and influenced by power relations in being hegemonic or contested. In this chapter, common sense ways of thinking about energy or the public are assumed to be patterns of beliefs akin to social representations that have become to a greater or lesser degree 'common sense'.

Technological change has received attention from sociologists, political scientists and geographers, who have critiqued a conceptualization of technology that sets it apart from society; who stress the non-monolithic nature of 'the public' (e.g. Walker, 1995); and emphasize how new technologies are embedded within, and shaped by, beliefs about what users are like, what they desire and want, what they will tolerate and what they are interested in. In relation to energy technologies, Marvin et al (1999) used the concept of 'technical development pathways' to describe how the gas, electricity and water meter technologies of the future could develop along markedly different paths. They emphasized how technological outcomes were not inevitable and pre-ordained, but shaped by the array of different 'logics' (implicitly suggesting different social representations) shaping technological development. Most critically for this chapter, they indicated how different pathways could result in metering devices being marketed and installed, which would provide very different technological contexts for individual behaviour. Whilst some might be designed to foster minimal user engagement, acting more or less on a 'plug and forget' basis, others could be designed to foster regular interaction with users, thus providing a quite different context for user response, awareness, motivation and action. This chapter extends this literature through a social-psychological analysis of pathways of energy, and specifically electricity, technology evolution at a superordinate or 'system' level of analysis, encompassing generating plant, grid supply and end-use technologies, drawing out different ways of representing system evolution and identifying how such representations may open up, or close down, opportunities for public engagement.

Energy systems and technologies in flux

Despite Thomas Edison's originally decentralized approach, across the 20th century 'large-scale technical systems' of energy generation, with a national grid of transmission and distribution networks of supply, were created in industrialized nations in which decision making was conducted centrally and at a remove from the public (Hughes, 1983). Despite its evident success in providing reliable electricity supply to all citizens, Amory Lovins (1977) characterized this system as a 'hard' energy pathway, critiquing the wisdom of many of its facets: large-scale generation plant sited at a spatial distance from points of use, centralized top-down energy governance and a preference for nuclear power. Since the 1970s, Lovins has consistently advocated the evolution of a 'soft' energy path with opposing facets: decentralized or distributed generation, greater levels of public participation and control and the increased use of renewable energy technologies (e.g. Lovins and Lehman, 2002). The dichotomy between single 'hard' and 'soft' energy pathways is an oversimplification of a highly complex subject with multiple dimensions and possible futures. Furthermore, the increased deployment of renewable energy technologies does not necessarily imply the adoption of other facets of the 'soft' energy pathway. Nevertheless, there are increasing signs that ideas in favour of more renewable energy, more public participation and smaller scale generation are circulating more widely in the UK and elsewhere, being adopted by key stakeholders in industry and government, and are likely to form an important part of a future 'low carbon' energy system.

Signs of this change include a UK government commitment to achieving a 60 per cent cut in carbon emissions by 2050, in comparison to 1990 levels, along with targets for electricity generation from renewable resources: 10 per cent by 2010 and 20 per cent by 2020. Key reports have pointed to the diminished importance of centralized supply systems in a decarbonized energy future (Anderson et al, 2005), as well as the likelihood of the '40 per cent house' having around two low-carbon energy generating technologies by 2050, such as solar photovoltaic (PV) panels or combined heat and power (CHP) plant, and exporting electricity to the grid (Boardman et al, 2005). The White Paper (Department of Trade and Industry (DTI), 2003, p18) described this future energy system as:

> *more diverse, where much of the energy is imported, but with increased amounts of offshore marine plants, wave, tidal and wind-farms... There is much more local generation, in part from medium to small local/community power plant, fuelled by locally grown biomass, from locally generated waste, from local wind sources, or possibly from local wave and tidal generators. These will feed local distributed networks, which can sell excess capacity into the grid. Plant will also increasingly generate heat for local use.*

Given the conventional, highly centralized system using nuclear and hydrocarbon resources and a national grid of supply networks, these technological visions, with a stronger emphasis upon 'medium to small local/community' generation and use, along with increased renewable energy, represent a significant departure from the norm. In 2050, it may be a commonplace to find smaller-scale, renewable energy technologies such as solar PV panels, solar hot water panels, small-scale wind turbines and micro CHP plant on most homes and buildings and in most communities in the UK. But while there is increasing consensus that centralized ('hard') energy systems need to change in order to effectively respond to environmental problems, there is far less awareness of, and agreement about, concomitant social aspects of energy system evolution, not least what role(s) the public holds as stakeholders in this process, and what the determinants of public acceptance of system evolution might be (Ekins, 2004).

Technological systems: Ways of representing energy and energy users

One reason for this lack of awareness of social aspects of energy system evolution might be that energy is a subject that may always have been conceived in multiple ways, with different groups or individuals approaching the subject with very different social representations of the role of the public or energy users. Stern and Aronson (1984, p15) asserted that 'there is no single socially shared concept of energy'. This is likely to be as true in the early 21st century as it was in the early 1980s. They identified four principle ways of understanding energy:

Table 4.1 *Summary of ways of representing energy*

Energy as:	Important properties	Central values	Interest groups
Commodity	Supply, demand, price	Choice, individualism, private sector provision of energy services	Energy producers, consumers with sufficient resources (fuel rich)
Ecological resource	Resource depletion, environmental impacts	Sustainability, frugality, choice for future generations, preference for renewables	Future generations, green movement
Social necessity	Availability to social groups, meeting essential needs	Equity, justice	The poor (fuel poverty) and other vulnerable social groups
Strategic material	Geopolitics, availability of domestic substitutes	National military and economic security	Military, energy suppliers

Source: Adapted from Stern and Aronson (1984)

- Energy as a commodity.
- Energy as an ecological resource.
- Energy as a social necessity.
- Energy as strategic material.

The essence of each of these is summarized in Table 4.1.

Whilst it is interesting to note the diversity of these various ways of framing energy issues, I would argue that these do not carry equal weight in energy policy making, and that the 'energy as commodity' has been, and continues to be, the dominant or hegemonic social representation of energy held by policy makers, most obviously indicated by the move to privatize and liberalize electricity and gas sectors in the UK. As a result of lobbying by various interest groups over the past 25 years, issues of environment and social justice are embedded within the policy mix, yet I would argue that they have not displaced the dominant position of the commodity view of energy.

The emergence of sustainable development as a policy goal in the 1990s has seen a new facet of the 'energy as social necessity' representation emerge, which I describe as 'energy citizenship' (Devine-Wright, 2004). This approach argues for the social necessity of public engagement and participation in processes of policy making and planning, driven by principles of local empowerment and action derived from Local Agenda 21 (LA21). This aspect is absent from Stern and Aronson's (1984) typology. Current discussions in the UK about a 'sustainable energy economy' or 'low carbon economy' reflect attempts to manage system evolution whilst invoking to greater or lesser degrees the different representations of energy specified above. Controversies over the value of different pathways (e.g. nuclear vs renewables; centralized vs decentralized) reflect the difficulties inherent in attempting to hold or balance commodity, security, ecological and social views simultaneously and the different interpretations of each adopted. But each viewpoint also explicitly or implicitly reflects different representations of energy users, and these are discussed in more detail below.

Centralized energy systems and representations of the public as consumer/deficit

The four different ways of representing energy identified by Stern and Aronson (1984) are embedded within, and have been shaped by, a particular kind of technical system: the centralized approach to energy generation and supply. Within this, it is possible to identify several ways of representing the public in relation to energy generation, supply and use:

- 'customers' or 'consumers';
- fuel 'rich' or 'poor';
- 'environmentally concerned'.

These are implied by 'energy as commodity', 'energy as social necessity' and 'energy as ecological resource' representations of energy. Cross-cutting each of these, the centralized system coexists with a commonly held 'deficit' view of the public as energy users – separated from, and minimally engaged in, energy systems over and above pressing a light switch. This has led to the design and deployment of a range of energy technologies, services and procedures, from meters to bills to regulatory institutions to power stations, that foster minimal public engagement (see for example, recent work on electricity bills: Boardman and Palmer, 2003; and on metering devices: Devine-Wright and Devine-Wright, 2006).

This is backed up by a body of research that has consistently indicated low levels of public awareness, understanding or interest in energy technologies. For example, social research has suggested that energy consumption is largely invisible and taken for granted (Hedges, 1991; Egan, 2002); that low levels of public awareness exist about energy prices (Kempton and Montgomery, 1982); there is deficient understanding of how energy technologies work (Kempton, 1986); that, despite rising levels of environmental concern, there is a general lack of awareness of the impacts of domestic energy consumption for climate change (Department of the Environment, Food and Rural Affairs (DEFRA), 2001). On the supply side, the 'out of sight and out of mind' (Pasqualetti, 1999) siting of power stations at distances from centres of population has left individuals poorly aware of where their electricity comes from and how the supply system works (Qualter, 1995), concerned about the health risks associated with transmission pylons and wires (Priestly and Evans, 1996), and often characterized as holding selfish and irrational 'NIMBY' (not in my back yard) reactions to proposed new generation plant, notably onshore wind turbines (Devine-Wright, 2005a).

In sum, it is suggested that the centralized energy system is embedded within, and has helped produce, a social representation of the 'energy public' that is overwhelmingly characterized by deficits: of interest, knowledge, rationality and environmental and social responsibility. Moreover, it is argued that this is a self-fulfilling prophesy – the more the representation is assumed to be common sense by decision makers, the more it is likely to lead to 'out of sight, out of mind' energy policies, and to institutions and technologies that foster its continuity, creating a context with limited scope for public engagement with the energy system. Imagining the likely implications of the centralized system and its related social representations of energy and energy users for future energy system evolution, one might speculate as follows:

In terms of governance: holding the view of the public as consumer/deficit suggests that decision making about system evolution is best left to the experts (that is to a bounded array of 'technocrats' already involved in managing the centralized system at the national level, including working groups involving government departments, regulatory bodies, industry and some academics) rather than being opened out to encompass more collective, deliberative processes directly with the public. Scepticism about the value of deliberative processes in energy system evolution would be consonant with this position.

In terms of technological change: designers, developers and installers of new energy technologies would aim to minimize public engagement since this would be assumed to increase the risk of resistance, delay, planning refusal and inefficient or incorrect use of technologies. Large-scale energy generation would be preferred and sited at a maximal distance from centres of population; for example, off-shore or in remote areas. New energy- demand technologies, including 'smartmeters', would be designed on a 'plug and forget' basis, aiming to minimize disruption to existing lifestyles; load-management devices would be embedded within existing appliances to work as independently as possible of the consumer so as to minimize inconvenience.

In terms of public acceptance: it would be assumed that the best way to ensure acceptance of new-energy technologies would be to get sufficient incentives (or benefits) in place and market them effectively to ensure consumer adoption; deal with NIMBY resistance to change by siting technologies away from centres of population and by obliging developers to compensate local residents, under the guise of local community economic benefits (e.g. DTI, 2005b); and prioritize policies to maintain low energy prices, consumer choice and reliable supply.

There are two issues that need to be discussed when considering these pathways of system evolution: whether the 'deficit' view is valid, and whether a pathway of system evolution based upon its core assumptions can be said to represent a more 'sustainable' energy system.

First, both deficit and related NIMBY views, despite being widely held, have been critiqued as an inaccurate account of public responses to new technologies on a number of different levels: whether the gap between 'expert' and 'lay' knowledge is best understood in terms of deficit/surfeit, in comparison to qualitatively different forms of thinking or knowledge practised by different groups (e.g. Irwin et al, 1999); whether new technologies are responded to by isolated individuals, or are socially constructed (Berger and Luckmann, 1967) by social actors through everyday interpersonal communication and exposure to mass media (e.g. Grove-White et al, 2000); and whether public acceptance is best secured through top-down, one-way information and awareness-raising campaigns funded by central government or industry in comparison to bottom-up, deliberative processes of public engagement (Grove-White et al, 2000).

Second, there is the issue of what 'sustainable' energy means, and who decides. If the most common or dominant way of thinking about the sustainable energy system of the future is one defined as basically with less environmentally negative consequences, then the main challenge is how to assimilate low-carbon (nuclear or renewable energy) technologies within the existing large-scale technical system. In terms of the scope for renewable energy development, this suggests integrating renewables within the conventional 'hard' energy pathway, favouring rapid and large-scale deployment within a 'streamlined' planning process with limited public involvement, minimizing the engineering challenge of intermittency to security of supply and maintaining low prices. To a degree, this is an accurate representation of policy and practice for wind energy in the UK and elsewhere in the early 1990s (Breuker, 2005), which favoured large-scale over smaller scale renewable energy development led by private utilities rather than communities and conceived as an asocial process of technology development.

Representing sustainable energy as minimizing environmental impacts suggests optimizing the balance between 'energy as commodity', 'energy as strategic resource' and 'energy as ecological resource' viewpoints, and playing down the importance of social aspects. However, this is an incomplete and unsatisfactory way of applying sustainable development to energy issues. Whilst there is no clear model available characterizing social aspects of a sustainable energy system (Tleubayeva and Devine-Wright, 2006), it is the case that principles of sustainable development, such as equity and participation as enshrined in UK and international sustainable development policy documents (e.g. DEFRA, 1999), suggest a pathway of system evolution where technological change is informed by, and embedded within, engagement with as wide an array of stakeholders as possible, including the public, at different levels – local, regional and national. This has been represented as the adoption of a 'paradigm change' in energy policy making, embracing both institutional dynamics of innovation processes and fostering societal engagement in implementation (Szarka, 2006).

Decentralized energy technologies and representations of the public as energy citizens

Circulating alongside this 'deficit' view, an alternative representation of the public can be identified involving quite different assumptions about public awareness, motivation and concern about energy, and it is likely to lead to very different pathways of technological change. This is described as 'energy citizenship' (Morris, 2001; Devine-Wright, 2004) in which the public are conceived as active rather than passive stakeholders in energy system evolution and where the potential for action is framed by notions of equitable rights and responsibilities across society for dealing with the consequences of energy consumption, notably climate change. Energy citizenship is not a new idea. Traces can be identified in writings on the virtues of alternative technology and 'small-scale' development, for example the seminal work of Schumacher (1974). What is novel is the degree to which it appears to be becoming an integral, conventional element of UK government energy policy, informed by wider policy on sustainable development, including the negative impacts of globalization and the benefits of 'localization' (e.g. Hines, 2000) in relation to food production and consumption, travel, water, waste and energy, and emerging ideas about sustainable consumption (Jackson, 2004).

Energy citizenship is a counterpoint to the social and psychological 'detachment' of the public from energy systems embedded within centralized systems and deficit views of energy users. It can be identified in a number of different sources or drivers for change. First, there is the emerging potential for smaller-scale energy generation, most obviously domestic scale devices, which could co-evolve with a more engaged and aware public or publics. Second, there is the view that a more sustainable energy system should imply or necessitate greater levels of public participation in energy decision-making, based upon a form of Local (Energy) Agenda 21. Lastly, there is a pragmatic view that public acceptance of technological change necessitates greater levels of engagement with the public about energy technologies, as such engagement may create better conditions for consensus to emerge about new development.

Whilst citizenship has conventionally been defined as the membership of a political community that entitles a subject to the exercise of rights and obliges the fulfilment of certain duties or responsibilities (Reeve, 1996), recent writing in environmental politics has begun to explore a wider notion of citizenship in relation to environmental problems. Dobson (2003), for example, has claimed that the principle responsibility or duty of environmental citizenship would be to 'ensure that (one's) ecological footprint does not compromise or foreclose the ability of others in present or future generations to pursue options important to them'. In a review of environmental citizenship literature, Barnett et al (2005) noted several dimensions of environmental citizenship: ascription of private responsibility for environmental problems, an emphasis upon environmental justice, and individuals responding to environmental problems through collective action. Energy citizenship is a view of the public that emphasizes awareness of responsibility for climate change, equity and justice in relation to siting controversies as well as fuel poverty and, finally, the potential for (collective) energy actions, including acts of consumption and the setting up of community renewable energy projects such as energy cooperatives.

Psychologists have been critical of the dominant 'model' or representation of the public held by policy makers and political scientists that views the person solely as a personal utility maximizer, focusing upon short-term, material gains or benefits (e.g. Tyler et al, 1986). Instead, psychological literature on citizenship suggests a range of values, beliefs and norms determining citizenship behaviours such as signing petitions or supporting particular energy policies. Taking value-belief-norm theory of support for environmental movements (Stern et al, 1999), Steg et al (in press) have empirically shown how biospheric values, an ecological worldview, awareness of negative environmental threats or consequences, ascription of personal responsibility and feelings of moral obligation shape public acceptance of higher energy prices. Other writers (e.g. Lubell, 2002) have suggested how perceptions of collective as well as personal cost and benefit can motivate acts of citizenship such as willingness to participate in cooperatives, echoing the subjective utility beliefs of Ajzen's Theory of Planned Behaviour (1991) at the community or group level of analysis. Other writers have focused upon processes of social identification as a motivational basis for civic participation: feelings of belonging in a group or social network (e.g. Stürmer and Kampmeier, 2003); perceived efficacy at personal and collective levels (Bandura, 1997) and perceived justice (Zoellner and Schweizer-Rees, 2005). These are explored in more detail in the following section, contextualizing energy citizenship in the development of micro-generation technologies and public participation in energy policy making and development.

Contexts of energy citizenship behaviour

Social and psychological aspects of micro-generation

It is likely that decentralized generation from homes and buildings, along with local power plant such as small-scale wind farms or district heating systems with CHP plant, will represent very different contexts for energy behaviour in the future. Deployment of micro-generation and smart metering technologies will transform buildings into power stations and offer unprecedented opportunities for 'in sight and mind' energy systems. These devices not only challenge accepted ways of imagining or talking about energy generation and supply, such as the utility of the concept of 'power station' in a decentralized energy future (Devine-Wright, 2004), but are also likely to substantially raise the salience of energy issues in everyday life, making people more aware of how heat and power is generated, supplied and consumed, and closing the current awareness gap between personal energy consumption and the consequences of such consumption for environmental problems such as climate change.

If this is the case, it could lead to elevated awareness of consequences, ascription of personal responsibility and personal norms that Stern et al (1999) identified as psychological determinants of pro-environmental behaviour. But raised awareness does not only suggest new contexts for shaping moral motivations for environmentally significant behaviours; it also suggests new potential for more self-interested energy behaviours. Real-time pricing and consumption feedback via the incorporation of information and communication technologies in smartmetering devices could radically alter the potential for economic tariffs offered for generating and consuming energy at different times of day and year. Purchase of shares in community renewable energy cooperatives offers a form of energy consumerism that is simultaneously self-interested, pro-environmental and civic-minded. The potential interconnectedness of energy systems, for example through community owned power plant or locally managed microgrids of heating and power supply systems, could 'socialize' the basis of energy use, linking pre-existing place and social identity processes with energy technologies, embedding energy technologies in social networks and enhancing social cohesion. Finally, micro-generation can foster feelings of control and perceived self-efficacy amongst energy users, currently minimized by centralized energy systems, symbolized by ideals of self-sufficiency.

Recent advocacy for micro-generation energy technologies highlight the potential of decentralization for greater public engagement. Van Vliet and Chappells (1999) contrast the role of energy 'consumers' with that of 'co-providers' who are not passive recipients of energy from a centralized system, but proactive agents of change in a more interdependent and evolving system of energy products and services. Dunn (2000), Hewitt (2001), Lovins and Lehman (2002), Rifkin (2002) and Vaitheeswaran (2005) alike focus upon potential economic, technical and environmental benefits of smaller scale, new and renewable technologies, with a lesser focus upon social benefits such as greater civic participation and empowerment. These writers take the position that system evolution of this kind will lead to greater social acceptance of new and emerging energy technologies, increased well-being and quality of life, particularly in developing countries, without already well-developed, centralized grid infrastructures. Other writers have taken a stronger political and sociological focus, advocating members of the public to take greater personal responsibility and control over energy generation and supply, for example by participating in the formation of public power corporations (Morris, 2001) and helping to renew ailing civic institutions, particularly at the local level through participation in community projects (Hoffman et al, 2004).

Whether one adopts a sceptical or supportive attitude to this body of advocacy, it is apparent that it represents a novel way of thinking about energy that employs metaphors of politics and change. Advocacy contributions allude to bottom-up control and system change. Local and small-scale energy technologies will give 'power to the people' (Hinshelwood, 2000; Hewitt, 2001; Vaitheeswaran, 2005), will 'decentralize power' (Greenpeace, 2005), signalling a 'micropower revolution' (Dunn, 2000) or 'energy revolution' (Greenpeace,

2005) and be illustrated by a 'microgeneration manifesto' (Green Alliance, 2004). For example:

> *Decentralising energy would democratise energy. By enabling local action and empowering individuals and communities as produc-ers, decentralisation has the potential to bring about a massive cultural change in our attitude to and use of energy.* (Greenpeace, 2005, p2)

Excitement about the socio-cultural and political implications of decentralized energy is not limited to advocates from the voluntary sector or environmental NGOs (non-governmental organizations). It is suggested by statements made by the UK energy minister Malcolm Wickes, when launching the official consul-tation on micro-generation (DTI, 2005c):

> *Climate change is often portrayed as a global problem requiring a global solution... Many are now starting to recognise that each and every one of us has a part to play... Let us be clear. Individuals as well as Governments and corporations can make a difference. And this is where microgeneration comes to the fore. Rooftop wind turbines, solar panels, heat pumps, bio-energy, micro-hydro ... these exciting technologies can help the individual to make a real difference to our climate. As someone once said – small is beautiful. And this applies just as much to power generation as it does to mobile phones. Before the advent of large-scale power stations, self-sufficiency in energy generation was the norm – water mills used to grind corn, coal-fired boilers providing heat. Of course I am not advocating a return to the early 1900s. But advances in technology means that products are now available that allow the individual to regain this self-sufficiency.* (Wickes, 2005)

The quotation suggests that adoption of micro-generation technologies by indi-viduals is conceived as a way in which individuals, rather than businesses or government agencies, can actively take responsibility for their role in mitigat-ing carbon emissions and, in doing so, contribute to solving environmental problems, clearly implicating notions of energy citizenship described above. From a psychological perspective, the motivation for doing so is attributed to a combination of environmental concern, ascription of personal responsibility (implicating Stern et al's (1999) value-belief-norm theory as important psycho-logical determinants of pro-environmental behaviour) and a desire for self-sufficiency or control, echoing in a number of ways the writings of Schumacher in the 1970s and the concept of perceived efficacy (Bandura, 1997).

Public participation in energy policy making and local development decisions

Stakeholder engagement has now become a commonplace of energy policy development (e.g. British Biogen, 1998; British Wind Energy Association (BWEA), 2002; DTI, 2005a). Although members of the public are not always characterized as stakeholders in such consultations, individuals were invited to contribute to the 'integrated stakeholder consultation process' conducted prior to the publication of the Energy White Paper (DTI, 2003) using specific methodologies such as internet-based questionnaires, focus groups and two-day deliberative discussion groups held in England, Wales and Scotland. The public are also implicated in recently revised planning guidance on renewable energy developments (Office of the Deputy Prime Minister (ODPM), 2004), which emphasizes:

> *Local planning authorities, regional stakeholders and Local Strategic Partnerships should foster community involvement in renewable energy projects and seek to promote knowledge of and greater acceptance by the public of prospective renewable energy developments that are appropriately located. Developers of renewable energy projects should engage in active consultation and discussion with local communities at an early stage in the planning process, and before any planning application is formally submitted.*

A number of initiatives led by regional and local government have been undertaken to promote civic engagement with, and community benefit from, renewable energy development. In Scotland, a 'concordat' was proposed by Highland councillors aiming to 'encourage industry to engage openly with and within the community affected; to work to assist the maximum direct/indirect community benefit and to divulge in confidence to the local renewable energy community trust, the profitability of operations' (Highland Council, 2003). Argyll and Bute Council (2004) announced an agreement with a developer that included activities such as 'renewable energy education with local communities' and ensuring that 'maximum benefit is achieved for the communities in the area'. In the south-west of England, the Government Office devised a 'Protocol on Public Engagement for Wind Energy Developments' (Devon Association for Renewable Energy (DARE), 2004), bringing together diverse stakeholder groups with the aim of reducing uncertainty caused by the varying approaches adopted by local authorities and renewable energy developers in the region for engaging the public and other stakeholders in energy development. The DTI are considering establishing a similar protocol applicable to the UK as a whole.

The admixture of reasons for promoting civic engagement with renewable energy developments highlighted in these local and regional initiatives are also indicated by statements from central government. A DTI report on community involvement in renewable energy projects (DTI, 2000) discussed the results of community involvement in a renewable energy project:

- 'Involvement will give the community some degree of control over the scheme.'
- 'A financial return should be generated, both to the community and investors.'
- 'If successful, involvement in a community venture will provide a sense of satisfaction.'

Such statements suggest that energy citizenship, in the form of community participation in energy development, will lead to a number of social-psychological impacts for the individuals and groups involved, including increased levels of self-efficacy (control and competence) at individual and collective levels, financial benefit for local people (self-interest), positive emotional responses and elevated self-esteem (satisfaction).

Putting such policy into practice, funded UK energy programmes include the Community Renewables Initiative (CRI) put forward by the Countryside Agency, which aims to provide advice and support to members of communities wishing to develop local renewable energy projects. Other examples of government-led support for 'bottom-up' collective energy action include Community Action for Energy, managed by the Energy Saving Trust, which aims to support community involvement and action for energy conservation. The magnitude of UK local energy action, and the extent of public interest and engagement in such activity, is suggested by the fact that there are more than 500 community renewable energy projects currently underway in the UK (Walker et al, forthcoming).

These are leading to the emergence of novel energy institutions, business structures and innovative finance mechanisms, which involve alliances between public, private and voluntary sectors and are manifest in energy social enterprises and cooperatives such as Sherwood Energy Village in Nottinghamshire (an industrial and provident society), Moel Moelogan in Wales, Baywind in Cumbria and Westmill Windfarm, Oxfordshire. They also reflect new roles for individuals as 'activists' or social entrepreneurs setting up local collective energy schemes (e.g. Adam Twine in Westmill, Oxfordshire). In South Wales, a range of participatory methodologies (most notably an independently run civic referendum in which all locals aged 16 or over living adjacent to a planned wind farm site were eligible to vote) were employed by a collective of local citizens (Awel Aman Tawe (AAT), 2001). It is notable that the cost of such participation was co-funded by the UK government (DTI) in the form of an evaluation study of the efficacy of different participation methodologies, and occurred independently of formal land-use planning procedures (AAT, 2001). Although it was not instigated or delivered by the local authority, it was designed to complement and enhance existing procedures in such a way as to enable greater levels of civic involvement in renewable energy decision making and planning than are the norm.

Energy citizenship and pathways of system evolution

Activities such as these suggest an alternative view of the public in relation to energy that is not fully captured by concepts such as 'consumer', 'energy user' or 'deficit'. The energy citizenship representation suggests that while members of the public frequently act out of self-interest, they can also behave as social and political actors concerned about the perceived legitimacy or fairness of decision making, and sometimes feeling responsible for the welfare of their local community, their children and future generations, and the environment, both locally and globally. Energy citizens can feel positive and excited about new energy technologies rather than apathetic and disinterested; be aware rather than ignorant of the scale of its potential impacts on political institutions, the environment and everyday lifestyles; and be willing to engage not just as individuals but as collectives in shaping technological change at local, regional and national levels. To summarize, this suggests the following beliefs about the public in relation to energy:

- that decentralized energy technologies can foster new ways of thinking and behaving about energy, ways that may be difficult to conceive within the mindset of the centralized system;
- that individuals may feel excited and positive about new energy technologies, rather than apathetic and disinterested;
- that individuals will want to take a more active role in generating heat and power, in supplying energy and in co-managing local distribution supply networks;
- that individuals are able and motivated to engage with the wider energy system via new energy technologies such as 'smartmeters';
- that individuals value at least a degree of self-sufficiency from the centralized system, as fostered by domestic and local 'power stations', or local 'micro-grids';
- that motivation to adopt micro-generation is at least in part based upon awareness of environmental problems such as climate change, ascription of personal responsibility to respond to such problems in a way that will make a difference and feelings of moral obligation to act;
- that individuals will be motivated and able to participate in local to national level political processes such as consultations on new energy policies;
- that individuals will wish to participate in local planning consultations concerning proposed energy developments;
- that local communities will accept renewable energy developments, if such developments are conducted in a manner that gives local people some degree of control as well as economic benefit.

Tracing the likely implications of a less centralized and more participatory energy system, one might speculate as follows:

In terms of governance: energy system evolution is best guided by sustainability principles, including social aspects such as public participation, local action, equity and justice alongside remedying poverty. Boundaries between 'expert' and 'lay' should be challenged and energy decision making opened out to encompass more collective, deliberative processes involving national, regional and local debate and methodologies such as citizens panels and juries. Policy makers should adopt a perspective on technological development that aims to ensure the co-production by all stakeholders of social consensus on system evolution, based upon the theme of equitable civic rights and duties for environmental protection and quality of life.

In terms of technological change: energy citizenship suggests maximizing rather than minimizing public engagement with system evolution, for example by siting or placing new energy technologies where they are most likely to engage the public's attention, and valuing smaller-scale in addition to larger-scale developments. This could include local power plant 'in people's back yards' (e.g. on roofs of new homes) as well as smartmeters at eye height in kitchens (as already put in place in the innovative zero-carbon Beddington Zero Emission Development (BedZED), London); the public are more effectively involved as stakeholders in land-use planning decisions; economic instruments are put into place to stimulate local entrepreneurial action for energy conservation and renewable energy generation, for example the development of share-owning cooperatives involving partnerships of private, public and voluntary institutions.

In terms of public acceptance: whilst incentivizing public engagement in system evolution (for example, by rewarding individuals for time spent responding to consultations or volunteering in community energy actions, or enhancing economic returns for energy generated by small-scale plant at local or building levels), energy policy simultaneously promotes concerted action at national, regional and local levels to raise awareness of the consequences of current patterns of energy production and consumption. More assertive leadership is provided by decision makers at all levels on the shared responsibility, rights as well as duties, held by all citizens in responding effectively to energy-related environmental problems such as climate change, with the potential for individual or household carbon allowances given serious consideration.

Despite the dangers of oversimplifying each position, Table 4.2 summarizes the essential differences between the perspectives outlined above.

Presenting these ideas in this form has the disadvantage of suggesting that these representations are dualistic opposites, and that the 'energy citizen' view will or should simply replace the 'consumer/deficit' as normative in UK energy policy. Instead, it is argued that all of these different facets of representing energy, and the public in relation to energy, are to different degrees already implicated in different aspects of UK energy policy and practice, and that past research on social representations of environmental beliefs (Castro and Lima, 2001) has demonstrated how change commonly involves not the 'replacing' of

Table 4.2 *A summary of facets of social representations of energy system evolution*

Facet	Evolution as centralized	Evolution as decentralized
Technological	Centralized Large-scale Automated, 'plug and forget' 'Hard'/technical	Decentralized Smaller-scale User engagement 'Soft'/socio-technical
Environmental	Continued use of hydrocarbon technologies (e.g. clean coal and carbon sequestration)	Use of renewables, and avoidance of less 'green' energy resources such as waste incineration and hydrocarbons
	Support for new nuclear plant	Rejection of new nuclear plant
Governance	Top-down Centralized institutions Private sector led	More bottom-up Greater role for local and regional institutions Community cooperatives and cross-sectoral partnerships
	Exclusive Representative democracy Values expert knowledge	Inclusive Participatory democracy Also values lay knowledge
Human	Consumer/deficit Ignorant Lazy Passive Individualistic Self-interested, personal utility maximizer, egoistic values Disempowered	Consumer/citizen Aware Motivated and engaged Active Socially embedded Motivated by a range of values, including biospheric and altruistic Empowered

one way of thinking with another, but the holding of what may be perceived as mutually incompatible positions simultaneously.

Such diversity of representation in UK policy and practice does result in an often confusing picture about who energy policy is for, to what degree the public should be involved in energy governance and what beliefs about the public are compatible with a more sustainable energy system. The many different institutions involved in shaping UK energy policy and practice, from Greenpeace to the Countryside Agency, the Renewables Power Association (corporate umbrella body) to the Royal Academy of Engineering, Number 10 to the Renewable Energy Foundation and the Department of Trade and Industry, representing voluntary, private, academic and public sectors, are likely to hold these views to different degrees, explicitly and implicitly. As a result, achieving consensus about how best to achieve a 'low carbon economy' or a 'low carbon society' will require a more explicit awareness by such institutions of the models of the public latent within particular viewpoints, policies and practices.

Challenges and opportunities in promoting energy citizenship

Whilst asserting that the energy citizenship representation of energy users is more compatible with the principles of sustainable development, it is also the case that there are a number of significant challenges standing in the way of wider acceptance and adoption of this viewpoint.

First, it is by no means clear that the public are willing to take up the enhanced, active role presumed for them. Although some evidence exists that members of the public hold positive beliefs about locally embedded renewable energy developments, seeking local energy supply, a share of profits and even a degree of ownership (Devine-Wright, 2005b), some scholars of community energy involvement (e.g. Hoffman et al, 2004) have noted the more general socio-cultural trend away from civic participation as indicated by measures of social capital such as voting and volunteering, thereby expressing some scepticism about the potential for local energy projects to invigorate local democracy. If such actions are more broadly in decline in society, it may be over-optimistic to hope that decentralized energy technologies will somehow be perceived and responded to in a very different way.

Second, there are formidable obstacles to innovation in energy systems. Some of these involve institutional barriers; for example, in a debate on microgeneration in the House of Commons (Hansard, 2005), David Heath MP commented:

> *those interested in hydroelectrics have forcibly pointed out the difficulties with the licensing system. They showed me the forms that they must fill in, which are astonishingly complex. There is virtually no difference between applying to run a small water turbine and applying to run Hinkley Point (nuclear power plant) in terms of the complexity of the information that is required... That makes it very difficult for someone who is not an expert even to attempt to apply. Could we introduce a threshold below which such activities are exempt as permitted development, which might apply not only to water turbines, but micro-wind turbines too? Such policies would certainly promote the use of microgeneration among householders.*

The quotation suggests that applying or maintaining institutional processes designed for a centralized system to decentralized technologies is inappropriate and will obstruct system evolution.

Third, the manner in which key institutions in the UK electricity industry represent the public will affect or constrain change. Empirical research suggests that it is the consumer/deficit representation of energy users, rather than that of energy citizenship, that is predominant within UK institutions involved in electricity supply, regulation, metering, consumer affairs and local energy management (Devine-Wright and Devine-Wright, 2005). In the context of personal interviews, when asked to describe the 'typical domestic electricity user' industry representatives responded with statements such as:

- 'The other thing then is do we have to do it? Because people are lazy. Have they got to do it? Why should they now?'
- '... most consumers don't really care... How much is it? £400 per year? How much per month? Phah [noise of not caring]... Not just complicated mechanisms an issue. Does not care.'
- 'People don't have much understanding and it takes a lot of time to understand the whole system it is you know you just turn on the light but then the mechanism is so complicated but people don't have the interest to know about that.'

Such statements suggest little awareness or enthusiasm on the part of key stakeholders in the UK electricity system for engaging with the public as energy citizens in energy system evolution.

Fourth, the fragility of current policies to support community involvement in renewable energy generation is suggested by continued uncertainty over the long-term funding of initiatives such as the CRI, the lack of centralized coordination of community energy action across government departments (Owens, 2004) and the fact that, even in the specific case of the AAT development, where a majority of local citizens voted in favour of a proposed community-owned wind energy development in an independently run referendum, the proposal has subsequently been refused planning permission by the local authority, indicating the marginal role such non-statutory yet participatory processes can play under current planning legislation.

Finally, on a more positive note, the potential to harness personal motivation for increased control, freedom and independence in energy supply and consumption may represent a significant psychological opportunity to promote evolution towards a decentralized energy system in a manner that promotes energy citizenship and the commodity representation of energy. The following quotation about decentralized generation from a UK industry representative suggests this view:

> ... *people would really like micro-CHP ... because they hate utilities they would see it [installing micro-CHP] as 'doing them down'. I am not quite sure what the reality of independence is but*

people see disrupting this as very subservient. You are the end of the wire. You get what you are given. You get this bill it might be right you never know. I think this a very lopsided one-sided arrangement. I think customers do see that anything that would level or even that relationship – they would quite like it.

Conclusions

Just as there are different ways of understanding energy, so also exist multiple representations of the public in relation to energy, which, in part, shape how new energy technologies and systems evolve. In this chapter, two different pathways of energy system evolution (centralized and decentralized) were identified and suggested to relate to two different forms of user representations (consumer/deficit and energy citizen) and two kinds of governance (representative and participatory democracy). Whilst such alternatives suggest dualistic options and either/or thinking, it is likely that both consumer and citizen representations of the energy public coexist to varying degrees, shaped by the values and practices of the individuals and institutions involved. It is argued that, whilst 'energy citizenship' is more reflective of the values of sustainable development, significant obstacles exist to putting it into practice in the UK, not least the dominant emphasis upon energy as a 'commodity', the necessity to change commonly held 'deficit' views and the challenges involved in motivating different social groups to put aside the legacy of the centralized system and engage in energy-related governance processes at local, regional and national levels.

Acknowledgements

I would like to acknowledge the helpful comment and insights of Joseph Murphy, as well as Hannah Devine-Wright, Gordon Walker, Bob Evans, Kate Burningham and Julie Barnett. In addition, I would like to acknowledge support by the Engineering and Physical Sciences Research Council (GR/S28082/01), as part of the Supergen Networks Consortium research project.

References

Anderson, K., Shackley, S., Mander, S. and Bows, A. (2005) *Decarbonising the UK: Energy for a Climate Conscious Future*, Tyndall Centre, UK
Argyll and Bute Council (2004) 'Renewable energy partnerships will benefit communities', press release from Argyll and Bute Council, 10 May
Awel Aman Tawe (2001) *Examining Approaches to Renewables Consultation: Lessons from the Awel Aman Tawe Community Wind Farm Project*, ETSU Report, K/BD/00236/REP

Ajzen, I. (1991) 'The theory of planned behaviour', *Organizational Behavior and Human Decision Processes*, vol 50, issue 2, pp179–211

Bandura, A. (1997) *Self-efficacy: Tthe Exercise of Control*, WH Freeman and Co, New York

Barnett, J., Doherty, B., Burningham, J., Carr, A., Johnstone, G. and Rootes, C. (2005) *Environmental Citizenship: Literature Review*, report to the Environment Agency, Bristol

Berger, P. L. and Luckman, T. (1967) *The Social Construction of Reality: A Treatise in the Sociology of Knowledge*, Anchor Books, New York

Black, J. S., Stern, P. C. and Elworth, J. T. (1985) 'Personal and contextual influences on household energy adaptations', *Journal of Applied Psychology*, vol 70, issue 1, pp3–21

Boardman, B. and Palmer, J. (2003) '4CE – Consumer choice and carbon consciousness: Electricity disclosure in Europe', final project report, ECI research report 28, Environmental Change Institute, University of Oxford, Oxford

Boardman, B., Darby, S., Killip, G., Hinnells, M., Jardine, C. N., Palmer, J. and Sinden, G. (2005) '40% House', Environmental Change Institute Report Number 31, ECI, University of Oxford, Oxford

Breuker, S. (2005) 'NIMBYism and institutional capacity for wind energy development: A comparison between The Netherlands and the UK', paper presented at the Locating Renewables in Community Contexts Conference, Open University, Milton Keynes, UK, 15 November

British Biogen (1998) *Wood Fuel from Forestry and Arboriculture: The Development of a Sustainable Energy Production Industry*, British Biogen, London

British Wind Energy Association (2002) *Best Practice Guidelines: Consultation for Offshore Wind Energy Developments*, BWEA, London

Castro, P. and Lima, M. (2001) 'Old and new ideas about the environment and science: An exploratory study', *Environment and Behavior*, vol 33, no 3, pp400–423

Department of the Environment, Food and Rural Affairs (1999) *A Better Quality of Life: A Strategy for Sustainable Development for the UK*, The Stationary Office, London

Department of the Environment, Food and Rural Affairs (2001) *The Environment in Your Pocket*, DEFRA, London

Department of Trade and Industry (2000) *Community Involvement in Renewable Energy Projects – a Guide for Community Groups*, DTI, ETSU K/GE/00014/36/REP

Department of Trade and Industry (2003) *Energy White Paper: Our Energy Future Creating a Low Carbon Economy*, DTI, London

Department of Trade and Industry (2005a) *Microgeneration Strategy and Low Carbon Buildings Programme: Consultation*, DTI, London

Department of Trade and Industry (2005b) 'Community benefits from wind power: A study of UK practice and comparison with leading European countries', report to the Renewables Advisory Board and the DTI, Report 05/1322, produced by Centre for Sustainable Energy with Garrad Hassan

Department of Trade and Industry (2005c) 'Micro generation strategy and low carbon buildings programme', Consultation, June, www.dti.gov.uk/consultations/files/publication-1505.pdf accessed 15 March 2006

Devine-Wright, H. and Devine-Wright, P. (2005) 'Representing the demand side: 'Deficit' beliefs about domestic electricity users', eceee 2005 Summer Study, Mandelieu, France, 30 May to 4 June, pp1343–1348

Devine-Wright, H. and Devine-Wright, P. (2006) 'Prospects for smart metering in the UK', in Jamash, T., Pollitt, M. and Nuttall, W. (eds) *Future Technologies for a Sustainable Electricity System*, Cambridge University Press, Cambridge

Devine-Wright, P. (2004) 'Towards zero-carbon: Citizenship, responsibility and the public acceptability of sustainable energy technologies' in Buckle, C. (ed) *Proceedings of Conference C81 of the Solar Energy Society*, UK Section of the International Solar Energy Society, 21 September, London, pp51–62

Devine-Wright, P. (2005a) 'Local aspects of renewable energy development in the UK: Public beliefs and policy implications', *Local Environment*, vol 10, no 1, pp57–69

Devine-Wright, P. (2005b) 'Beyond NIMBYism: Towards an integrated framework for understanding public perceptions of wind energy', *Wind Energy*, vol 8, no 2, pp125–139

Devine-Wright, P., Hunter, S., Walker, G., Fay, H. and Evans, B. (2005) 'Energised communities? The politics and practice of community-led sustainable energy initiatives', paper presented to the 6th Biannual Conference on Environmental Psychology, Bochum, Germany, 19 September

Devon Association for Renewable Energy (2004) 'Invitation to workshops on 13th or 19th May 2004: Developing a south west protocol on public engagement for wind energy developments', internet communication, 10 May 2004

Dobson, A. (2003) *Citizenship and the Environment*, Oxford University Press, Oxford

Dunn, S. (2000) *Micropower: Tthe Next Electrical Era*, Worldwatch Institute, Washington, DC

Egan, C. (2002) *The Application of Social Science to Energy Conservation: Realizations, Models and Findings*, American Association for an Energy Efficient Economy, Report E002, Washington, DC

Ekins, P. (2004) 'Step changes for decarbonising the energy system: Research needs for renewables, energy efficiency and nuclear power', *Energy Policy*, vol 32, pp1891–1904

Green Alliance (Joanna Collins) (2004) *A Microgeneration Manifesto*, September, Green Alliance, London

Greenpeace (2005) *Decentralising Power: An Energy Revolution for the 21st Century*, Greenpeace, London

Grove-White, R., Macnaghten, P. and Wynne, B. (2000) *Wising Up: The Public and New Technologies*, a research report by the Centre for the Study of Environmental Change, Lancaster University, Lancaster

Guy, S. and Shove, E. (2000) *A Sociology of Energy, Buildings and the Environment: Constructing Knowledge, Designing Practice*, Routledge, London

Hansard (2005) 'Local Energy Generation', House of Commons Hansard Debates for 6 June 2005

Hedges, A. (1991) *Attitudes to Energy Conservation in the Home – Report on a Qualitative Study*, HMSO, London

Hewitt, C. (2001) 'Power to the people: Delivering a 21st century energy system', Institute of Public Policy Research, London

Highland Council (2003) 'Concordat sought from renewable energy developers', press release from the Highland Council, 31 March

Hines, C. (2000) *Localisation: a Global Manifesto*, Earthscan, London

Hinshelwood, E. (2000) 'Whistling in the wind: The role of communities in renewable energy development', Network for Alternative Technology and Technology Assessment, Newsletter 127 (Sept-Oct), pp17–20

Hoffman, S., Pippert, A. and Noble, M. (2004) 'Community-based energy: Concepts and case-studies', paper presented to the 18th Biannual Conference of the International Association of People-Environment Studies, Vienna, 7 July

Hughes, T. (1983) *Networks of Power: Electrification in Western Society, 1880-1930*, the John Hopkins University Press, Baltimore and London

Irwin, A., Simmons, P. and Walker, G. (1999) 'Faulty environments and risk reasoning: The local understanding of industrial hazards', *Environment and Planning A*, vol 31, no 7, pp1311–1326

Jackson, T. (2004) 'Motivating sustainable consumption: A review of evidence on consumer behaviour and behavioural change', a report to the Sustainable Development Research Network

Kempton, W. (1986) 'Two theories of home heat control', *Cognitive Science*, vol 10, no 1, pp76–90

Kempton, W. and Montgomery, L. (1982) 'Folk quantification of energy', *Energy*, vol 7, no 10, pp817–827

Lovins, A. (1977) *Soft Energy Path: Toward a Durable Peace*, Penguin, London

Lovins, A. and Lehmann, A. (2002) *Small is profitable: The Hidden Economic Benefits of Making Electrical Resources the Right Size*, Rocky Mountain Institute, Old Snowmass

Lubell, M. (2002) 'Environmental activism as collective action', *Environment and Behavior*, vol 34, no 4, pp431–454

Lutzenhiser, L (1993) 'Social and behavioral aspects of energy use', *Annual Review of Energy and the Environment*, vol 18, pp247–289

Marvin, S., Chappells, H. and Guy, S. (1999) 'Pathways of smart metering development: Shaping environmental innovation', *Computers, Environment and Urban Systems*, vol 23, pp109–126

Morris, D. (2001) *Seeing the Light: Regaining Control of Our Electricity System*, Institute for Local Self-Reliance, Minneapolis, Minnesota

Moscovici, S. (1984) 'The phenomenon of social representations', in Farr, R. and Moscovici, S. (eds) *Social Representations*, Cambridge University Press, Cambridge, pp3–69

Office of the Deputy Prime Minister (2004) 'Planning policy statement 22: Renewable energy', The Stationary Office, Norwich

Owens, G. (2004) *Community Engagement in Energy through Energy Mutuals: Interim Findings*, Mutuo, London

Pasqualetti, M. J. (1999) 'Morality, space and the power of wind-energy landscapes', *The Geographical Review*, vol 90, pp381–394

Priestley, T. and Evans, G. W. (1996) 'Resident perceptions of a nearby electric transmission line', *Journal of Environmental Psychology*, vol 16, pp65–74

Qualter, A. (1995) 'A source of power: Young children's understanding of where electricity comes from', *Research in Science and Technological Education*, vol 13, no 2, pp17–186

Reeve, A. (1996) 'Citizenship', in McLean, I. (ed) *Concise Dictionary of Politics*, Oxford University Press, Oxford, p69

Rifkin, J. (2002) *The Hydrogen Economy*, Polity Press, Cambridge

Schumacher, E. (1974) *Small is Beautiful: Economics as if People Mattered*, Harper and Row, New York

Steg, L., Dreijerink, L. and Abrahamse, W. (in press) 'Factors influencing the acceptability of energy policies', *Environment and Behavior*

Stern, P. (2000) 'Toward a coherent theory of environmentally significant behavior', *Journal of Social Issues*, vol 56, no 3, pp407–424

Stern, P. and Aronsen, E. (1984) *Energy Use: The Human Dimension*, National Academy Press, Washington, DC

Stern, P., Dietz, T., Abel, T., Guagnano, G. A. and Kalof, L. (1999) 'A value-belief-norm theory of support for social movements: The case of environmentalism', *Human Ecology Review*, vol 6, no 2, pp81–97

Stürmer, S. and Kampmeier, C. (2003) 'Active citizenship: The role of community identification in community volunteerism and local participation', *Psychologica Belgica*, vol 43, pp103–122

Szarka, J. (2006) 'Wind power, policy learning and paradigm change', *Energy Policy*

Tleubayeva, M. and Devine-Wright, P. (forthcoming) 'Towards an environmental psychology of sustainable energy', *Zeitschrift Umweltpsychologie*

Tyler, T. R., Rasinski, K. A. and Griffin, E. (1986) 'Alternative images of the citizen: Implications for public policy', *American Psychologist*, vol 41, no 9, pp970–978

Vaitheeswaran, J. (2005) *Power to the People: How the Coming Energy Revolution Will Transform an Industry, Change Our Lives and Maybe Even Save the Planet*, Earthscan, London

Van Vliet, B. and Chappells, H. (1999) 'The co-provision of utility services: Resources, new technologies and consumers', in Shove, E., Southerton, D. and Chappells, H. (eds) *Consumption, Everyday Life and Sustainability*, A Reader for the European Science Foundation Summer School, 21–26 August

Walker, G. (1995) 'Renewable Energy and the Public', *Land Use Policy*, vol 12, no 1, pp49–59

Walker, G., Hunter, S., Devine-Wright, P., Evans, B., Hunter, S. and Fay, H. (forthcoming in 2007) 'Harnessing community energies: Explaining and evaluating community-based localism in renewable energy policy in the UK', Special Issue of *Global Environmental Politics*

Wickes, M. (2005) Speech given to the MicroPower Conference, London, 7 July, www.dti.gov.uk/ministers/speeches/wicks070705.html accessed 5 December 2005

Zoellner, J. and Schweizer-Rees, P. (2005) 'Acceptance of wind energy plants – exemplified by the counties Aurich (Lower Saxony) and Ohrekreis (Saxony-Anhalt)', paper presented at the 6th Biannual Conference of Environmental Psychology, University of the Ruhr, Bochum, Germany, 19 September

Section III
TECHNOLOGY AND SUSTAINABILITY: CONTEXTUALIZED ACCOUNTS

Chapter 5

Governance Lessons from Green Niches: The Case of Eco-Housing

Adrian Smith

Introduction

Ideas under the label alternative technology (AT) were an early expression of sustainable technology. AT emerged in the 1970s, advocated by a social movement with a particularly radical approach to technology development; to specific forms of technology; and to the social goals that technology must facilitate (Winner, 1979; Smith, 2004). Housing was an early concern for AT activists, and many of the housing ideas espoused by the movement remain alive amongst green builders today. This chapter is concerned with those green building ideas and activities. They represent a vision for green housing quite different from the homes most of us live in.

Why and how should we take notice of these ideas and activities? Well, sometimes associated initiatives become celebrated, prize-winning exemplars of sustainable development. The Beddington Zero Emission Development (BedZED) is a recent example. It is a housing development in Beddington, South London where net imports of energy are zero. It has won many accolades,[1] attracted many visitors, and been used by policy makers as a backdrop for launching policy initiatives (e.g. a Department of Trade and Industry (DTI) photovoltaics (PV) programme). The development (82 sustainable homes) is the kind of thing many policy makers would like to see replicated. Sustainable homes like these provide the kind of 'ready made', practical solutions for policy problems, like climate change, and help ground policy rhetoric and aspiration (Lovell, 2004).

The Hockerton Housing Project[2] in Nottinghamshire is another example. This too has become an exemplary sustainable housing development, with on-site renewables and water systems supporting a row of six low-energy, earth-sheltered, passive solar dwellings. Such schemes attract media publicity and official approval (Hockerton was opened by Construction Minister Nick Raynsford). And they become objects for building research and best practice guides (e.g. Building Research Establishment, 2002). Such attention suggests there is a desire to learn from these niche housing developments.

Recent interest in green niches has also come from theorists interested in governance for sustainable technologies. The strategic creation of innovative, greener niches has been proposed as a new approach for sustainable technology governance (Schot et al, 1994; Kemp et al, 1998; Hoogma et al, 2002; Loorbach and Rotmans, 2006). In essence, the niche-based approach advocates the planned and protected creation of niche situations in which novel technical artefacts and user practices can come together in more sustainable forms (Kemp et al, 1998). The ambition is to create lessons from these 'socio-technical' niches and to use them to help diffuse sustainable practices more widely in society.

Of course, simply because the niche concept and associated ideas are new to theorists does not mean green niches are a completely new phenomenon.[3] As the opening reference to AT implies, activists have been trying to create more sustainable practices for over 35 years, with mixed success (Winner, 1979; Pursell, 1993; Jamison, 2002; Smith, 2004). Wider recognition of these green niches by society, government and business has fluctuated over this period. Current theoretical and policy interest raises their saliency once more. Whilst it is true that eco-housing was not created as a 'strategic niche', it is the case that green building activists were creating exemplars with the purpose of pressing widespread changes in housing. Their attempts do therefore have relevance for the new strategic niche management theory, which shares a similar sense of mission.

This chapter argues that drawing lessons from niches is not as straightforward as we might hope. Nevertheless, progress is possible. In the following section, niche-based approaches to sustainable technology governance are introduced. The question of socio-technical context is raised as an important consideration in the potential for this governance approach. The point is reinforced in the subsequent section, in which the characteristics of the green building movement are introduced. Green builders operate in a very different socio-technical context to mainstream volume house-builders – a point summarized in the penultimate section of the chapter. The chapter concludes by considering the implications for governance, the challenges that translating practices between different contexts poses, and some tentative proposals for policy reform.

Niche-based approaches and the socio-technical perspective in sustainable technology governance

Shove (1998) has noted how building research tends toward an exclusive abstraction of the technological and economic performance of elements of exemplary dwellings (e.g. a solar heating system). She argues that the very different 'socio-technical contexts' in which more conventional houses are built and used are ignored by such abstract technical analyses, and thus important impediments for the adoption of green housing practices (like solar heating) are subsequently overlooked (Shove, 1993; see also Rohracher, 2001). An approach concerned with socio-technical context would look to the guiding principles, industrial structure, user relations, policy, knowledge and social meanings that shape technology use in specific situations or classes of situation.

In taking the socio-technical view, however, one must be careful not to study the embedding and structuring effect of prior socio-technical practices to the exclusion of studying opportunities for new practices. Shove and others identify how existing socio-technical contexts close down space for alternative possibilities. If the socio-technical perspective is to be used in a proactive and prospective fashion, then it ought to be able to spot processes by which contexts are destabilized and space for alternatives open up. How do existing practices become problematic? How do they become disembedded? How do alternative practices exploit this space and work to reconfigure the socio-technical? In short, it would help to see some examples of socio-technical agency to complement the examples of socio-technical structuring. The green building movement and the eco-house niche it has created is one such example.

The point made in this chapter is that we must not be ignorant of the socio-technical processes creating green niches and their contexts. Actors drawn to sustainable housing solutions for, say, a regulatory imperative for 'low carbon' housing risk missing the deeper story behind the exemplars, whose broader ecological values and vision for housing is quite distinct. Co-option of green housing elements 'tends to overlook the social processes behind the design and construction of the sustainable houses, in particular the beliefs and motivations of the project team' (Lovell, 2004, p52).

Like sustainable housing initiatives before it (e.g. the low-energy homes in Milton Keynes in the 1980s), BedZED is being monitored and evaluated, reports are published on its performance, and it is serving as a basis for best practice guides. There is certainly plenty to learn from this innovative development. However, looking at things as they stand, as exemplars for wider practice, we must not forget the unique circumstances that lead to their creation. Some of the values, processes and actors involved in BedZED are different compared to more conventional housing developments. It is important that we remember this. Housing designs are 'part and parcel' of the context in which they are embedded (Leopold and Bishop, 1983; Hooper and Nicol, 1999).

In the case of BedZED, some of the unique circumstances behind its creation include a team of architects led by a determined individual (Bill Dunster), whose prior commitment extended to applying green design in the construction of his own home. They also include partnership with an innovative environmental advocacy and solutions-based organization committed to bioregional ideas for local sustainability – the Bioregional Development Group. Together they had the knowledge and motivation to build differently. For example, they went to great lengths to try and source reclaimed steel and other construction materials (Lazarus, 2002), and trained contractors in the skills needed to build their designs. They were helped in this by a client willing to consider extra-market values, interested in sustainability issues, and with concern for the life-cycle operation of its buildings (the Peabody Trust social housing landlord). Similarly, the Hockerton Housing Project was an eco-housing initiative whose process diverged from the norm. It was self-built by a community committed to green building ideas, willing to learn the necessary skills for constructing their homes, who had a material interest in the operational and life-cycle costs of the building (i.e. no developer–occupant split), and benefited from links with a pioneering green architect who lived locally. Such circumstances count. They open up opportunities for introducing new ideas, social arrangements and technological practices. This brings one back to Shove's point about the significance of contexts and histories, and the way they influence which socio-technical configurations are considered to 'work' and are valued under given circumstances.

Niche-based governance approaches like strategic niche management (SNM) seek to accelerate the influence of exemplary green solutions upon the mainstream by being more sensitive to the full socio-technical context. Advocates urge the planned and protected creation of niche situations in which novel technical artefacts and user practices can come together in more sustainable forms (Kemp et al, 1998). The ambition is to derive lessons from the novel 'socio-technical' practices in the niche, and to act upon these lessons in such a way as to help similar practices diffuse more widely in the mainstream. These socio-technical lessons relate not only to the narrow technical and economic aspects of green housing, such as water systems, but also to the kinds of social practices and meanings upon which those technologies are predicated, such as active management of water use. Wider lessons are also sought relating to the institutional reforms (e.g. training, markets, regulations) that can help niche forms of housing 'work' beyond niche contexts, and so diffuse more widely (Hoogma et al, 2002; Smith, 2004).

Such lessons have to be acted upon (embedded). A constituency of support is necessary. This becomes easier as the alternative socio-technical practices become more efficient, effective and credible – a process helped by the recruitment of resourced, capable and influential actors. Commitment and participation in strategic niche management is thus a 'collective endeavour' of 'state policy-makers, a regulatory agency, local authorities (e.g. a development agency), non-governmental organizations, a citizen group, a private company, an industry organization, a special interest group or an independent individual' (Kemp et al, 1998, p188). This socio-technical constituency has to create a climate in which niche practice appears a reasonable expectation for the future (Basalla, 1988). It has to persuade resourced actors that their interests and values can be reframed and best met through the alternative arrangements in the niche, compared to the older practices extant in the wider socio-technical regime. It is this networked, multi-stakeholder approach that suggests SNM is more a governance approach than a specific policy instrument or task of government. Indeed, embedding niche lessons will require coordination across a variety of policy instruments (e.g. fiscal incentives, regulatory measures, education and training, public procurement).

However, there is a paradox to the SNM social learning ambition. Niches in tune with the incumbent regime are more likely to diffuse (Weber et al, 1999), but will not demand very great changes in socio-technical practice; whilst radical niches, like those studied here, will not diffuse much at all. Highly divergent sustainable niches will have to offer considerable positive feedback, in terms of development potential and scope for profitable application, before 'mainstream' actors break from the existing regime and move into the sustainable niche (Smith, 2003). A question remains as to precisely how incumbent regimes (including policy reforms) are able to act upon lessons about sustainability generated by green niches. At which juncture, it is time to proceed with the case study. It represents an acid test for niche-based approaches since it deliberately involves particularly radical initiatives in sustainable development. This chapter contends that differences across socio-technical contexts appear to be a key issue affecting the degree of learning and diffusion of practices.

The green building movement and its socio-technical characteristics

The numbers of eco-houses built in the UK each year are small, and difficult to pin down precisely. Brinkley estimates around 100 eco-houses are built each year, without elaborating how he arrived at the estimate (2002, p218). One survey put the total number of 'sustainable housing schemes' in the UK at 400, without listing them, and provided details for 80 of the best, all of them small-scale (White, 2002). Whatever the precise number, it seems clear that eco-housing remains a very small niche. It compares with around 190,000 new dwellings built each year and a total stock of 26 million dwellings in the UK.[4] Nevertheless, policy support is increasingly being applied to the promotion of more sustainable practices for the hundreds of thousands of homes proposed in the large housing schemes planned for growth zones like Thames Gateway and elsewhere.[5] There is a desire amongst policy makers for these volume housing projects to provide sustainable homes and communities (Office of the Deputy Prime Minister (ODPM), 2005). How can the eco-housing experience inform this mainstream interest in sustainability?

The figures above put the contribution from building new, greener houses into perspective. It will take over 130 years to replace the existing stock of dwellings at existing build rates. So, whilst this chapter is concerned about the movement of green building ideas into the mainstream construction of housing, an even bigger challenge is to refurbish and improve the performance of existing buildings. Some of the ideas set out in this chapter about translating green building practices across contexts remain relevant, but the refurbishment issue merits special attention beyond this contribution.

The origins of eco-housing in the UK can be traced back to the 1970s, when alternative technology activists began thinking about housing and the environment. A few architectural schools (e.g. Cambridge, Hull and the Architectural Association in London) provided bases for people to develop ideas and gave them space for practical experimentation. One iconic example was the autonomous home built by the Street Farmers' radical eco-architecture group in the fields of Thames Polytechnic in 1972. 'Autonomy' was an important early theme in green building – a theme that encapsulated many of the issues that remain of concern to green builders today. As students graduated they joined other activists in building eco-homes or renovating existing houses.

Early activists financed themselves by becoming involved in government research programmes and demonstration projects in low-energy homes (which emerged in the wake of the energy crises), as well as trying to initiate their own projects and green architectural practices. It was really a practical attitude, and an impatience to get on and build eco-houses, and learn from the experience, that characterized the early green building movement. Green builders took advantage of public funds for job creation schemes and grants available for renovation and housing cooperatives in order to create more radical eco-housing projects. Early green builders Brenda and Robert Vale explained this practical attitude thus:

> *One live, working experiment, however impractical if it were applied universally, will transmit an idea far better than a shelf full of theoretical reports. Something that can be seen and touched and shown to work to some degree arouses curiosity, and curiosity in turn leads to solutions.* (Vale and Vale, 1975, p18)

This attitude lends itself to a desire for eco-houses to both inspire and debate housing sustainability. Initiatives were well documented in the alternative press, such as *Undercurrents* magazine, and served as test beds for ideas being disseminated by green builders through books, articles and TV series (e.g. Vale and Vale, 1975; Clarke, 1976; McLaughlin, 1976; Borer and Harris, 1994).

In many cases there are direct links between these earlier activities and initiatives today – for example, pioneers continue practicing and training others. Today, a loose but much broader network of builders, architects, activists and clients continue to experiment and produce homes echoing earlier concerns. Green builders communicate via specialist publications, associational organizations, events and training programmes (e.g. *Building for a Future* magazine; the Association for Environment Conscious Building; self-build training courses; and the advocacy and design work of green architects and activist builders, like Architype, Gaia Architects). There is an element of mission within these networks. This is not solely a niche market. It includes the advocacy of green ideas and techniques through training, and the public promotion of green houses as practical demonstration projects. It seems reasonable to give this activity the label green building *movement* in order to denote the spirit of collective advocacy involved in green housing.

As the green building movement evolved, so a number of salient principles and practices emerged. Although early initiatives sometimes performed poorly (e.g. solar heating systems), this did not invalidate these efforts in the minds of activists; it simply illustrated a need for further commitment, experimentation and development.

Green building is not a monolithic school of architecture and building: practitioners disagree over trade-offs between various goals (e.g. earth-sheltered constructions with high thermal mass versus lightweight, insulated timber designs). Even so, there remains a sufficiently distinctive collection of overarching values, ideas and practices from which a socio-technical niche can be discerned.

Autonomy has already been mentioned as an early goal, and reflected the ideals of some in the wider AT movement, who considered the ecological society as being best served by socio-technical practices that facilitated decentralized, cooperative living (see Boyle and Harper (1976) for debate about the practicability and desirability of this ecological vision). The ideal for autonomous housing is 'a house operating independently of any inputs except those of its immediate environment. The house is not linked to the mains services of gas, water, electricity or drainage, but instead uses the income-energy sources of sun, wind and rain to service itself and process its own wastes' (Vale and Vale, 1975, p7). Housing technologies were sought that might offer the prospect for occupants to live 'off grid' and facilitate green lifestyles. An activist in 1975 described their attempts at autonomy thus:

> *Through our building activities we have a good mechanism for the application of some alternative technology hardware. For example, one of the schemes currently underway includes a solar roof as part of an improvement grant scheme. In another case, involving the renovation of six small cottages into four new units we have actually managed to get approval for a methane digestor – not to mention a possible solar panel and wind generator: this is also part of a standard improvement grant scheme. We envisage that the largest of the four new units will be about 50% energy autonomous for a negligible extra capital cost.* (John Potter, COMTEK, quoted in *Undercurrents*, Issue 11, p9)

In addition to environmental autonomy was an interest in social autonomy, expressed in a concern for technologies and techniques that could be 'understood and practised by people without recourse to specialised training' (Vale and Vale, 1975). There was interest in the idea of 'dweller control' over the house-building process (Turner, 1976) and concomitantly in housing technologies susceptible to user participation, control and even self-build.

Even if autonomous housing is forgotten today, associated technologies and techniques retain interest amongst green builders because they are still considered to reduce dependency on distant, external resource inputs. These include rainwater harvesting; water recycling and on-site wastewater treatment; superinsulation of the building fabric; material selection on locality and environmental grounds; passive solar design; heat and electricity storage; small-scale wind energy, PVs and other distributed micro-generation technologies in the home; heat recovery and heat pumps. Today, in some cases, the environmental appeal of these technologies is augmented by mass market potential, in contrast to AT interest in decentralized, self-reliant ecological lifestyles.

Bringing these elements together in eco-houses requires a different approach to housing design, construction and operation. One is less free to draw upon external resources to power and service a housing structure that normally takes any form irrespective of location, but which in eco-housing must be sensitive to the site and resources. The eco-house becomes a working machine in which lifestyles have to be considered carefully and matched with the supply systems built into the house. So, for example, cisterns for rainwater collection and use are not only sized adequately, but also are sited to make full use of gravity, in order that electronic pumping loads are kept low. The layout of buildings, and even angle of glazing, is set to make full use of the low sun in winter, whilst shading the high sun in summer. Site specificities count. Rooms are allocated according to use over the day and year, and the proximity this requires with respect to thermally massive walls, solar conservatories, natural ventilation airways, and the services of water supply, use and treatment. In short, form follows environment to a greater extent than high-input conventional housing.

Design follows material life-cycle principles as far as possible. The sourcing of materials, preferably as local as possible, has been a key concern. It involves care for the environmental footprint embodied in building elements. Natural, local materials are preferred. Techniques using natural materials include cob (mixing earth and straw), strawbale construction, rammed earth, timber and use of lime as a setting agent in mortars, renders and concrete (Borer and Harris, 1994; Jones, 2002). Alternatively, some green builders have been trying to reuse construction materials and reclaimed elements in their projects. Attempts have been made to source items such as doors and structural steel. Merchants in reclaimed building material are gradually beginning to emerge. Obstacles include the absence of test procedures and robust standards of performance for reclaimed elements, and tight commercial and time pressures discouraging demolition contractors from reclaiming materials.

Concern for material sustainability has led some green builders to reconsider vernacular forms of housing. That is, learning from traditional practices and techniques that out of necessity were restricted to local materials and low energy and water inputs for services. Solutions to old material constraints are reinterpreted under the new social desire for environmental restraint. Traditional vernaculars consequently inspire some green builders, and adaptations in building techniques and materials are made, such as natural ventilation techniques rather than mechanical air conditioning.

Technical novelties in the niche involve new or renewed skills from green builders. They have to be able to integrate the various technologies, and use construction techniques different to those evident in more conventional, volume house-building situations. Superinsulation and heat recovery, for example, require levels of air tightness much higher than in normal housing. Similarly, roofs designed to collect rainwater, rather than shed it rapidly, must be exceptionally watertight, and the stored water has to be managed carefully in order to ensure it is potable and available.

Eco-houses can also place different demands on the occupants. Some favoured technologies require more active relationships – such as monitoring power levels in batteries, checking water levels in cisterns, closing blinds over sun-spaces during evenings, maintaining grey water treatment systems. If a passive solar house becomes a few degrees colder in winter then comfort might be sought using technologies like jumpers and warm clothing rather than a conventional heating system. Not all green households are so ascetic, and well-designed eco-houses need not be hard work. The point remains, however, which is that the values and perspective of householders has to approach that of the designers if the eco-house is to work.

Within green building, this socio-technical matching of design and use has been eased by the fact that many eco-houses are bespoke projects, and households have the commitment and inclination necessary. Enthusiasm for ecological principles inclines users to be (at least initially) more patient, tolerant or supportive in adapting to the demands of the working relationship involved between occupant and eco-house. Such involvement has been facilitated by an attachment to self-build or client involvement in projects (Broome, 1996). The small-scale nature of developments also permits experimentation. Compared to the development of a large housing estate, problems in the single eco-house can be corrected more easily and with less pervasive consequences.

Indeed, green builders acknowledge the importance to innovation of learning from mistakes. Tough lessons were one outcome of early AT initiatives in housing. Indeed, US-based autonomous housing activist Mike Reynolds has called for 'forums of failure' where green builders can experiment. His designs are the product of '30 years of failure. You learn by failure. We're asking politicians to give us situations where we can fail'.[6] Over time, performance does improve. And yet developments today, like BedZED, continue to experience teething difficulties over socio-technical performance. The niche-based policy view would see this as a valuable part of a broad learning process. There are limits, of course. Clients have to be happy with the finished product, and too many failures simply give green building approaches a bad reputation in the wider industry. However, a degree of openness towards trial and error is in sharp contrast to the situation for volume house-builders, where making the same mistake on the scale of hundreds of houses across a large project can leave the developer open to considerable liabilities.

Cost considerations feature in all projects. Eco-housing concepts still have to be financed if they are to be built, and sometimes the capital costs of designs are higher. However, where additional costs can be met, they are often justified by savings in operation, or by appeal to environmental externalities, or offset against wider network costs avoided (e.g. superinsulation and lower or no utility bills) (Vale and Vale, 2000). At other times, green values lend themselves to a very different kind of calculation, such that costs, whilst an important constraint, are nevertheless traded-off differently, and marginally higher costs are tolerated for green features, or offset through self-building.

Here, green building principles imply a different set of criteria for judging the efficacy of ecological construction. Green builders challenged narrow economic measures from the outset (e.g. *Architectural Design* 1972, vol 7, p420). Evaluation is extended to concern for total operating costs over the life-time of the building, as well as the initial material and construction costs. Lifetime criteria count in green building. Even where life-cycle paybacks are small, the extra costs are accepted on the grounds of more diffuse environmental values. One green household even justified spending £15,000 on PV panels (bringing only £150 energy saving each year) by comparing their green expenditure with the amounts other households spend on stylish kitchens (Lovell, 2004, p49).

Clearly, green builders are operating in a socio-technical niche very different from the mainstream regime for volume house-building.[7] Life-cycle cost considerations are not so deeply embedded in volume house-building, where the split between developer and user is felt more keenly. Materials are shipped in as required without much thought given to embodied energy or resources, other than to the extent that this is partially reflected in the price of materials. Volume builders use standard designs (e.g. a pattern book of twenty or so different house designs) and well-known, tried-and-tested construction techniques (e.g. brick and block) in order to keep costs down. Standardization facilitates the easy use of subcontracted labour, and permits the bulk purchase of materials through central supply offices. Such attachment can leave developers unaware of new technological developments elsewhere, or wary of pursuing innovations.[8] There is little opportunity for occupants to become involved in volume housing design. Moreover, occupants are anticipated by volume house-builders in a very passive and conservative fashion. Homes are marketed through internal fixtures and fittings rather than environmental performance.

If the green building movement were to serve a strategic niche function then lessons would have to navigate quite a divide in socio-technical practice. That socio-technical divide is illustrated in summary form in Table 5.1. Somehow, innovations in the green niche would have to be translated into meaningful lessons for the mainstream regime.

Under pressure for environmental improvements, building regulations have for many years attempted to improve the energy performance of buildings. They are currently being extended to a wider set of sustainable building considerations. However, these are based on judgements of what is deemed a reasonable demand upon the mainstream socio-technical regime (Raman and Shove, 2000).

In contrast, green building practices can rub against existing regulations – which are designed with the mainstream housing socio-technical regime in mind. The use of reclaimed materials, like structural steel, and natural materi-

Table 5.1 *Comparing the green building socio-technical niche with the volume house-building regime*

Socio-technical feature	Green building	Volume house-builder movement
Guiding principles		
Values	Ecology	Profit and loss
Design principles	Green vernacular	Standard patterns (e.g. limited
	Adapt to site-specifics	designs) of developers choosing
		Centralized teams
Technologies		
Hardware	Novel	Tried and tested
	Small-scale/autonomous services	Grid/central services
Materials	Natural and reclaimed materials	Routine, bulk purchasing
	Green building supplies	Listed suppliers
Innovation	Step changes	Incremental
Industrial structure		
Process	Bespoke building	Speculative building
	Specialist builders	Subcontracted labour
Skills	Mix of craft-based and speciality skills, e.g. renewables	Standard industry practice Mass production
Costs	Life-cycle costs	Construction costs
	Premium for sustainable features	Profit from contracted price
Risk	Single house – learn from correcting faults	One fault on many dwellings – large liabilities
Scale	Single dwellings or small groups	Larger estates
User relations		
Household assumptions	Active commitment to a green life style	Passive & conservative consumers
User involvement	High-user involvement or self-build	Purchaser of property
Policy		
Regulations	Land use planning and building regulations can be a constraint	Land use planning and building regulations are followed
Knowledge		
Search criteria	Knowledge relevant to reducing the ecological footprint of homes	Knowledge relevant to existing competencies and business practice
Meaning		
Commitment	Sustainable values and green life styles	Housing markets and building regulations

Note: Socio-technical dimensions taken from Geels (2005).

als, like straw bale, can worry building inspectors since their regulatory framework is unfamiliar with such novelty. Unless there has been a precedent locally, 'the process of obtaining a permit can be a lengthy and laborious process of dialogue, education, and planning' (Bainbridge et al, 1994, p47; Rosen, 2004). Regulatory mismatches simply underscore the different socio-technical context in operation in the green building niche. In advance of any widely disseminated record of performance, green builders have to make an extra effort to get their novel designs and materials passed by building control regulations. In contrast, volume house-builders are largely followers of building regulations like energy efficiency, which they lobby hard to influence – and then fail to comply with in as many as one third of new developments (Raman and Shove, 2000; Environmental Data Services (ENDS), 2005).

Of course, this simple contrast between green builders and volume house-builders necessarily skims over a number of subtleties, but it is sufficient for the purpose of this chapter, which is to point out the considerable difference in socio-technical practices that produce eco-houses and volume houses respectively. So how might mainstream lessons about sustainable housing design be drawn from green niches that diverge so radically from the mainstream?

Discussion – Lessons for governance

A small green niche in eco-housing in the UK, produced by the green building movement, offers practical lessons for sustainable housing. The key challenge for governance is translating this particular framing of sustainability from an originating, green building socio-technical context that is very different from the target, mainstream house-building socio-technical context. Reinterpreting problems and adapting deep green lessons to mainstream requirements proves extremely challenging. As one interviewee put it:

> *Most green houses are one-offs, they're bespoke buildings and they happen because an individual wants a building like that, and there's someone there who can do it; but if we tried to replicate that into the hundreds, let alone the thousands and tens of thousands of buildings that are needed! It's not possible to do a typical green building and replicate it thousands of times over. The issue ... is how do we get the volume building sector to take on green building principles, but they are still buildable and fit the volume housing market.* (interview)

Given this situation, governance for sustainable technologies must support translations between niche and mainstream. This support and translation can take a number of forms, but here the focus is on two possibilities in particular: (1) adapting lessons and practices; (2) altering socio-technical contexts. Each of these is elaborated on below.

Translation 1: Adapting lessons

The first translation involves the more conventional idea of technology transfer, in the sense that a specific socio-technical practice is taken out of its originating context and inserted into a different context. This is what we see when policy makers hold up eco-houses as exemplars for a policy goal, like climate change or water conservation. They wish to see certain socio-technical practices in the eco-house replicated more widely, such as greater use of active solar heating, or more grey water recycling.

In order to be successful, there must be sufficient flexibility for these practices to be considered to 'work' and add value under more mainstream contexts. Do these practices make sense to mainstream developers? Are they profitable? Can it be installed easily, given the skills and routines of contractors? Are these innovations the kinds of things that count in developer considerations and requirements? How easily can institutions and infrastructures be reformed to facilitate transfer? How disruptive of supply chains are these new socio-technical practices, and can they open up new business opportunities for suppliers? These are some of the considerations that will determine whether a socio-technical practice arising in a green niche is considered also to work in volume house-building situations.

Governance processes that negotiate changes to building regulations might be considered to follow this mode of translation. In regulations, builders are required to meet certain environmental standards.[9] Additional to government regulations – whose implementation is reliant upon actors beyond the state – are voluntary codes for improving environmental performance created and adopted by firms, professional associations and other bodies (e.g. accreditors of environmental management systems). It is in this sense that regulations and codes can be considered as governance. However, this kind of translation and associated mode of governance is not particularly demanding because it does not demand deep deliberation on the problem of sustainable housing. Standards and codes are negotiated on the basis of what is judged to be a reasonable demand, given mainstream socio-technical contexts (Raman and Shove, 2000). In other words, regulation looks at translating green practices that do not pose too much disruption (relatively speaking) for mainstream socio-technical contexts. Governance processes that include the building of new coalitions behind alternative problem framings are largely absent. Governance is relatively thin here because it does not seek to transform the criteria against which niche socio-technical practices are deemed to 'work' in mainstream contexts.

So, under this first mode of translation, governance is likely to help only those practices that fit easily into the mainstream context for house-building, or that can be added on without too much cost or difficulty. If highly insulative glazing can be found at the right price it will be installed. If PV is required it will be bolted on – even in advance of more sensible energy conservation measures (Liddell and Grant, 2003). However, sometimes even relatively straightforward practices, like greater wall insulation, can pose a challenge if standards become too tight. Cavity spaces may become too great for traditional brick-and-block build methods. Alternative, prefabricated wall materials may perform better but require new supply chains, skills and installation techniques on-site. Obviously such considerations become even more acute for more unusual green build techniques, like rammed earth or strawbale.

The governance lesson here is that it is important to understand the differences in socio-technical context in order to better identify which greener practices have sufficient flexibility to be considered to 'work' under both contexts. However, the kinds of practice that are sufficiently flexible to work under such divergent contexts may not be particularly green – they cannot embody the green context that produced them (i.e. underpinning values and performance criteria) too strongly, since this would limit their transferability. Transferability requires them to be able to 'slot into' the mainstream practices, or be susceptible to being added on, without too much disturbance. As such, add-on technologies like PV might be more attractive than fundamental reorientations like autonomy. Unfortunately, under this kind of translation you may get diffusion but little innovative buy-in. House-builders and households will continue to be regulation following rather than voluntarily over-complying in search of sustainable development.

Translation 2: Altering contexts

The second kind of translation open to governance recognizes the difference in context more profoundly, and seeks to understand the values, principles and activities that create green housing. Governance processes might then try to inculcate in the mainstream some of the values, principles and framings held in the green niches. That is, try to bring the mainstream socio-technical context closer to that behind the green building movement. This is a more challenging goal because it would imply some kind of buy-in from mainstream actors, including customers, who might then become more inclined to innovate. Green elements would become a standard part of housing practice and a motivation for future experimentation and innovation in housing. This could be encouraged through governance processes that support intermediary developments that bring green builders and mainstream developers together. In short, governance must bring the mainstream volume house-building world into sustained contact with the green building niche.

In some respects, BedZED is an example of an intermediary development that is doing this, since it involved mainstream firms in building services (Arup), structural engineering (Ellis and Moore), and construction management (Gardiner and Theobald). Mainstream frameworks can pose challenges when contractors are brought into greener housing projects, since novelty in the latter can undermine competences rooted in the former. At BedZED, mainstream contractors had to get to grips with the demands of the sustainable designs, learn from the experience, and in this way expand their capacity for engaging in projects for sustainable development.[10] For example, the project had to convene special workshops for contractors in order to explain the special airtightness requirements for the project, and feedback lessons from the construction of early units into that for subsequent units. This adds time and effort to construction (Ramshaw, 2004, p13). Training has to provide an accommodation between any specialist demands in green building techniques and the skill base of the workforce available.

Similarly, the Hockerton Housing Project exposed a regional housing developer, Gusto Homes, to green building ideas and practice to such an extent that it inspired a reorientation of the business. Some of the practices at Hockerton now feature in the more conventional homes built by Gusto. Gusto build to standards greener than regulations require, and incorporate features such as rainwater collection, solar water heating and mechanical heat recovery ventilation. These have added a premium of around 10 per cent to the homes at their award-winning Millennium Green development.

Stamford Brooke is another project that approximates to the idea of an intermediary development. It is a project led by the National Trust (a landowning conservation charity) for 650 houses on land it owns in Cheshire. The Trust's core concern for building conservation and traditional construction vernaculars mean it has an affinity with the green building movement and an interest in sustainability (interview evidence). At Stamford Brooke the Trust was required to use mainstream developers, but remained keen to push for green standards of construction. To this end they encouraged and cajoled the developers into building to regulatory standards expected in ten years time. The process was helped by a technical committee including green building practitioners. This committee has kept pressing the developers and pointing to examples, techniques and suppliers that could meet these green requirements. In this way, developers were made aware of elements of the green building movement that could prove useful in the future, and might even be incorporated in other developments today (e.g. high-insulation windows, low-flush toilets).

In effect, these examples are like stepping-stones between niche and mainstream. They provide spaces where the practicability for volume house-builders to operate more like green builders can be explored. Viewed in this light, we can re-conceive initiatives like BedZED as instances of developments, the values, processes and circumstances of which actually bring contrasting socio-technical contexts together. Green builders and mainstream developers become aware of the principles, framings, criteria and constraints that the other operates under. Governance processes might be innovated to try and support these intermediary developments.

In practice, the split between the above two kinds of translation is less stark than it appears. In trying to transfer a green socio-technical practice into the mainstream, some kind of socio-technical changes will be required. The difference is in the degree of involvement in translation by actors from each context, and the degree of change being deliberated: is it about transferring practices or deliberating upon fundamental re-framings? One advantage of creating learning situations like BedZED and Stamford Brooke is that volume house-builders can come into contact with green building ideas on a more practical basis and learn through doing. As a result, there might be scope for a deeper internalization of elements of the green building vernacular, such that more conventional translation (e.g. through building regulations) appears less daunting and proceeds more effectively. Such insights have relevance beyond eco-housing – wherever the goal is to explore how green niches can help mainstream practices be reoriented more sustainably. The insight provided by the analysis here is to look for creative clashes between socio-technical contexts in specific developments.

How might governance processes do this in a practical sense? Here are some tentative suggestions requiring further research:

- More imaginative facilitation and process criteria either in publicly funded programmes, or through regulatory frameworks, could provide a lead. The history of the green building movement suggests there will always exist activists who seek out opportunities to build as sustainably as possible. More bureaucratic public authorities and technical committees are unlikely to be able to practice this kind of nimble, green entrepreneurship. Nor can they appreciate and internalize all the values constituting green building. Governance could certainly give such values room to breathe.
- Risky new projects could be underwritten with public funds, or public land made available to innovative green community initiatives (access to land being a key constraint for many grass-roots groups).
- Public authorities could help by being sympathetic to designs and techniques that sit awkwardly with existing building controls and planning regulations. Perhaps even relaxing controls temporarily, without implying general precedents, and under careful monitoring.
- Space for failure as well as success has to be provided.

However, this kind of intervention will only help nurture green building initiatives; it will not translate lessons for the mainstream. It is the intermediary developments that do this, and here innovations in governance are required. We have already discussed the potential for intermediary developments to bring actors from the two contexts together. Alternatively, training policy could support 'green sabbaticals' that would cover salary costs for likely change-agents from mainstream firms to spend a period of time working alongside activists in green niches, and then disseminating the lessons drawn from the experience. Such experiences ought to aim to build mutual understanding, and respect for the goals of radical sustainable development.

A final kind of governance reform that could encourage greater engagement from the mainstream would be to reform the way public policy is developed. This has been suggested by the Sustainable Consumption Roundtable (SCR) in the context of making food retailing more sustainable, but might be usefully applied to niche-mainstream situations too. The Roundtable noted how mainstream firms have little incentive to devote finite capital in green projects when more conventional business investments yield higher returns:

> For early movers on sustainability the opportunity cost of ignor-
> ing this fundamental business principle can be highly damaging...
> What is needed is an approach that gives encouragement to the
> early movers to demonstrate what is possible on a menu of issues,
> with a clear commitment to enact well-designed policy measures if
> the rest of the sector does not follow. (SCR, 2005, pp1, 4)

The 60-year history of an organic niche in the food context (Smith, 2006), and
the 30-year history of the eco-housing niche discussed here, both suggest that
pioneering movers on sustainability have existed for a long time. What the SCR
suggests is the need to encourage involvement in niche experimentation by early
movers from the mainstream. That can be done if government commits to
reforming regulations in step with the sustainability activities of leading players.
This will boost first-mover advantages. In other words, it will create an incentive for mainstream involvement in niches because it has the supportive
attention of policy makers and assurances that this provides an advantage in
the governance of the sector.

Conclusion – Translating between niche and mainstream

This chapter has noted how innovative green housing developments can sometimes attract widespread approval without widespread emulation. Policy
makers hold them up as examples in good practice that embody their policy
goals, whether for low carbon emissions, or efficient water usage, or resource
productivity, etc. This chapter has argued that such exemplars are often products of a niche socio-technical context quite different from the mainstream
housing context, in which it is hoped some reproduction of good practice will
take place. The point was illustrated by elaborating the development of ideas in
the green building movement in the UK over the last 30 years. The green niche
was then contrasted with the volume house-building context. Ideas for translating lessons and practices between these two contexts were presented.
Considered in this translation light, existing policies, such as building regulations, can be understood differently. They seek to transfer socio-technical
practices that have sufficient flexibility to translate easily between contexts. An
additional, and more ambitious, governance strategy would seek to try and
transform the mainstream socio-technical context itself. It would try and steer
that change closer to the values and guiding principles that exists currently in
green niches.

Of course, whilst it is essential to understand opportunities for translating
sustainability lessons between different socio-technical contexts, and to remember the values that inspired and underpinned the creation of niche green
initiatives, it is also wise to recognize constraints for learning. What works on a
small, niche scale may not do so on a mass scale. Nor can one naively ignore
those business, government and social actors that have a powerful material

interest in mainstream socio-technical regimes. Implicit in SNM is a rational model of governance, in which niche lessons will be taken up and acted upon consensually. A more argumentative model would see those lessons being variously taken up, rejected or ignored by different actors, and debated and reshaped to suit their material and economic interests. We see some evidence for this in the slow and limited reforms to building regulations. In practice, green niches are likely to be only a *source* of debatable ideas for mainstream sustainable development, not a *model* for mainstream transformations. This chapter has explored how anyone interested in niche-based approaches to the governance of sustainable technologies might engage in those debates. How those debates play out in practice will constitute what sustainable development actually means for mainstream housing.

Acknowledgements

This chapter draws upon work funded by the Economic and Social Research Council in the UK. It benefits from the time practitioners, policy makers and academics have given freely to discuss their experiences and provide their perspectives on the topic. I am grateful to them and to participants in the Governance of Sustainable Technologies research network, towards which this chapter was a contribution and which benefited from network discussions. The network was organized by Joseph Murphy, whose editorial comments on an earlier draft of this chapter were particularly helpful.

Notes

1   Including the shortlist of the prestigious Stirling Prize of the Royal Institute of British Architects.

2   Winner of the 2001 Solar Prize for solar construction by the European Solar Association.

3   Whilst the proactive creation of green niches is new in sustainable technology theory, it derives from a perspective on technology development deriving from evolutionary economics.

4   Statistics from Office of Deputy Prime Minister website (www.odpm.gov.uk accessed 27 April 2005).

5   Over the next ten years the Thames Gateway project plans to construct 120,000 new homes; and the growth zone around Milton Keynes and the South Midlands anticipates over 133,000 new homes.

6   Presentation to the International Earthship Summit, University of Brighton, 29–31 October, 2004.

7   In what follows, the mainstream socio-technical regime has been characterized using secondary sources (e.g. Leopold and Bishop, 1983; Colquhoun, 1999; Hooper and Nicol, 1999; Barlow, 2000; Housing Forum, 2002;).

8   See: www.cabe.org.uk/news/press/showPRelease.asp?id=669 accessed 28 October 2004.

9   In practice, they earn points for different kinds of improved building performance, which means they have a degree of flexibility over how they incorporate environmental considerations into their building, and they must attain an overall score for the house to be deemed adequate.

10 Arup, for example, are now working with the Shanghai Industrial Investment Corporation to develop a sustainable city on the island of Dongtan in the mouth of the Yangtze River. Of course, businesses can be involved simultaneously in relatively sustainable and unsustainable projects. The point made here is that involvement in greener projects stretches their capabilities, making them able to meet client, regulatory and public demands for more sustainable practices when and where they arise.

References

Bainbridge, D., Steen, A. and Steen B. (1994) *The Straw Bale House*, Green Books, Totnes

Barlow, J. (2000) *Private Sector Housebuilding: Structure and Strategies into the 21st Century*, Council of Mortgage Lenders, London

Basalla, G. (1988) *The Evolution of New Technology*, Cambridge University Press, Cambridge

Borer, P. and Harris, C. (1994) *Out of the Woods: Environmental Timber Frame Design for Self Build*, Centre for Alternative Technology Publications, Machynlleth

Boyle, G. and Harper, P. (1976) *Radical Technology*, Wildwood House, London

Brinkley, M. (2002) *The Housebuilder's Bible* (5th Edition), Burlington Press, Foxton

Broome, J. (1996) 'Making sustainable homes', *The Architects Journal*, 7 November, pp48–50

Building Research Establishment (2002) *General Information Report 89 – BedZED*, BRE, Watford

Clarke, R. (1976) *Technological Self-Sufficiency*, Faber & Faber, London

Colquhoun, I. (1999) *RIBA Book of 20th Century British Housing*, Butterworth Heineman, Oxford

Environmental Data Services (2005) 'Flouting of building regulations undermines energy efficiency gains', *ENDS Report* no 360, January, pp13–14

Geels, F. (2005) *Technological Transitions and System Innovations*, Edward Elgar, Cheltenham

Hoogma, R., Kemp, R., Schot, J. and Truffer, B. (2002) *Experimenting for Sustainable Transport: The Approach of Strategic Niche Management*, Spon Press (Taylor and Francis), London.

Hooper, A. and Nicol, C. (1999) 'The design and planning of residential development: House types in the speculative housebuilding industry', *Environment and Planning B: Planning and Design*, vol 26, pp793–805

Housing Forum (2002) *The Housing Forum Demonstration Projects Report*, Housing Forum, London

Jamison, A. (2002) *The Making of Green Knowledge*, Cambridge University Press, Cambridge

Jones, B. (2002) *Building with Straw Bales: A Practical Guide for the UK and Ireland*, Green Books, Totnes

Kemp, R., Schot, J. and Hoogma, R. (1998) 'Regime shifts to sustainability through processes of niche formation: The approach of strategic niche management', *Technology Analysis and Strategic Management*, vol 10, no 2, pp175–195

Lazarus, N. (2002) *BedZED Construction Materials Report 1*, Bioregional Development Group, London.

Leopold, E. and Bishop, D. (1983) 'Design philosophy and practice in speculative housebuilding: Part 1', *Construction Management and Economics*, vol 1, pp119–144

Liddell, R. and Grant, N. (2003) 'Eco-minimalism: Getting the priorities right', *Building for a Future*, vol 12, no 3, pp10–13

Loorbach, D. and Rotmans, J. (2006) 'Managing transitions for sustainable development' in Olsthoorn, X. and Wieczorek, A. (eds) *Understanding Industrial Transformation: Views from Different Disciplines*, Springer, Dordrecht

Lovell, H. (2004) 'Framing sustainable housing as a solution to climate change', *Journal of Environmental Policy & Planning*, vol 6, no 1, pp35–55

McLaughlin, T. P. (1976) *A House for the Future*, Independent Television Books, London.

Office of the Deputy Prime Minister (2005) *Creating Sustainable Communities: Delivering the Thames Gateway*, ODPM, Wetherby

Pursell, C. (1993) 'The rise and fall of the appropriate technology movement in the United States, 1965–1985', *Technology and Culture*, vol 34, no 3, pp629–637

Raman, S. and Shove, E. (2000) 'The business of building regulation', in Fineman, S. (ed) *The Business of Greening*, Routledge, London

Ramshaw, J. (2004) 'Signed, sealed and delivered: Achieving airtightness', *Ecotech – Sustainable Architecture Today*, vol 9, July, pp12–17

Rohracher, H. (2001) 'Managing the technological transition to sustainable construction of buildings: A sociotechnical perspective', *Technology Analysis & Strategic Management*, vol 13, no 1, pp137–150

Rosen, N. (2004) 'Tread carefully', *The Guardian – Society*, 30 June, pp14–15

Schot, J., Hoogma, R. and Elzen, B. (1994) 'Strategies for shifting technological systems: The case of the automobile', *Futures*, vol 26, no 10, pp1060–1076

Shove, E. (1993) 'Technical possibilities and building practices: The realities of passive solar design', paper presented to the 3rd European Conference on Architecture, Florence, 17–21 May

Shove, E. (1998) 'Gaps, barriers and conceptual chasms: Theories of technology transfer and energy in buildings', *Energy Policy*, vol 26, no 15, pp1105–1112

Smith, A. (2003) 'Transforming technological regimes for sustainable development: A role for alternative technology niches?', *Science and Public Policy*, vol 30, no 2, pp127–135

Smith, A. (2004) 'Alternative technology niches and sustainable development', *Innovation: Management, Policy & Practice*, vol 6, pp220–235

Smith, A. (2006) 'Green niches in sustainable development: The case of organic food in the UK', *Environment & Planning C: Government and Policy*, forthcoming

Sustainable Consumption Roundtable (2005) 'Sustainable consumption: The role of food retail', Roundtable Submission on the FISS (Food Industry Sustainability Strategy), www.sd-commission.org.uk/publications/downloads/Roundtable_submission_on_the_FISS.pdf accessed 15 March 2006

Turner, J. F. C. (1976) *Housing by People: Towards Autonomy in Building Environments*, Marion Boyars, London

Vale, B. and Vale, R. (1975) *The Autonomous House*, Thames and Hudson, London

Vale, B. and Vale, R. (2000) *The New Autonomous House*, Thames and Hudson, London

Weber, M., Hoogma, R., Lane, B. and Schot, J. (1999) *Experimenting with Sustainable Transport Innovations: A Workbook for Strategic Niche Management*, University of Twente Press, Twente

White, N. (2002) *Sustainable Housing Schemes in the UK*, Hockerton Housing Project, Hockerton

Winner, L. (1979) 'The political philosophy of alternative technology: Historical roots and present prospects', *Technology in Society*, vol 1, pp75–86

Chapter 6

Micro-Generation: A Disruptive Innovation for the UK Energy System?

Raphael Sauter and Jim Watson

Introduction

The connection of large numbers of distributed generators to the electricity system is essential to meet the UK government's targets for renewable energy (10 per cent of electricity supplied by 2010) and combined heat and power (10GW of CHP installed by 2010). In its recent micro-generation consultation (Department of Trade and Industry (DTI), 2005) the UK government confirmed the Energy White Paper's (DTI, 2003) aspiration for larger contributions from renewable energy sources beyond 2010 in response to climate change and energy security concerns. In many other countries too, there is a trend towards smaller scale sources of generation (e.g. International Energy Agency (IEA), 2002; Pehnt et al, 2006). A variety of drivers has been identified for the expected growth in micro-generation technologies, including environmental concerns (particularly the need to reduce carbon emissions), worries about the insecurity of energy supplies, the development of new energy service companies and programmes to tackle fuel poverty.[1]

One of the most radical implications of the expected growth in distributed generation is the possibility of micro-generation of electricity in individual homes. This could be by means of micro CHP units instead of central heating boilers, or by small-scale renewable technologies such as photovoltaic (PV) panels or micro-wind turbines. In the UK, micro CHP units with capacities of less than 5KWe (kilowatt electricity) could achieve an installed capacity of 300–500MWe (megawatt electricity) by 2010 as compared to zero in 2002 (Department of the Environment, Food and Rural Affairs (DEFRA), 2004). The potential micro CHP market for the UK is considerable, with around 17 million gas-fired central heating systems and 1.3 million gas boilers sold every year (Crozier-Cole and Gareth, 2002).

If they are installed in sufficient numbers, domestic micro-generation technologies could be highly disruptive for current energy systems (Fleetwood, 2001; Adner, 2002). By blurring the boundary between energy supply and demand these technologies could change consumer-provider relationships, and enable consumers to play a more active role in energy service provision (Chappells et al, 2000; Collins, 2004). They could raise awareness of energy consumption and therefore result in different consumption patterns or lower the amount of electricity consumed (Dobbyn and Thomas, 2005). They also present a new set of challenges for the electricity system. Micro-generation technologies might foster fundamental changes in system architecture, operation and control (*The Economist*, 2000).

The main aim of this chapter is to analyse the potential disruptiveness of micro-generation for the system of electricity provision. As some of the more rhetorical literature about micro-generation suggests, the extent of disruptiveness depends on what perspective is taken. It leads to the question of what or who might be disrupted? The chapter examines this question in the light of the large technical systems (LTS) framework that was developed by Thomas Hughes. This framework provides a basis for considering the electricity system as a whole, including its technologies, institutions, regulations and actors. It consequently broadens the firm-based analysis of disruptiveness that is most prevalent in the literature. The paper argues against a general framing of micro-generation as being 'radical' or 'disruptive'. Such a framing might create unnecessary resistance in the existing energy system. Instead it tries to identify particular system components and actors that may indeed be radically affected by micro-generation, and to outline governance implications.

The chapter comprises three main parts. The first outlines the main features of LTS and examines the extent of inertia within these systems. Drawing on the historical LTS perspective, the second part outlines the range of possible impacts of change – from incremental to radical impacts – from an *ex ante* perspective. It builds on an approach that considers the impact on innovating firms, and extends this to include broader impacts on socio-technological systems. It also places particular emphasis on the consumer's role in these systems. The third part of the paper applies this broader framework to the case of micro-generation with reference to the UK energy market. It considers a number of different models for micro-generation deployment and conducts an initial analysis of disruptiveness with respect to a wide range of possible impacts. This analysis shows that different models of deployment will have different patterns of disruptiveness. The chapter will conclude with implications for governance strategies for the market uptake of micro-generation technologies.

The electricity system as a large technical system

The study of LTS has become increasingly important during the past two decades (e.g. Hughes, 1983; Mayntz and Hughes, 1988; Davies, 1996). These systems – which include air traffic control, electricity supply industries and rail networks – tend to consist of a complex network of new and old technologies, bespoke equipment and organizational relationships. Large technical systems are singled out as a distinct category since they have unique characteristics. According to Thomas Hughes, a pioneer in this area, they have three distinct features (Geyer and Davies, 2000):

- A set of components that can be both technical (e.g. power stations, transmissions lines) and non-technical (distribution companies, environmental laws).
- A set of horizontal and vertical interconnections between the components. This means that changes in one component often lead to changes in others.
- A control component that sets out the way in which the economic and wider social performance of the system is regulated. Control is exercised by management and economic systems (e.g. wholesale power markets), technical systems (e.g. control technologies) and regulatory systems (e.g. through regulators).

Hughes' work on the LTS concept was focused on the invention and development of an LTS, its transfer to other societies and system growth. The latter was subsequently further investigated (Mayntz and Hughes, 1988). LTS research then focused on the question how to change an existing LTS (Summerton, 1994a) and on the governance of an LTS in the context of a changing environment characterized by the questioning of the economic performance of hierarchical systems, a distrust of centralized governmental action and the decreasing acceptance of LTS by the public (Coutard, 1999).

System inertia and barriers to change

The defining features of a typical LTS identified by Hughes have far-reaching consequences for the operation and development of the system. These consequences are particularly important for those proposing to make radical changes to current technical systems – in our case, those seeking to radically shift the UK energy system to incorporate micro-generation. As Thomas Hughes points out, achieving such a radical shift is not merely a technical challenge. It also faces considerable opposition since it challenges the institutional and organizational arrangements of the current system.

> *Large scale technology, such as electric light and power systems, incorporate not only technical and physical things such as generators, transformers and high-voltage transmission lines, but also*

utility companies, electrical manufacturers and reinforcing institutions such as regulatory agencies and laws... Large technological systems represent powerful vested interests... Numerous persons develop specialised skills and acquire specialised knowledge appropriate for the system of which they are part... [They] construct a bulwark of organisational structures, ideological commitments, and political power to protect themselves and the systems.
(Hughes, 1983, p2)

It is therefore necessary to further investigate these barriers to change, in order to understand what radical change means to an existing LTS. Based on Hughes' study, the following main barriers for change of an existing LTS can be distinguished: technology, institutions (including regulations) and actors or social groups, which are all interconnected. At the technological level, the electricity system has been characterized by central power plants that are horizontally integrated via dispatch systems. It has also been vertically integrated on the supply and demand side. The provision structure is vertically organized around central power plants through infrastructures such as gas pipelines and the electricity network. Electricity is transported through the transmission and distribution network to the consumption points, largely in a one-way direction from the central power plant to the consumer.

At the institutional level, hierarchical and centralized organization around an LTS, such as state bureaucracies and industries, have led to new forms of organization; institutions reflect these new systems and are even organized around them (Mayntz, 1993) with the underlying objective to protect LTS as their *raison d'être*. In this context Winner (1999) points out that technologies have been used to settle political issues in a particular community or are adapted to a certain political context. Winner therefore doubts if the creation of new administrative hierarchies is a necessary consequence of particular technological systems. Rather, the type of hierarchy is a political choice. As this paper will illustrate, a number of different organizational structures could be used to support the deployment of micro-generation.

Both companies and political administrations may be opposed to radical changes due to internal organizational inertia or 'cultural lock-in' of big organizations (Foster and Kaplan, 2001). Incumbent industries may oppose disruptive changes to the current systems since their products, knowledge and marketing have been developed for the existing market and LTS (Tushman and Anderson, 1986). The institutional embedding process of technology can be understood as the alignment of supporting institutions to the system and a resulting, mutual reinforcing interdependence. This techno-institutional lock-in of the existing energy system has also been described as 'Techno-Institutional Complex' (TIC) (Unruh, 2000).

Actors' behaviour is not only limited or enabled by technology and institutions, but also by societal values (e.g. Mayntz and Scharpf, 1995). The symbolic value of LTS has played an important role in the construction process of national electricity systems: it has been argued that large hydropower stations have contributed to building Swedish nationalism (van der Vleuten, 2004), while in France, nuclear technology has been closely linked to the idea of the 'grande nation' and French national identity (Hecht, 1998).

The embedded character of socio-technical systems has led to an 'entrenchment' of big technological systems that makes it difficult to keep them under social control (Collingridge, 1992) and to introduce deliberate change. Similarly, Walker (2000) identified 'entrapment' as a systemic facet of LTS. Thus, changes in these systems are rather incremental to optimize the existing system and are often described as path-dependent. In recent years the advent of liberalization and re-regulation has started to challenge this structure, though many of the technical aspects of vertical integration and centralization remain. LTS are inherently averse to radical change. The following section will explore how changes in these systems could occur in spite of these barriers.

Changes in an existing LTS

To explain changes in an existing LTS, Hughes developed the concept of 'reverse salients' that can occur only if the system follows specific goals such as economic efficiency. If components (technical or non-technical) of the system do not comply with the system's goals, they constitute reverse salients. In an efficiency-seeking system these are inefficiencies caused by internal or external factors. Under this logic, component changes occur to remedy these systemic imperfections and consequently maintain and stabilize the existing LTS in the longer term. These changes or corrections are incremental. However, they can also constitute the 'nucleus of a new system' (Hughes, 1983, p81). If the corrected component does not fit with other system components, they will have to adapt, which may lead to a new system.

Climate change policy adds an additional system goal: the reduction of CO_2 emissions in energy generation and consumption. Climate change could therefore create reverse salients within the existing LTS, where innovations correct the electricity system into a more low-carbon direction (Winskel, 2002). Domestic micro-generation can be seen as such an innovation. The question is, however, what the consequences for the other system components will be. Does micro-generation fit into the existing system as a new component, or is it rather the 'nucleus of a new system' and therefore a radical change to the existing electricity system?

With respect to system change Summerton (1994b) stresses the 'undoing of closure', that is, the opening of entrenched structures as a prerequisite for system 'reconfiguration' – a term that already indicates its incremental approach. She distinguishes between three possible reconfigurations: first, a territorial expansion and interconnection of similar systems across political borders; second, the crossing of functional system boundaries, for example between the energy system and communication system, which results in a 'second order system' (Braun and Joerges, 1994; van der Vleuten, 2004); and finally, reorganization as a consequence of liberalization and the end of former monopolies. While these reconfigurations are incremental in nature, since they are supposed to improve the existing system, 'abrupt innovation' can result from a series of incremental changes over time (Summerton, 1994b).

If these reconfiguration concepts are applied to the case of micro-genera-tion, micro-generation technologies are unlikely to expand the electricity system beyond the current territorial or political borders (at least in industrialized countries). Instead, these technologies will decentralize and localize the electric-ity infrastructure. They could also help foster the creation of a second order system that is based on the electricity system and the communication technol-ogy system. Different operational configurations of micro-generation that are incorporated in the models set out later in this chapter could increase the use of communication/control technologies to manage the energy system, and there-fore replace existing control mechanisms.

Furthermore, the reorganization of the electricity system underway in terms of privatization and re-regulation contributes to the undoing of closure at the level of institutions and actors. Both on the supply and demand side, micro-generation could broaden the number of actors and therefore change the institutional arrangement. On the supply side, as Walt Patterson has pointed out, micro-generation will increase the role of system participants who have hitherto existed on the fringes of the energy system. These include 'architects, civil engineers, building service engineers … not to mention electrical and gas engineers and information technology specialists' (Patterson, 1999, p161). On the demand side, liberalization and the introduction of competition made it possible for consumers to become active consumers or even 'co-providers' (van Vliet, 2004).

From this perspective micro-generation is both the result and source of changes in the existing electricity LTS. The central question of this chapter is whether the changes induced in the system by micro-generation will go beyond incremental changes: will micro-generation be disruptive to the electricity system, as has been claimed by a number of different studies (e.g. Patterson, 1999; Dunn, 2000; Fleetwood, 2001; Adner, 2002)? The framing of new tech-nologies such as domestic micro-generation as radical or disruptive is a central point in the analysis of its potential market uptake. Stakeholder perceptions of whether a technological innovation is incremental or radical – whether it actu-ally is or not – could influence its market adoption or rejection (Hall and Kerr, 2003).

Unlike incremental innovations, radical innovations are at variance with the existing system; they disrupt and destroy (Abernathy and Clark, 1985). Christensen used the term 'disruptive innovations' (Christensen, 1997), defined as creating 'an entirely new market through the introduction of a new kind of product or service' (Christensen and Overdorf, 2000). Studies dealing with disruptive innovations are mainly concerned with the question of how these innovations enter the mainstream market and the implications for companies' strategies (e.g. Utterback and Acee, 2003). Other studies try to clarify the defi-nition of 'incremental' and 'radical' innovations. However, they are focused on product research (Garcia and Calantone, 2002) or on the technical aspect of inventions (Dahlin and Behrens, 2005).

In the following section we develop a framework to assess the impact of new technologies on an existing LTS in terms of their disruptive or incremental nature by drawing upon the LTS and innovation literature.

Towards an understanding of radical system change

To understand the disruptiveness of micro-generation for the electricity system, this chapter builds on Abernathy and Clark's (1985) matrix on the impact of new innovations on firms, as previously suggested by Hofman (2003). This matrix is helpful for the analysis since it assesses the impact of a technological innovation on different main features of the electricity system. In its original version, it considers two sets of factors – those that influence the technological capabilities of the firm and those that influence the firm's relationship with its customers. For each factor, general descriptions of incremental and radical impacts of new innovations are provided.

Abernathy and Clark acknowledge the limitations of this approach. They state that 'technological innovation may influence a variety of economic actors in a variety of ways, and it is this variety that gives rise to differing views of the significance of changes in technology' (Abernathy and Clark, 1985, p4). For this reason, their original focus on the innovating firm is not sufficient for the consideration of more systemic impacts of micro-generation. This criticism has also been acknowledged by many other recent studies taking a more systemic perspective (e.g. Hall and Kerr, 2003; Geels et al, 2004).

In their analysis of the innovation dynamics of fuel cell technology, Hall and Kerr (2003) point out that this narrow perspective is 'myopic'. Analysing the impact of fuel cell technology on the automobile, they suggest that all stakeholders or actors affected by a technological innovation should be included in the analysis of whether it is incremental or radical.

Consequently new more systemic categories are introduced along the above-identified main features of the electricity LTS into Abernathy and Clark's matrix. Instead of the focus on technological capabilities and customer relationships, the adapted matrix includes three domains of innovation: technical, non-technical and control components. Technical components are the design and embodiment of electricity generation technology, electricity network design and metering issues. Non-technical components include the ownership of the network and generation units, the structure of system participants, supply chain or installers' network, consumer-supplier relationship and skills (including labour, managerial and technical). Finally, the control components are analysed in terms of the regulatory setting (e.g. distribution charges), load management (through the settlement system), the wholesale market and the financial framework.

Following Abernathy and Clark, general descriptions of incremental and radical impacts of new innovations are provided in Table 6.1. The table includes a new third column which identifies actors that are most affected by each inno-

Table 6.1 *Some impacts of micro-generation innovation on the existing electricity LTS*

Domain of innovation	Range of impact of innovation		Actors affected
	Incremental	Radical	
Technical components			
Design/embodiment of electricity generation technology	Improves/perfects established design	Leads to the application of new design (e.g. PV, Stirling engine etc)	Manufacturers, installers, consumers, builders
Electricity network design	Strengthens existing network structure	Demands new system components (e.g. decentralized networks)	DNO, suppliers, regulator, telecom. Industry
Metering	Builds upon existing meters	Replaces existing metering infrastructure	Suppliers, DNO, regulator
Non-technical components			
Network ownership	Keeps existing ownership structure	Radically changes the ownership structure (e.g. microgrids)	Network operators, suppliers
Generation ownership	Keeps existing ownership structure	Radically changes the ownership structure (e.g. to consumers)	Generators, suppliers, consumers
Structure of system participants	Strengthens existing structure between incumbent players	Leads to new market entry (independent micro-generators)	All
Supply chain/ installers' network	Uses existing structures	Destroys existing channels	Product supplier, installers
Consumer–supplier relationship	Strengthens existing relationship	Radically changes traditional relationship (e.g. consumers generate own power)	Consumers, suppliers, regulator
Skills (labour, managerial/ technical)	Extends viability of existing skills (e.g. links between electrical and heating engineers)	Destroys value of existing expertise (e.g. installation of hydrogen fuel cell systems)	Manufacturers, installers, architects
Control components			
Regulatory setting	Strengthens existing regulation structures	Disrupts and creates new regulation structures (e.g. for energy services)	Regulation authority, all market participants
Load management	Builds on established procedures	Introduces new dispatch/settlement procedures	Network operators, suppliers
Wholesale market	Strengthens existing market structures	Creates new markets (e.g. decentralized markets)	Network operators, suppliers
Financing	Builds upon existing financial arrangements	New market of financial services (e.g. to finance energy services)	Suppliers, consumers, banks

Source: Our elaboration, based on Abernathy and Clark (1985)

vative impact. The lists of actors identified in the table are not exhaustive, but include those that are likely to be involved and/or affected most by the diffusion of micro-generation technologies.

As previously noted, micro-generation could be disruptive to a wide variety of actors: firms that produce power generation, transmission and distribution equipment, electricity network operators (e.g. Distribution Network Operators (DNOs)), regulatory institutions, energy suppliers, consumers and so on. The number and type of actors affected depends, however, on the national context and its market concentration and organization. The innovation matrix for micro-generation developed in this chapter is designed to be applicable to different contexts in order to allow comparative studies in the future. However, the empirical results in this paper refer to the UK context.

The explicit inclusion of actors in the broadened matrix underlines the fact that perception influences judgements about whether micro-generation is considered to be radical or disruptive. If it is perceived as radical innovation that destroys existing markets, it is likely to face resistance from some system participants. This perception will, however, depend on how micro-generation units are owned, installed and operated. The distinction between the different domains of innovative impact helps to identify those parts of the system that will be particularly disrupted – and higher resistance might therefore be expected. These individual impacts contribute to an overall picture of the 'systemic' disruptiveness of micro-generation.

Models of micro-generation deployment

To examine the extent to which micro-generation technologies could be disruptive in the light of the adapted matrix, it is important to take into account some different possibilities for their deployment and use (Watson, 2004). In particular, these different possibilities imply a variety of roles for consumers and energy suppliers, but also finance actors, DNOs and others. They also have different implications for existing institutions, and for other parts of the electricity system, including its technical infrastructure (Sauter et al, 2005).

Three alternative models for deployment have been developed for this task that suggest a wide range of consumer and energy supplier roles. The main aim was to develop these models with a different degree of consumers' financial and behavioural involvement. They represent three rather 'extreme' models in terms of the consumer–supplier relationship, and the role each side might play. Consumer behaviour ranges from a passive role to a 'co-provision' role (van Vliet, 2004). The former role does not imply substantial changes in behaviour as a result of having micro-generation installed in the home. The latter sees consumers as becoming more active participants in the electricity system as self-providers of energy services. The dynamic nature of the three models is reflected in Figure 6.1. It shows on the horizontal axis the company's role (between the current role as main energy supplier to a more passive back-up role) and on the vertical axis the consumer's role (ranging between passive consumer and co-producer).

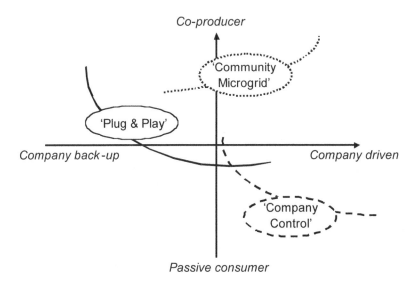

Figure 6.1 *Deployment models for micro-generation technologies*

The 'Plug & Play' model is inspired by the idea that micro-generation might allow consumers to become partly independent of conventional energy suppliers. Consequently the consumer takes the initiative to purchase, install and operate the unit. The micro-generation unit is owned and financed by the home-owner. Within this model, consumers might change their consumption pattern due to a higher awareness of energy issues gained during the purchasing and installation process. They might also do so for economic reasons in response to the reward they are offered for any exported electricity: they might choose to maximize their revenue through exporting as much electricity as possible into the grid under a scheme of attractive export rewards, or they could choose to maximize their on-site consumption, particularly if export rewards are low (i.e. they reduce their electricity bill through lower consumption of imported electricity). Technically, this leads to the requirement of an import-export or additional generation meter – possibly read remotely. This could also include half-hourly data collection linked to time-of-day pricing if the micro-generator was able to sell electricity at the real-time market price. This would have a potential impact on the control components of the system.

The 'Company Control' model is based on the notion that companies might use fleets of micro-generators as a substitute for central power generation – that is, as a virtual power plant.[2] This model involves a more passive consumer who only provides the 'site' in its home for the micro-generation unit, which is owned by an energy service company (ESCO) or traditional energy utility. As opposed to Plug & Play, under this approach the company is the driving force for the micro-generation installation – for example, promoting through marketing to its existing customer base. The micro-generation unit is operated according to the company's needs so as to help balance supply and demand,

and to avoid buying electricity from the wholesale market.[3] The needs of the consumer – particularly for hot water and heating in the case of micro CHP – must also be taken into account to some extent. Technically, this model requires real-time remote control over the unit, involving a multifunction meter with information about the operation mode (import, export) and a facility to send control signals to the micro-generator to optimize the supply-demand balance.

In the third model, consumers and institutions at the regional or local level in a particular geographical area decide to pool their resources to develop a 'Community Microgrid'. The Community Microgrid model could be set up by the local community and consumers to provide the energy services required, as suggested elsewhere (Devine-Wright, 2004). The micro-generation units are connected to the microgrid, which potentially implies a high level of consumer involvement on two different levels. They have primary control over their unit, but also will help to guarantee the supply-demand balance within the microgrid. Their incentive to do this stems partly from the fact that they may own shares in the community energy company. Since micro-generated electricity fed into the grid goes to the nearest load, this arrangement avoids the export and settlement in the wider distribution grid, where it is only valued – if at all – at the wholesale electricity price. As under Plug & Play, a high awareness on energy issues or economic incentives may lead to changes in consumption patterns. Technically it has similar implications to Company Control.

Table 6.2 summarizes the three deployment models, distinguishing between their social, economic and technical characteristics. In the following section, these different models will be tested against the developed matrix set out in Table 6.1. For each model, it is assumed that a significant number of UK households have micro-generation units installed.[4]

Micro-generation models and disruptiveness in the UK context

The UK has a particularly long history of electricity and gas liberalization, and its energy industries have a specific configuration of actors. These include a strong regulatory body (Ofgem – the Office of Gas and Electricity Markets), an electricity generation and supply market that is increasingly characterized by a few large vertically integrated companies, organizational separation of transmission and distribution companies, and a high rate of switching between energy suppliers by consumers. Switching has now reached over 50 per cent, and household customers can switch their energy supplier every 28 days. A large share of electricity generation is contracted to the large suppliers and not traded in the wholesale market. The transmission system is managed by National Grid, whereas the distribution network is owned by 12 DNOs in England and Wales, two in Scotland and one in Northern Ireland.

Although there is currently no major micro-generation policy framework in place in the UK, some regulatory barriers have been removed. For example, simplified connection and metering standards have been introduced. Ofgem and the DTI have both issued consultations on their future approach to micro-

Table 6.2 *Models for the deployment of micro-generation*

	Plug & Play	Company Control	Community microgrid
A) SOCIAL			
Agency	Consumer	Company Energy supplier	Community energy company
Ownership	Consumer Homeowner	Energy supplier (potential ownership shift to customer at the end of financing contract)	Community energy company (with private wire network) owned by community / citizens
Consumer involvement	Consumer may adjust behaviour depending on income structure	Passive consumer, but provides 'site' for micro-generation unit	Consumer possibly adjusts behaviour & may have financial stake in energy company
B) ECONOMIC			
Up-front financing	Cash Bank loan Finance packages	Company: balance sheet Customer: lease payments; premium energy price; contracting (mCHP)	Company: balance sheet Customer: lease payments; premium energy price
Income for MG owner	Avoid power import Generation reward Export reward	Avoids buying electricity at system buy price Avoids grid losses	Retail price for micro-generated electricity since direct supply via private wires
Implications for Consumers	Financial savings over medium/long-term	No up-front costs and energy service contract	No up-front costs, energy service contract and potentially influence on company strategy
Energy supplier	Loss of sales Potential new market for home energy services	Avoidance of buying wholesale electricity and lower grid losses	Direct supply of micro-generated electricity to customers via private networks
DNO	Loss in income from use of system charges?	Loss in income from use of system charges?	n.a.
C) TECHNICAL			
Operation mCHP	On-site balance according to domestic heat demand	System balance as additional component to on-site balance	Shared operational interest
PV, micro wind Metering Communication & control	Weather dependent Import-Export meter – possibly read remotely Possibly consumer access to time-of-day pricing information	Weather dependent Remote multifunction meter Facility for control signals to micro-generator Integration into company balancing systems	Weather dependent Import-export meter – possibly read remotely Facility for control signals Consumer access to time-of-day pricing information

Source: Authors' elaboration

generation (DTI, 2005). The DTI strategy – which was published in April 2006 – might include economic incentives for micro-generation deployment and measures to remove barriers in areas such as planning. Ofgem's work is much more technical and incremental, and it is unclear whether this will have a significant impact on micro-generation deployment.

One area that is unlikely to be addressed by these policy and regulatory initiatives is the current fiscal framework for energy investment in the UK. Existing fiscal rules distinguish between investments on the energy supply side and investments on the demand side – particularly in domestic households (Chesshire, 2003). Whereas consumers have no access to tax or depreciation allowances for investments in micro-generation, companies investing in central generation are able to use enhanced capital allowances. They are also able to pass on any sales tax (VAT) through to their customers, whereas household consumers have to pay VAT for any micro-generation units they buy. Some micro-generation technologies now attract a lower rate of VAT than the standard rate of 17.5 per cent.

With regard to the supply chain for micro-generation, the picture varies from technology to technology. The UK boiler market is dominated by a supply chain that goes from the manufacturer via merchants and/or retailers to the installer. There are around 100,000 registered installers in the UK (Society of British Gas Industries (SBGI), 2003), most of which have no experience with micro CHP technology because deployment is at such an early stage. For solar PV technology, there is now a relatively small network of specialist companies and installers in the UK as a result of a modest government support programme. Micro-wind is a largely untested technology, with very few trained installers, though suppliers have concluded deals with at least two major utilities to supply this technology.

Following on from this brief outline of the UK context, the matrix of impacts of micro-generation outlined in Table 6.1 can be applied to the three deployment models in Table 6.2. This results in three different patterns of disruptiveness for micro-generation, as summarized in Figure 6.2. These patterns have been generated by assigning quantitative indicators of disruptiveness to each innovative impact. These indicators are on a scale of zero to three. A score of zero for a particular impact of micro-generation stands for no change, a score of one indicates an incremental change, and a score of three denotes a disruptive impact.

It is important to acknowledge that this quantitative scoring process is inherently subjective, and the results from it should be treated with some care. Judgements have been made about the breadth of each type of innovative impact that micro-generation might cause. In addition, the scoring process has tried to take into account impacts on the system as a whole, including those for a variety of actors. In some cases, it has been difficult to reach an aggregate score across these actors, which shows the need for further research that would have to distinguish impacts for different actors. In view of these limitations, the results presented here are tentative. They provide an indication of whether micro-generation deployed under a specific model is likely to be disruptive for

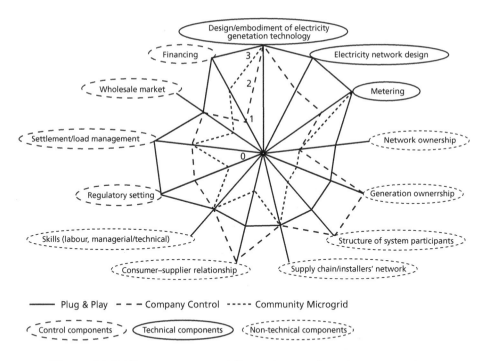

Figure 6.2 *Different patterns of disruptiveness for micro-generation*

the electricity LTS. They also suggest which specific impacts are likely to be the most disruptive.

Overall, the Plug & Play model of micro-generation is likely to be particularly disruptive to the consumer–supplier relationship, while Community Microgrid implies the most radical changes across the system as a whole. The Company Control model is rather incremental and strengthens some features of the current LTS – particularly the dominant position of the incumbent energy companies.

In all of the models, the impact on 'design/embodiment of electricity generation technology' is similar, due to the shift from central power plant based electricity generation to decentralized power plants. They are independent of the financial or operating framework. Also, supply chain and skills will have to change considerably under all approaches. However, the quality of these changes will be rather different. While under Plug & Play the current manufacturer-merchant/retailer-installer will have to include a new product (which has proven to be radical in the case of condensing boilers), under Company Control the suppliers are likely to build up a new (or extend their existing) installers' network. The need for new skills is similar for all models. All of the models require considerable new technical skills (e.g. for installing micro CHP systems instead of conventional boilers), new managerial skills (in particular for Community Microgrid). To a greater or lesser degree, each model also suggests significant investments in transmission and distribution infrastructure to support this new architecture. The settlement system will have to adapt for all models – but to a greater extent under Community Microgrid.

While Plug & Play will be particularly disruptive at the non-technical level in terms of changes in generation capacity ownership and consumer–supplier relationship, it will also imply major changes in the metering infrastructure.

Under a Company Control model, the most disruptive implications of micro-generation occur at the technology and control level. Considerable changes might be required to network design and organization, such as real-time monitoring, multifunction meters and communication tools that allow remote control of micro CHP units. This model is characterized by a continuing dominance of electricity generation by incumbent electricity companies (albeit through micro-generation rather than centralized generation). However, it is possible that these companies will offer new energy services to consumers as a quid pro quo for hosting micro-generation in their homes. In the context of the relatively high switch rate of UK households, this may represent an option for energy suppliers to strengthen their customer relationship over a longer period. It is also possible that more conventional and incremental incentives will be offered, such as simple change in tariff or export rewards linked to a supply contract. In this model, the non-technical components such as consumer–supplier relationship, ownership and structure of system participants will only change incrementally because consumers continue to have a passive role.

Community Microgrid is the most disruptive model to the electricity system. Micro-generation has radical implications in all three domains. For example, micro-generation deployment requires significant changes to control components due to the need for new regulatory and governance arrangements to enable the development of integrated microgrids. Since the consumer's role changes both at the 'micro' level (within their own home) and at the 'macro' level (through the ownership of shares in the community energy company), more intensive modes of communication are required. To cope with these new challenges the consumers also need a considerably deeper knowledge of the energy system and its functions.

Conclusions

This chapter has examined the potential disruptiveness of micro-generation for the existing electricity system. Since the framing of a technological innovation might create barriers within this system, it is of crucial importance to analyse to what extent and under which circumstances domestic micro-generation might be disruptive. This analysis has implications for the governance of an electricity system with a substantial share of micro-generation technologies.

The chapter has built on the concept of LTS to broaden out the firm-based analysis of disruptiveness that has often been used. It has developed an *ex ante* framework for the analysis of the impact of technological innovation on the existing large technical system for electricity. It has set out three models for micro-generation deployment and presented their specific patterns of disruptiveness.

It suggests that micro-generation is not inherently disruptive for the electricity system. Micro-generation's impact on the system depends heavily on the model of deployment, the driving forces behind deployment and the consequent arrangements for ownership, financing, operation and technological integration. For each of the models, some impacts are likely to be disruptive whilst others will be more incremental. In order to distinguish the level at which each impact will occur, different domains of innovation were identified. This provided a clearer picture of what and who might be disrupted by a substantial uptake of micro-generation in the UK.

The deployment models have highlighted different kinds of impact, and differences in the extent to which these impacts might be incremental or radical. Whilst the consumer driven Plug & Play model is more disruptive for the relationship between system participants (e.g. consumers and suppliers), the company-driven Company Control model implies more radical changes at the technology level since it requires more sophisticated load management solutions. Community Microgrid is the most disruptive of the three models, with potentially radical impacts across the electricity system.

This chapter provides some implications for the governance of an electricity system that incorporates large numbers of micro-generators. Such a system has additional goals: for example, for CO_2 reduction and decentralized provision. Under some of the deployment models discussed in this chapter, this system will include a larger, more diverse range of actors. As discussed in the Introduction to this book, the functional approach to governance is relevant to such scenarios. Higher levels of complexity in socio-technical systems requires a shift to governance that includes an increased role for non-governmental actors. The State fulfils a coordinating (or regulatory) function. The DTI's current work to develop a micro-generation strategy is a good example of this coordinating function in action.

This chapter has shown that such a shift is not inevitable even if micro-generation becomes significant. An expansion of micro-generation driven by incumbent energy companies will require no major change to the existing governance structure for the electricity system. Most of the changes required could be technical in nature. However, Plug & Play and Community Microgrid will involve a considerable number of new actors (e.g. regional market operators, new types of energy company) and/or old actors in a new position in the system (e.g. consumers acting as co-producers).

Under any of these models, the impacts of micro-generation could go beyond the LTS for electricity provision. They may have knock-on effects on other technical systems, such as those for housing design/construction and for telecommunications. The governance of micro-generation will need to take these effects into account.

Finally, a mass-market for micro-generation will only be possible with further changes in existing regulations. These changes might include measures to level the playing field between micro-generation and central generation, through changes in taxation regimes, for example, or changes in the wholesale market structure. They could also include policies to encourage consumers to invest, perhaps by offering grants or by regulations that encourage energy suppliers to operate as energy service companies. Further research will be required to test the robustness of these preliminary conclusions. This would test further the extent to which micro-generation might be disruptive for the UK electricity system by capturing the views of key electricity system actors. It could also broaden the analysis beyond the UK to explore how this disruptiveness might vary across different national contexts.

Notes

1   In the UK a household is defined as being in fuel poverty where it would need to spend more than 10 per cent of its income on energy to maintain a satisfactorily warm home. Although fuel poor households in the UK fell from 5.5 million in 1996 to 2.25 million in 2002 due to improved incomes and falling energy costs, fuel poverty might rise again with recent energy price increases.
2   For more information about an example of a 'virtual power plant' in this context, see the EU-funded project 'The Virtual Fuel Cell Power Plant' at: www.cogen.org/projects/vfcpp.htm.
3   The function to dispatch (start-stop) the micro-generator depends on the technology: while micro CHP linked to sufficient hot water storage has a certain operational flexibility within the domestic heat demand, PV and micro wind depend on the weather conditions.
4   The meaning of 'significant numbers' is open to interpretation. For this paper, it has been assumed that the mid-range scenario set out by the DTI System Impacts of Additional Micro-generation (SIAM) study has been followed (Mott MacDonald, 2004). This suggests that 8 million micro-generation units are installed by 2020.

References

Abernathy, W. J. and Clark, K. B. (1985) 'Innovation: Mapping the winds of creative destruction', *Research Policy*, vol 14, pp3–22
Adner, R. (2002) 'When are technologies disruptive? A demand-based view of the emergence of competition', *Strategic Management Journal*, issue 23, pp667–688
Braun, I. and Joerges, B. (1994) 'How to recombine large technical systems: The case of European organ transplantation', in Summerton, J. (ed) *Changing Large Technical Systems*, Westview Press, Boulder, pp25–51
Chappells, H., Klintman, M., Linden, A. L., Shove, E., Spaargaren, G. and van Vliet, B. (2000) 'Domestic consumption, utility services and the environment', Final Report of the DOMUS Project, funded by the European Commission DG XII, February
Chesshire, J. (2003) 'Energy efficiency projects and policies for step changes in the energy system: Developing an agenda for social science research', ESRC Seminar, March, Policy Studies Institute, London.
Christensen, C. M. (1997) *The Innovator's Dilemma: When New Technologies Cause Great Firms to Fail*, Harvard Business School Press, Boston

Christensen, C. M. and Overdorf, M. (2000) 'Meeting the challenge of disruptive change', *Harvard Business Review*, March–April, pp66–76

Collingridge, D. (1992) *The Management of Scale: Big Organizations, Big Decisions, Big Mistakes*, Routledge, London

Collins, J. (2004) *A Micro-Generation Manifesto*, Green Alliance, London

Coutard, O. (ed) (1999) *The Governance of Large Technical Systems*, Routledge, London

Crozier-Cole, T. and Gareth, J. (2002) 'The potential market for micro CHP in the UK', report to the Energy Saving Trust

Dahlin, K. B. and Behrens, D. M. (2005) 'When is an invention really radical? Defining and measuring technological radicalness', *Research Policy*, vol 34, pp717–737

Davies, P. A. (1996) 'Innovation in large technical systems: The case of telecommunications', *Industrial and Corporate Change*, vol 5, pp1143–1180

Department of the Environment, Food and Rural Affairs (2004) *The Government's Strategy for Combined Heat and Power to 2010*, DEFRA, London

Devine-Wright, P. (2004) 'Towards zero-carbon: Citizenship, responsibility and the public acceptability of sustainable energy technologies', in Buckle, C. (ed) Proceedings of Conference C81 of the Solar Energy Society, UK section of the International Solar Energy Society, 21 September, London, pp51–62

Department of Trade and Industry (2003) *Our Energy Future: Creating a Low Carbon Economy*, The Stationery Office, London

Department of Trade and Industry (2005) *Microgeneration Strategy and Low Carbon Buildings Programme: Consultation*, DTI, London

Dobbyn, J. and Thomas, G. (2005) 'Seeing the light: The impact of micro-generation on our use of energy', Sustainable Consumption Roundtable, London, www.sd-commission.org.uk/news/download_pdf.php?attach_id=281HF20-NHIXD0M-HGM DMHZ-KSA3R0Z accessed 24 October 2005

Dunn, S. (2000) *Micropower: The Next Electrical Era*, Worldwatch Institute, Washington

Fleetwood, T. (2001) 'An investigation into the disruptive capacity of distributed power technologies', MSc dissertation, Manchester School of Management, Manchester

Foster, R. and Kaplan, S. (2001) *Creative Destruction: Why Companies that are Built to Last Underperform the Market and How to Successfully Transform Them*, Doubleday, New York

Garcia, R. and Calantone, R. (2002) 'A critical look at technological innovation typology and innovativeness terminology: A literature review', *The Journal of Product Innovation Management*, vol 19, pp110–132

Geels, F. W., Elzen, B. and Green, K. (2004) 'General introduction: System innovation and transition to sustainability', in Elzen, B., Geels, F. and Green, K. (eds) *System Innovation and the Transition to Sustainability: Theory, Evidence and Policy*, Edward Elgar, Cheltenham, pp1–16

Geyer, A. and Davies, A. (2000) 'Managing project-system interfaces: Case studies of railway projects in restructured UK and German markets', *Research Policy*, vol 29, pp991–1013

Hall, J. and Kerr, R. (2003) 'Innovation dynamics and environmental technologies: The emergence of fuel cell technology', *Journal of Cleaner Production*, vol 11, pp459–471

Hecht, G. (1998) *The Radiance of France: Nuclear Power and National Identity after World War II*, MIT Press, Cambridge.

Hofman, P. S. (2003) 'Embedding radical innovations in society', paper for the 11th Greening of Industry Network Conference, San Francisco, October, 2003, www.prosus.uio.no/english/business_industry/condecol/gin_peter.pdf accessed 11 October 2006

Hughes, T. P. (1983) *Networks of Power Electrification in Western Society, 1880–1930*, Johns Hopkins University Press, Baltimore

International Energy Agency (2002) *Distributed Generation in Liberalised Electricity Markets*, IEA/OECD, Paris

MacDonald, M. (2004) *System Integration of Additional Micro-generation*, DTI, London

Mayntz, R. (1993) Große technische Systeme und ihre gesellschaftstheoretische Bedeutung, Kölner Zeitschrift für Soziologie und Sozialpsychologie, pp97–108

Mayntz, R. and Hughes, T. (eds) (1988) *The Development of Large Technical Systems*, Westview Press, Boulder

Mayntz, R. and Scharpf, F. W. (1995) 'Der Ansatz des akteurzentrierten Institutionalismus', in Mayntz, R. and Scharpf, F. W. (eds) *Gesellschaftliche Selbstregelung und Politische Steuerung*, Campus, Frankfurt a.M., pp39–72

Patterson, W. (1999) *Transforming Electricity*, Earthscan, London

Pehnt, M., Cames, M., Fischer, C., Praetorius, B., Schneider, L., Schumacher, K. and Vo, J. P. (eds) (2006) *Micro Cogeneration: Towards Decentralized Energy Systems*, Springer, Heidelberg

Sauter, R., Watson, J. and Hughes, L. (2005) 'Metering, communication and control technologies for micro-generation', STP, Working Paper 2005/1' www.sustainabletechnologies.ac.uk/PDF/Working%20papers/109_1.pdf

Society of British Gas Industries (2003) *Micro CHP - Delivering a Low Carbon Future*, SBGI, www.sbgi.org.uk/index.php?fuseaction=sbgi.articleDetail&con_id=8010453 accessed 15 March 2006

Summerton, J. (ed) (1994a) *Changing Large Technical Systems*, Westview Press, Boulder

Summerton, J. (1994b) 'Introductory essay: The systems approach to technological change', in Summerton, J. (ed) *Changing Large Technical Systems*, Westview Press, Boulder, pp1–21

The Economist (2000) 'The dawn of micropower', *The Economist*, 5 August

Tushman, M. L. and Anderson, P. (1986) 'Technological discontinuities and organizational environments', *Administrative Science Quarterly*, vol 31, pp439–465

Unruh, G. C. (2000) 'Understanding carbon lock-in', *Energy Policy*, vol 28, pp817–830

Utterback, J. M. and Acee, H. J. (2003) 'Disruptive technology', presented at the Keith Pavitt Conference, University of Sussex, UK, 14 November 2003, www.sussex.ac.uk/Units/spru/events/KP_Conf_03/documents/Utterback_Acee.pdf

van der Vleuten, E. (2004) 'Infrastructures and societal change: A view from the large technical systems field', *Technology Analysis & Strategic Management*, vol 16, pp395–414

van Vliet, B. (2004) 'Shifting scales of infrastructure provision', in Southerton, D., Chappells, H. and van Vliet, B. (eds) *Sustainable Consumption: The Implications of Changing Infrastructures of Provision*, Edward Elgar, Cheltenham, pp67–80

Walker, W. (2000) 'Entrapment in large technology systems: Institutional commitment and power relations', *Research Policy*, vol 29, pp833–846

Watson, J. (2004) 'Co-provision in sustainable energy systems: The case of micro-generation', *Energy Policy*, vol 32, pp1981–1990

Winner, L. (1999) 'Do artefacts have politics?', in MacKenzie, D. and Wajcman, J. (eds) *The Social Shaping of Technology*, Open University Press, Buckingham, pp28–40

Winskel, M. (2002) 'The "Dash for Gas" in the British electricity supply industry', *Social Studies of Sciences*, vol 32, no 4, pp565–599

Chapter 7

The Rationale for Policy Interventions from an Innovation Systems Perspective

Tim Foxon

Introduction

As discussed in the introductory chapter and in many of the other contributions to this volume, a number of trends have come together in recent years leading to a shift away from the traditional centralized, top-down, technocratic model of how national governments function to a more fluid, decentralized and participative model of governance. However, it is recognized that national governments still have a key role to play within this new landscape, but face the challenge of trying to shape the context and manage complexity and plurality rather than being able to control other actors more directly. This raises the question of the rationale for government interventions in this changed arena. This chapter explores how ideas from innovation systems (IS) thinking have begun to explore the idea of 'systems failures' as a rationale for public policy intervention, which includes, but goes beyond, the traditional idea of 'market failure'. The market failure approach is based on mainstream neo-classical economic thinking, and this language, and the ideas that it incorporates, are still largely used by policy makers.

The next section provides a brief review of the innovation systems approach, leading on to a discussion of the 'systems failure' argument. The fourth section looks at the links to the governance and 'social shaping of technologies' literatures. In the fifth section I draw on initial lessons from the transition approach to innovation, now being applied to innovation in energy policy by the Dutch government. The sixth section highlights some common themes and argues for moves towards a co-evolutionary theoretical framework and in the conclusion I discuss ways forward.[1]

Innovation systems approach

We begin by briefly reviewing the IS approach and its main theoretical findings (for a longer review of this and other approaches to understanding innovation, see Foxon, 2003).

The IS approach was developed in the late 1980s and early 1990s by a group of scholars drawing on institutional and evolutionary economic thinking. This approach emphasizes that innovation is a dynamic process, arising out of the interactions between different actors, and involving knowledge flows as well as market interactions. Rather than being categorised as a one-way, linear flow from research and development (R&D) to new products, innovation is seen as a process of matching technical possibilities to market opportunities, involving multiple interactions and types of learning (Freeman and Soete, 1997). This more systemic and dynamic picture of the innovation process emphasizes the role of feedbacks, which either amplify or inhibit technology-push and market-pull drivers, (Kline and Rosenberg, 1986).

The concept of a (national) system of innovation was first developed by Chris Freeman (1987), working at the Science and Technology Policy Research Unit (SPRU), in a pioneering study of the then successful Japanese economy in the late 1980s. Freeman stressed the positive role of government, working closely with industry and the science base, to create a vision and provide long-term support for the development and marketing of the most advanced technologies; the integrated approach to R&D, design, procurement, production and marketing within large firms; and the high level of general education and scientific culture, combined with thorough practical training and frequent updating in industry.

Two major studies in the early 1990s by Lundvall (1992) and Nelson (1993) analysed national innovation systems in more detail. Lundvall (1992) defined a national system of innovation as constituted by 'the elements and relationships which interact in the production, diffusion and use of new, and economically useful, knowledge ... either located within or rooted inside the borders of a nation state' (Lundvall, 1992, p2). He stressed the role of interactions between users and producers, facilitating a flow of information and knowledge linking technological capabilities to user needs, and relying on mutual trust and mutually respected codes of behaviour. Innovation is thus seen as a process that is ubiquitous and cumulative, involving new combinations of knowledge, produced through various forms of learning. These include: learning-by-doing – increasing the efficiency of production operations through experience gained (Arrow, 1962a); learning-by-using – increasing the efficiency of use of complex systems through experience (Rosenberg, 1982); and learning-by-interacting –

increasing efficiency of the system through user–producer interactions. Even activities aimed specifically at contributing to innovation, such as R&D, referred to as searching, generally look for alternatives (in terms of products, processes, markets, etc) close to the ones already well known to the organization, leading to the idea of technological trajectories (Dosi, 1982, 1988).

Nelson (1993) conducted a major empirical study and comparison of the national innovation systems of 15 countries. They concluded that 'to a considerable extent, differences in innovation systems reflect differences in economic and political circumstances and priorities between countries'. These differences reflected the differences in the institutional set-ups between the countries, including systems of university research and training and industrial R&D, financial institutions, management skills, public infrastructure and national monetary, fiscal and trade policies.

The IS approach was taken forward by the Organisation for Economic Co-operation and Development (OECD) (1999, 2002), who have undertaken further empirical and comparative analyses of national and regional IS. They characterize these systems in terms of the different actors and institutions (small and large firms, users, governmental and regulatory bodies, universities, research bodies), the interactions and flows of knowledge, funding and influence between them, and the incentives for innovation created by the institutional set-up. The development of IS theory and its policy applications have interacted and co-evolved over this period, though much remains to be done (Mytelka and Smith, 2002). Recent work by the OECD on governance of IS is discussed below.

In summary, IS approaches emphasize three aspects of innovation processes. First, that innovation occurs through systemic, dynamic and non-linear processes, involving multiple interactions between a range of actors with different roles within the system. Second, actors exhibit 'bounded rationality' (Simon, 1955, 1959); that is, they are limited in their ability to gather and process information relevant to decision making. This implies that innovation processes exhibit inherent uncertainties, and that expectations of future technological and market opportunities and policy and regulatory frameworks play an important role in actors' behaviour. Third, institutions, in the sense of social rule systems, are seen to play an important role in creating incentives or barriers to the rate and direction of innovation.

The 'systems failure' argument

The IS approach thus presents a much more complex picture of the innovation process than the old linear model of innovation. The linear model dovetailed well with the dominant neoclassical economic framework to provide a rationale for innovation policy, usually understood as public support for R&D. The rationale for this is that, since new knowledge is often easy to copy, innovators cannot always appropriate the full benefits of their investment in knowledge creation, and so private firms may lack the incentives necessary to undertake socially efficient levels of innovative activity. In economic terms, the social returns to innovation exceed the private returns (Arrow, 1962b), and so some innovative activity has the characteristics of a public good, in that it is non-rival and non-excludable. Innovation is generally non-rival in that, once created, its use by one agent does not reduce the amount/quality available for use by others, and hence it is not desirable to ration access to it. It is non-excludable since, once supplied, it is hard to deny access to other users. This means that it will be undersupplied by the market, which cannot exclude non-paying free riders. These features provide a rationale for public support for innovation, particularly at the early stages of R&D when new products or services are far from market.

In contrast, environmental policy has largely dealt with addressing the market failure of negative environmental externalities – environmental by-products of consuming or producing activities that affect third parties but are not reflected in market transactions and prices (Pigou, 1932). This provides a rationale for cost-effective environmental policy measures to 'internalize' these externalities: via 'the polluter pays' principle, through the use of policy instruments such as 'market-based' or 'economic' instruments (like taxes or emissions trading schemes) and other instruments (like emission or technology standards, voluntary agreements or assignments of property rights).

The IS approach presents a challenge for policy makers in formulating the rationale for policy interventions, particularly relating to environmental sustainability. Policy makers may be seen directly as actors within the innovation system; for example, as providing funding for R&D, and as contributing to the outcomes of policy-making processes, such as taxes, regulations and incentives, which form part of the institutional framework for the innovation system (van der Steen, 1999). Thus, in addition to policy outcomes providing direct incentives or barriers to firms pursuing innovation towards sustainability, government actions and rhetoric also influence firms, economic and environmental regulators, consumers and other actors indirectly – for example, by creating more or less positive expectations for sustainable innovation to be worth pursuing. The systems approach also highlights that both innovation and environmental market failures are complex and need to be addressed together.

Thinking about how to formulate an alternative rationale for policy interventions has focused on the notion of 'systems failure' – particularly in the work of Charles Edquist (1994, 2001) and Keith Smith (1992, 2000). This argues that the current concept of 'market failure', understood as a comparison between conditions in the real world and those of an ideal or optimal market system, is no longer appropriate. Instead, the concept of 'systems failure' is proposed as a rationale for policy interventions (Edquist, 1994, 2001; Smith, 2000). This advocates undertaking concrete empirical and comparative analyses, using IS concepts, to identify systems failures that can be rectified. In this approach, two conditions are identified that must be fulfilled for public intervention to be justified in a market economy (Edquist, 2001):

1. A problem must exist; that is, a situation in which market mechanisms and firms fail to achieve objectives that have been socially defined, through a public policy process.
2. The state and its agencies must have the ability to solve or mitigate the problem (i.e. the issue of potential government and bureaucratic failure must be addressed).

In many cases, this concept of systems failure leads to similar or identical policy prescriptions to the concept of market failure, for example the use of market-based instruments to internalize negative environmental externalities. The crucial difference, however, is that it does not presume that public policy interventions can recreate ideal market solutions, which are assumed to have maximal economic efficiency. It is now recognized that markets are based on sets of legal and institutional rules, such as those guaranteeing private property and contractural arrangements (North, 1990; Hodgson, 1993; Williamson, 2000). These rules are often designed to provide incentives for socially desirable types of behaviour that go beyond promoting pure economic efficiency. The task facing policy makers is to design the rules so that they do not lead to excessive costs on private firms and individuals, or create unnecessary levels of bureaucratic intervention. The systems failure approach is designed to help policy makers identify cases where changes to rule-systems could lead to more effective achievement of social objectives without excessive costs or unnecessary bureaucracy. This approach is particularly relevant to the analysis of dynamic socio-economic systems, such as those involving radical innovation, where it is difficult or impossible to identify equilibria where optimal market solutions would pertain. In such cases, systems failures may be identified through empirical analyses of the effectiveness of current systems and comparative analyses of the effectiveness of systems operating under different legal and institutional rules.

Smith (2000) identifies four areas of systems or systemic failure, which could provide a rationale for specific policy interventions:

1. *Failures in infrastructure provision and investment.* Both physical infrastructures, such as for energy and communications, and science-technology infrastructures, such as universities, technical institutes and regulatory agencies, are important parts of innovation systems. However, because of their large scale, indivisibilities and very long time horizons of operation, they are unlikely to be sufficiently provided by private investors, and so there is a case for public support for infrastructure provision.
2. *Transition failures.* Because existing firms, especially small firms, are necessarily quite limited in their technological capabilities and horizons, they are likely to experience great difficulties in responding to technological changes due to developments outside firms' area of expertise, changes in technological opportunities or patterns of demand that push the market into new areas of technology, or major shifts in technological regimes or paradigms. Public policies may be used to help firms to cope with such changes.

3. *Lock-in failures.* Path dependence, due to system or network externalities, combined with the fact that technologies are closely linked to their social and economic environment, can lead to 'lock-in' of existing technologies, creating barriers to the innovation and adoption of new technologies (Arthur, 1989). New technologies must compete not only with an existing dominant technology, but also challenge the overall technological and institutional system in which it is embedded. This requires public policies to generate incentives for new technologies or technological systems, and to overcome barriers created by the prevalence of incumbent technology or system.

4. *Institutional failures.* The set of public and private institutions, regulatory systems and the policy system creates a framework of opportunities and barriers to innovation by firms. Hence, the performance of these institutions and systems in regard to innovation should be monitored and assessed, and if they are judged to be creating unnecessary barriers, this would provide a rationale for policy changes or interventions.

Smith (1992) also stresses that policy making should take an adaptive approach, and look for design and formulation of institutional arrangements that promote business experiments and generate a greater connectedness between organizations generating knowledge (e.g. universities) and those applying such knowledge (e.g. firms). As other aspects of technological and institutional systems co-evolve, this also suggests that a continuous learning approach to improving policy processes and measures may be needed to cope with continuous dynamic change (Foxon, 2004).

This approach seems particularly relevant for the social and environmental challenges of sustainability. Public policy actors have a key role in creating the right incentive structures to address these challenges and facilitating the involvement of stakeholders in developing and implementing such structures. However, a systems approach should not be perceived as having an 'anti-market' bias (OECD, 2002) and market mechanisms still play a key role in promoting innovation, along with non-market interactions, such as knowledge networking.

The concept of systems failure was applied in our study of UK renewable energy innovation systems and resulting policy implications. This study identified systems failures relating to technologies moving from the demonstration to pre-commercial (e.g. for wave and tidal power) and pre-commercial to supported commercial (e.g. offshore wind) stages of development (Imperial College Centre for Energy Policy and Technology (ICEPT) and E4Tech, 2003; Foxon et al, 2005b). We argued that these failures provide a case for more specific policy interventions to support renewable technologies, for example through providing revenue support to help create niche markets.

A broader policy challenge is raised by the techno-institutional lock-in of current high carbon, fossil-fuel based energy systems (Unruh, 2000, 2002; Neuhoff, 2005; Foxon, 2006). The need to promote innovation of more sustainable technologies, such as renewable energy technologies, through addressing the systemic failures associated with the lock-in of unsustainable technologies, was addressed in our research (see note 1). We developed a set of guiding principles for policy processes to promote sustainable innovation (Foxon et al, 2005a), which incorporates many of the above ideas:

- Stimulate the development of a sustainable innovation policy regime that brings together appropriate strands of current innovation and environmental policy and regulatory regimes.
- Apply systems thinking and practice, engaging with the complexity and systemic interactions of innovation systems and policy-making processes.
- Advance the procedural and institutional basis for the delivery of sustainable innovation policy.
- Develop an integrated mix of policy processes, measures and instruments that cohere to promote sustainable innovation.
- Incorporate policy learning as an integral part of sustainable innovation policy process.

Links to governance and 'social shaping of technology' literatures

In this section, we explore some of the links between the above ideas on IS, resulting from research on the concept, with the literatures on governance and 'social shaping of technology', as outlined in the introductory chapter.

Understanding policy-making processes

As described in Chapter 1, governance refers to the changing practices relating to 'an increasingly complex state–society relationship in which network actors are prominent in policy making and the state's primary role is policy coordination rather than direct policy control' (Bache and Flinders, 2004). The recognition and improved understanding of these changing practices creates the potential to move beyond the old dichotomy of looking for either state or market solutions to societal problems. We argue that the systems failure argument fits well with this new thinking.

The current conventional stated rationale for policy interventions is to correct for 'market failures'. For example, the UK Treasury's paper outlining the argument for the use of economic instruments to internalize costs of environmental damage into market prices states that 'If the Government intervenes to correct these market failures efficiently, it will achieve better environmental outcomes, as well as greater overall economic efficiency' (HM Treasury, 2002, p1). It may be argued that this approach is fine as far as it goes, but that it raises a number of difficulties, which may be traced back to the implicit adherence to the principles of neoclassical economics. The framing of the rationale typically suggests that, if the government can find the right intervention, it can recreate the conditions for a perfect market solution. These assumptions underlie the fundamental theorems of welfare economics

(Arrow and Debreu, 1954), which state that, in perfectly competitive markets, the equilibrium reached by trading between buyers and sellers at market prices will be economically efficient, and that such an efficient equilibrium can always be reached from a given starting allocation of resources. There are a number of arguments that may be raised as to why these theorems fail to describe accurately markets in the real world (e.g. Bowles, 2004, Chapter 6). The point we want to make here is that government interventions are framed in terms of trying to recreate a theoretical model of how markets deliver economically efficient solutions.

One difficulty is that in problems relating to sustainability, particularly the intersection of environment and innovation, governments are trying to correct for multiple market failures. For example, Grubb and Ulph (2002) identify six types of innovation market failure, which interact in a complex way with each other and with the market failure relating to the public-good nature of environmental benefits. In these circumstances, it is unreasonable to expect governments to recreate perfect market solutions, or even to come up with 'second best' solutions. If and when the resulting interventions fail to deliver policy objectives, this may lead to a backlash against all government interventions. Hence, neither markets nor governments can be expected to deliver optimal solutions, but most observers agree that at least some government interventions can have positive social benefits. So, a clear rationale for such interventions, or a framework for determining such a rationale, is needed.

One way of making progress, that is consistent with the systems approach, would be to focus on policy-making processes, rather than individual policy measures. This recognizes that policy making is an ongoing process of assessment, debate, intervention and evaluation, which may be guided by economic insights, but should not be dominated by such insights.

In our research, we investigated the implications of the understanding of IS for sustainable innovation policy processes. In developing our analytical framework, we examined how this understanding relates to theoretical and empirical conceptions of policy-making processes (Foxon et al, 2004). These seek to explain variation between policy sectors and between countries, relative stability or change in policy making and hence effectiveness and causes of policy success and failure.

John (1998) identified five broad theoretical approaches to explaining policy variation, change and effectiveness:

1. Institutional approaches – which emphasize the structures and constraints imposed by the formal and informal institutions that together form the 'social rules' of a system (e.g. March and Olsen, 1989; North, 1990).
2. Network approaches – which emphasize how interactions between actors and institutions influence policy outputs and outcomes (e.g. Marsh and Rhodes, 1992).
3. Socio-economic approaches – which emphasize how socio-economic factors influence the decisions of public actors and affect policy outputs and outcomes (e.g. Ham and Hill, 1984).

4. Rational choice theory – which emphasizes individual actors acting in their own rational self-interest, with collective decisions arising out of bargaining between actors, which can be analysed using game theory (e.g. Ward, 1995).
5. Ideas-based approaches – which emphasize the importance of ideas and advocacy in political debate, and the actors, such as non-governmental organizations (NGOs), think tanks and academics, that are involved in the development and promotion of ideas (e.g. Majone, 1989).

Each of these approaches has been criticized for presenting a limited view. A more complete theoretical picture would synthesize elements from them. For example, it would view policy-making processes as influenced both by the development of ideas and arguments and by power struggles between different interest groups, in which actors act both to maximize their interests within current institutional rule systems and, where possible, to change rules and institutions to their benefit. Kingdon (1995) has developed a useful partial synthesis, based on a concept of adaptive policy making. He argues that in the policy process there are three parallel 'streams' of activity – the 'problem' stream, the 'policy proposal' stream and the 'political' stream – and two key steps: getting problems on to the policy agenda, a step which is dominated by political activity; and generating a set of alternative solutions to be considered, a step which is dominated by civil servants and analysts/researchers. He argues that the separate streams of problems, policies and politics come together at certain critical times: when policy windows are open. Items reach the policy agenda because a problem comes to the fore, either through normal political events, such as annual budgets, or through focusing events, such as a crisis or disaster; or because a change in the political stream, such as a new administration, leads to a change in priorities. The set of alternatives is generated by attaching proposals, previously formulated in the policy stream, to the problem that has now reached the agenda via the window opened by the problem event or political event.

A further criticism of many theoretical approaches to the policy-making process is that they tend to concentrate on policy formation and neglect the issue of policy implementation, which is arguably as important in influencing the effectiveness of policies in practice (Hill, 1997). Implementation is also crucial to the question of the extent to which success or failure of policies feed back into further policy making, a vital element in policies that seek to promote sustainability.

Some of these ideas are starting to be discussed in policy-making circles, even if they have not yet reached a more general public discourse. For example, a recent OECD project built on the organization's earlier work on IS to produce a report on *Governance of Innovation Systems* (OECD, 2005). This recognizes that governance is an 'interactive process involving various forms of partnerships, collaboration, competition and negotiation' and that these are shaped by the institutional settings in which they occur. This implies that individual policy domains, such as economic policy, innovation policy and environmental policy, may have their own communities with specific preferences, ideologies and backgrounds, leading to distinct imperatives and rationales for action. Hence, policy for sustainable development may have different or even opposing objectives and imperatives to the fundamental economic growth imperative that usually underlies innovation policy. This leads the OECD report to posit a more evolutionary view of policy making (OECD, 2005, p25). We explore such evolutionary views in the following sections.

Evolutionary economic and sociological explanations of technological change

As suggested in the first section, the IS approach arose out of institutional and evolutionary economic thinking. A key text in this thinking is Nelson and Winter's (1982) *Evolutionary Theory of Economic Change*. This developed an understanding of economic actions, particularly relating to technological change, based on Herbert Simon's (1955, 1959) insight that economic actors display 'bounded rationality', that is, they are limited in their ability to access and process information, and hence look for satisfactory or 'satisficing' solutions. From this, Nelson and Winter (1982) introduced the fundamental notion of the 'routine', which could be any technical, procedural, organizational or strategic process used by a firm as part of its normal business activities, for example, its R&D strategy or a particular production profile. They argued that routines change in an evolutionary process in firms searching for better techniques or processes that satisfy their chosen criteria, such that successful routines, and the firms that employ them, are selected by the process of market competition. Since profit making may be only one of a number of criteria used in the search process, alongside, for example, developing innovative solutions or building market share, and the fact that the market and knowledge environment is dynamic, it can not be assumed that firms are profit-maximizing entities. Furthermore, it can not be assumed that markets involving actors with bounded rationality will reach optimal equilibria. Hence, in an evolutionary economic approach, the standard assumptions of the neoclassical picture underlying the 'market failure' argument no longer hold, and so something like the 'systems failure' rationale for intervention is needed.

In an interesting paper, MacKenzie (1992) has suggested that evolutionary economic approaches could form a bridge between economic and sociological understanding of technological change processes. He highlights the analogies between the process of searching for and selecting satisficing routines, and the sociological notions of 'closure' and creation of stable networks. Both approaches emphasize the importance of expectations in influencing which technological areas are explored, leading to persistent patterns or trajectories of technological change, which could be understood as self-fulfilling prophecies, or social institutions. An example of this is provided by Moore's Law, developed in the late 1960s by semiconductor pioneer Gordon Moore, who proposed that the computing power of microchips would double roughly every 18 months. This law subsequently helped to guide the rate of development of microchips by the computing industry. In the next section, we discuss a practical example of a government trying to apply an evolutionary and systems-based approach in practice.

The role of policy in the Dutch transition approach

An evolutionary based approach to policy making, known as 'transition management' or the 'transition approach', is now being undertaken by the Dutch government, following ideas developed by Dutch academics for the 4th Netherlands Environmental Policy Plan, published in 2000. Jan Rotmans, Rene Kemp and colleagues (Rotmans et al, 2000, 2001; Kemp and Rotmans, 2001) argued that persistent environmental problems, such as climate change, require a systems approach to policy making, in order to stimulate transitions towards more sustainable systems. This approach is designed to be shaping or modulating, rather than controlling, to be oriented towards long-term sustainability goals and visions, and to be iterative and flexible, and so to have a steering philosophy of goal-oriented incrementalism (Kemp and Loorbach, 2005).

This approach is now being applied to innovation in energy policy by the Dutch Ministry of Economic Affairs (Ministry of Economic Affairs, 2004). Five transition paths have been formulated and developed using a participatory approach, coordinated and facilitated by the ministry. This involves stakeholders working in public–private project teams, led by industry. For each area, visions for the future and medium-term (20 year) strategic goals were developed (Where do we want to go?), 'transition paths' were formulated (How are we going to get there?) and 'transition experiments' proposed (How are we going to travel the paths?). This is based on a 'learning-by-doing' approach – undertake experiments, design learning goals into experiments, feed back lessons into subsequent measures. This builds on earlier ideas by these authors of promoting change through the support of niches in which new technologies have the space to develop, at least partially protected from the dominant socio-technical regime (Kemp et al, 1998).

The Ministry of Economic Affairs (2004) sees the transition approach as a way of dealing with uncertainties and avoiding apparent certainties. The government is not 'choosing' specific options, but organizing its policy around a cluster of options: the transition paths. These enable the government to give direction to the market, whilst giving market players the opportunity to develop their own products based on their own market analysis, ambitions and entrepreneurship. It argues this requires a new form of concerted action between market and government ('policy renewal') involving:

- Relationships built on mutual trust – Stakeholders want to be able to rely on a policy line not being changed unexpectedly once adopted, through commitment to the direction taken, the approach and the main roads formulated. The government places trust in market players by offering them 'experimentation space'.

- Partnership – Government, market and society are partners in the process of setting policy aims, creating opportunities and undertaking transition experiments, for example through ministries setting up 'one stop shops' for advice and problem solving.
- Brokerage – The government facilitates the building of networks and coalitions between actors in transition paths.
- Leadership – Stakeholders require the government to declare itself clearly in favour of a long-term agenda of sustainability and innovation that is set for a long time, and to tailor current policy to it.

As described by Kemp and Loorbach (2005), the transition management approach was informed largely by insights from the innovation literature and evaluation studies of innovation policy and environmental policy instruments, and developed somewhat independently from the literature on governance. However, they argue that there are clear links to different governance approaches, as follows:

- Soft planning instead of comprehensive planning – Transition management consists of government acting to secure circumstances that will enhance the potential for achieving societal goals by promoting innovation and mitigating negative effects.
- An exercise in incrementalism – Transition management is an incrementalist strategy for changing functional systems. This has the advantages that it appears less disruptive to existing special interests, the costs of taking a wrong step are kept low, it reduces the danger of lock-in to unwanted paths, and it allows lessons learned to inform further steps. These benefits from incrementalism have long been advocated in economic policy debates, in terms of the idea of 'muddling through' (Lindblom, 1960, 1979). It also fits well with an evolutionary understanding of change happening through a long series of 'trial and error' steps.
- Adaptive governance – Transition management closely relates to ideas of adaptive management, policy or governance (Lee, 1993; March and Olsen, 1995), as a strategy for political institutions to cope with the problems of ignorance, conflict and ambiguity facing attempts at intelligent change. However, it emphasizes that learning and adaptation needs to occur at a system level, as well as at an individual level.
- Interactive governance – Transition management seeks to move from an older model of participation by different groups to a more genuinely interactive model of actors working together and mutually adapting towards a set of collectively chosen long-term goals through a common process.
- Multi-level governance – Transition management can be seen as a form of multi-level governance, comparable to the wider concept of decision making being shared by governments and other actors, organized at different territorial levels and interacting through trans-boundary and trans-national networks.

These ideas have close links to those of multi-level and metagovernance, discussed in Chapter 1. As with transition management, metagovernance recognizes that, due to a number of converging trends including market liberalization, individualism and globalization, the state often no longer has the ability to deliver particular outcomes, but may still be able to influence the conditions whereby desired outcomes may occur, through the use of incentives and creating common spaces. As described by Jessop (1998, 2004), this involves 'the design of institutions and generation of visions which can facilitate not only self-organisation in different fields but also the relative coherence of the diverse objectives, spatial and temporal horizons, actions, and outcomes of various self-organizing arrangements'.

Towards a co-evolutionary approach

This paper has argued that the idea of systems failure as a rationale for public policy intervention, coming from IS theory, avoids some of the problems associated with the notion of market failure, and resonates with ideas from the governance and social shaping of technology approaches. We argue that there are some key themes, which all these approaches share, and that further development of these themes could be fruitful.

The first theme is the idea of systems or networks. The starting point for the IS approach is that innovation arises not just from the actors and institutions that make up the system, but through their interactions. The systems concept arose originally in the context of engineering and information sciences, whereas network is the equivalent social science concept. The governance literature sees policy making through complex networks of interacting actors and institutions as a third type of decision-making process, alongside state hierarchies and markets (Bache and Flinders, 2004). Importantly, systems or networks are seen as dynamic entities, evolving over time. Recent thinking in complex systems theory emphasizes that, though the exact behaviour of complex systems over time is uncertain, it makes sense to examine properties of the system, such as robustness under perturbations, and resilience and adaptability to changing environmental conditions (Forrest et al, 2005).

The second theme is that of adaptability or learning. As suggested by some of the proponents of the systems failure argument, and exemplified by the transition approach, policy making should take an adaptive approach in this new arena. It is possible for policy makers and stakeholders to agree on certain long-term policy objectives but not on exactly how these will be reached. Lack of perfect foresight on the part of governments, markets or actors means that the future is fundamentally uncertain, and this requires actors to learn or adapt to changing conditions, whilst pursuing their goals. Applied to governments, this implies the need for policy learning, that is, the recognition that there is a need for feedback from the implementation of policies to future policy development, and to establish clear processes by which this can occur (Foxon et al, 2005a). In this context, governance processes are seen as an endogenous part of innovation systems (van der Steen, 1999).

The third theme, we argue, is that of evolutionary theorizing. As we discussed above, evolutionary economic thinking is the implicit basis for the IS approach and, it was argued, could form the bridge to the social shaping of the technology approach. Recent work by Richard Nelson, one of the pioneers of evolutionary economics, has begun to explore the co-evolution of technologies and institutions as a fruitful way of developing this bridge (Nelson and Sampat, 2001; Nelson, 2005). Nelson identifies institutions as 'social technologies' – standardized patterns of behaviour that have evolved as useful and productive ways of undertaking particular social or economic tasks. They evolve in the context of a range of factors, including organizational and governance structures, and the broad system of norms, beliefs, and rules of the game, that constitute the institutional environment. Of course, institutions, considered from a number of perspectives, are central to debates on governance (North, 1990; Jessop, 2001; Acemoglu, 2004; Parto, 2005). Physical technologies can also be seen as evolving in this context, through improved understanding and adaptation to user needs. Furthermore, technologies and institutions co-evolve, so that the evolution of technologies influences that of institutions, and vice versa. The theoretical basis for the co-evolution of technologies and institutions, and the idea that IS forms the setting for this co-evolution, have begun to be investigated (Nelson, 2002; Foxon, 2004).

The first two themes of systems and adaptability arise naturally in evolutionary approaches and, though they do not necessarily require an evolutionary theoretical basis, we argue that these approaches are worthy of further investigation.

Conclusions and ways forward

This paper has discussed a number of theoretical ideas: innovation systems, systems failure, approaches to understanding policy-making processes, evolutionary economic and sociological explanations of technological change, and the transition approach, and argued for systems failure as a rationale for public policy interventions. We conclude by looking at both analytical and practical ways of taking these ideas forward.

The analytical challenge relates to the need to develop a stronger theoretical grounding for these ideas, linking systems change, new forms of governance and sustainability transitions. This will also need to engage with a range of heterodox economic thinking, from ecological, evolutionary and institutional economics, which has the potential to link these ideas to important questions of costs and allocation of resources, in a richer way than the mainstream neoclassical economic picture. We suggest that the approach of analysing 'co-evolution of technologies and institutions' could provide a way forward towards a richer theoretical and analytical picture. This has the potential to incorporate ideas from systems and complexity theory, as well as to see the role of governments as endogenous to IS.

The practical challenge relates to the need to engage with real-world policy processes. Despite the move towards governance described in this and other chapters, the dominant framing of government interventions to promote sustainability is still the language of correcting for market failure. As we have argued, this framing is based on outdated concepts from neoclassical economic theory, which assume that markets can deliver optimal welfare solutions, if only imperfections in the market can be corrected. The systems failure idea presented here could form a framing for government actions that is more compatible with the new ideas of governance, innovation systems and sustainability.

As described above, the development of IS theory and its policy applications have interacted and co-evolved. The application of the systems failure rationale for policy intervention, not least in the context of promoting sustainable innovation, could represent a further fruitful step in this co-evolution.

Acknowledgements

This paper draws on fruitful interactions in the course of our Sustainable Technologies Programme (STP) project with colleagues, particularly Peter Pearson, Zen Makuch, Macarena Mata, Robert Gross and Frans Berkhout, and stakeholders who attended our sustainable innovation policy workshops. The author would also like to thank the other members of the STP Governance of Sustainable Technologies Network, particularly Joseph Murphy and Adrian Smith, for useful discussions and helpful comments and suggestions on earlier versions of this paper.

Notes

1   This Chapter is based on ideas developed in the course of a research project under the ESRC Sustainable Technologies Programme on 'Policy drivers and barriers for sustainable innovation'. This project engaged with policy makers and other stakeholders through a series of workshops and case studies, and produced guidance for improving sustainable innovation policy processes (Foxon et al, 2005a). The project findings are reported in various papers (Foxon et al, 2004, 2005a, b) and in the final monograph (Foxon et al, 2005c).

References

Acemoglu, D. (2004) 'Understanding institutions', Lionel Robbins Lectures, London School of Economics, 23–25 February 2004

Arrow, K. (1962a) 'The economic implications of learning by doing', *Review of Economic Studies*, vol 29, pp155–173

Arrow, K. (1962b) 'Economic welfare and the allocation of resources for invention', in Nelson, R. (ed) *The Rate and Direction of Inventive Activity*, Princeton University Press, Princeton, pp609–625

Arrow, K. and Debreu, G. (1954) 'Existence of an equilibrium for a competitive economy', *Econometrica*, vol 22, no 3, pp265–290

Arthur, W. B. (1989) 'Competing technologies, increasing returns, and lock-in by historical events', *The Economic Journal*, vol 99, pp116–131

Bache, I. and Flinders, M. (2004) 'Multi-level governance and British politics', in Bache, I. and Flinders, M. (eds) *Multi-level Governance*, Oxford University Press, Oxford

Bowles, S. (2004) *Microeconomics: Behavior, Institutions and Evolution*, Russell Sage Foundation, Princeton University Press, Princeton

Dosi, G. (1982) 'Technological paradigms and technological trajectories', *Research Policy*, vol 11, pp147–162

Dosi, G. (1988) 'Sources, procedures, and microeconomics of innovation', *Journal of Economic Literature*, vol 26, pp1120–1171

Edquist, C. (1994) 'Technology policy: The interaction between governments and markets', in Aichholzer, G. and Schienstock, G. (eds) *Technology Policy: Towards an Integration of Social and Ecological Concerns*, Walter de Gruyter, Berlin

Edquist, C. (2001) 'Innovation policy – a systemic approach', in Archibugi, D. and Lundvall, B-A. (eds) *The Globalizing Learning Economy*, Oxford University Press, Oxford

Forrest, S., Balthrop, J., Glickman, M. and Ackley, D. (2005) 'Computation in the wild', in Park, K. and Willins, W. (eds) *The Internet as a Large-Scale Complex System*, Oxford University Press, Oxford

Foxon, T. J. (2003) *Inducing Innovation for a Low-carbon Future: Drivers, Barriers and Policies*, Carbon Trust, London

Foxon, T. J. (2004) 'Innovation systems as the setting for the co-evolution of technologies and institutions', paper presented at the Organisations, Innovation and Complexity: New Perspectives on the Knowledge Economy Conference, University of Manchester, 9–10 September 2004

Foxon, T. J. (2006) 'Technological lock-in and the role of innovation', in Atkinson, G., Dietz, S. and Neumayer, E. (eds) *Chapter in Handbook of Sustainable Development*, Edward Elgar, Cheltenham

Foxon, T. J., Makuch, Z., Mata, M. and Pearson, P. (2004) 'Informing policy processes that promote sustainable innovation: An analytical framework and empirical methodology', STP Working Paper 2004/4, www.sustainabletechnologies.ac.uk/PDF/Working%20papers/106b.pdf accessed 16 October 2006

Foxon, T. J., Pearson, P., Makuch, Z. and Mata, M. (2005a) 'Transforming policy processes to promote sustainable innovation: Some guiding principles', report for policy makers from STP project, ESRC Sustainable Technologies Programme, 7 March 2005

Foxon, T. J., Gross, R., Chase, A., Howes, J., Arnall, A. and Anderson, D. (2005b) 'UK innovation systems for new and renewable energy technologies: Drivers, barriers and systems failures', *Energy Policy*, vol 33, no16, pp2123–2137

Foxon, T. J., Pearson, P., Makuch, Z. and Mata, M. (2005c) *Policy Drivers and Barriers for Sustainable Innovation*, ICEPT Monograph 2005/1, www.sustainabletechnologies.ac.uk/Projects/policy.htm accessed 16 October 2006

Freeman, C. (1987) *Technology and Economic Performance: Lessons from Japan*, Pinter, London

Freeman, C. and Soete, L. (1997) *The Economics of Industrial Innovation* (3rd Edition), Pinter, London

Grubb, M. and Ulph, D. (2002) 'Energy, the environment and innovation', *Oxford Review of Economic Policy*, vol 18, no 1, pp92–106

Ham, C. and Hill, M. (1984) *The Policy Process in the Modern Capitalist State*, Harvester Wheatsheaf, Brighton

Hill, M. (1997) *The Policy Process in the Modern State*, Prentice Hall, Brighton

Hodgson, G. (1993) 'Evolution and institutional change: On the nature of selection in biology and economics', in Maki, U., Gustafsson, B. and Knudsen, C. (eds) *Rationality, Institutions and Economic Methodology*, Routledge, London

HM Treasury (2002) *Tax and the Environment: Using Economic Instruments*, HM Treasury

Imperial College Centre for Energy Policy and Technology and E4Tech (2003) 'The UK innovation systems for new and renewable energy technologies', Report for UK DTI, June 2003, www.dti.gov.uk/energy/renewables/policy/iceptheukinnovation.pdf

Jessop, B. (1998) 'The rise of governance and the risk of failure', *International Social Science Journal*, vol 50, no 155, pp29–45

Jessop, B. (2001) 'Institutional re(turns) and the strategic-relational approach', *Environment and Planning A*, vol 33, pp1213–1235

Jessop, B. (2004) 'Multi-level governance and multi-level meta-governance', in Bache, I. and Flinders, M. (eds) *Multi-level Governance*, Oxford University Press, Oxford pp49–74

John, P. (1998) *Analysing Public Policy*, Continuum, London

Kemp, R., Schot, J. and Hoogma, R. (1998) 'Regime shifts to sustainability through processes of niche formation: The approach of strategic niche management', *Technology Analysis and Strategic Management*, vol 10, no 2, pp175–195

Kemp, R. and Rotmans, J. (2001) 'The management of the co-evolution of technical, environmental and social systems', in Weber, M. and Hemmelskamp, J. (eds) *Towards Environmental Innovation Systems*, Springer Verlag, Heidelberg

Kemp, R. and Loorbach, D. (2005) 'Governance for sustainability through transition management', draft paper (version 1 February 2005, earlier version presented at EAEPE Conference, 7–10 November 2003, Maastricht, the Netherlands)

Kingdon, J. (1995) *Agendas, Alternatives and Public Policies*, HarperCollins College Publishers, New York

Kline, S. and Rosenberg, N. (1986) 'An overview of innovation', in Landau R. (ed) *The Positive Sum Strategy: Harnessing Technology for Economic Growth*, pp275–306

Lee, K. N. (1993) *Compass and Gyroscope: Integrating Science and Politics for the Environment*, Island Press, Washington DC

Lindblom, C. (1960) 'The science of "muddling through"', *Public Administration Review*, vol 19, pp79–88

Lindblom, C. (1979) 'Still muddling, not yet through', *Public Administration Review*, Nov/Dec, pp517–526

Lundvall, B-A. (ed) (1992) *National Systems of Innovation: Towards a Theory of Innovation and Interactive Learning*, Pinter Publishers, London

MacKenzie, D. (1992) 'Economic and sociological explanations of technological change', in Coombs, R., Saviotti, P. and Walsh, V. (eds) *Technological Change and Company Strategies: Economic and Sociological Perspectives*, Academic Press (reprinted in MacKenzie (1996))

MacKenzie, D. (1996) *Knowing Machines: Essays on Technical Change*, MIT Press, Cambridge, MA

Majone, G. (1989) *Evidence, Argument and Persuasion in the Policy Process*, Yale University Press, New Haven

March, J. and Olsen, J. (1989) *Rediscovering Institutions*, Free Press, New York

March, J. and Olsen, J. (1995) *Democratic Governance*, Free Press, New York

Marsh, D. and Rhodes, R. (eds) (1992) *Policy Networks in British Government*, Clarendon, Oxford

Ministry of Economic Affairs (The Netherlands) (2004) *Innovation in Energy Policy – Energy Transition: State of Affairs and Way Ahead*, www.energietransitie.nl

Mytelka, L. K. and Smith, K. (2002) 'Policy learning and innovation theory: An interactive and co-evolving process', *Research Policy*, vol 31, pp1467–1479

Nelson, R. (1993) *National Innovation Systems: A Comparative Analysis*, Oxford University Press, New York

Nelson, R. (2002) 'Technology, institutions and innovation systems', *Research Policy*, vol 31, pp265–272

Nelson, R. (2005) *Technology, Institutions and Economic Growth*, Harvard University Press, Cambridge, MA

Nelson, R. and Winter, S. (1982) *An Evolutionary Theory of Economic Change*, Harvard University Press, Cambridge, MA

Nelson, R. and Sampat, B. (2001) 'Making sense of institutions as a factor shaping economic performance', *Journal of Economic Behaviour & Organization*, vol 44, pp31–54

Neuhoff, K. (2005) 'Large-scale deployment of renewables for electricity generation', *Oxford Review of Economic Policy*, vol 21, no 1, pp88–110

North, D. C. (1990) *Institutions, Institutional Change and Economic Performance*, Cambridge University Press, Cambridge

Organisation for Economic Co-operation and Development (1999) *Managing National Innovation Systems*, OECD, Paris

Organisation for Economic Co-operation and Development (2002) *Dynamising National Innovation Systems*, OECD, Paris

Organisation for Economic Co-operation and Development (2005) *Governance of Innovation Systems*, vol 1, Synthesis Report, OECD, Paris

Parto, S. (2005) '"Good" governance and policy analysis: What of institutions?', MERIT-Infonomics Research Memorandum Series 2005-001, University of Maastricht

Pigou, A. (1932) *The Economics of Welfare* (4th Edition), Macmillan, London

Rosenberg, N. (1982) *Inside the Black Box: Technology and Economics*, Cambridge University Press, Cambridge

Rotmans, J., Kemp, R., van Asselt, M., Geels, F., Verbong, G. and Molendijk, K. (2000) Final report of the study 'Transitions and Transition Management' for the 4th National Environmental Policy Plan of The Netherlands, October 2000, ICIS & MERIT, Maastricht

Rotmans, J., Kemp, R., and van Asselt, M. (2001) 'More evolution than revolution: Transition management in public policy', *Foresight*, vol 3, no 1, pp15–31

Simon, H. A. (1955) 'A behavioral model of rational choice', *Quarterly Journal of Economics*, vol 69, pp1–18

Simon, H. A. (1959) 'Theories of decision making in economics', *American Economic Review*, vol 49, pp258–283

Smith, K. (1992) 'Innovation policy in an evolutionary context', in Saviotti, P. and Metcalfe, J. S. (eds) *Evolutionary Theories of Economic and Technological Change: Present Status and Future Prospects*, Harwood Academic Publishers, Reading

Smith, K. (2000) 'Innovation as a systemic phenomenon: Rethinking the role of policy', *Enterprise & Innovation Management Studies*, vol 1, no 1, pp73–102

Unruh, G. C. (2000) 'Understanding carbon lock in', *Energy Policy*, vol 28, pp817–830
Unruh, G. C. (2002) 'Escaping carbon lock in', *Energy Policy*, vol 30, pp317–325
van der Steen, M. (1999) *Evolutionary Systems of Innovations*, Van Gorcum Press, The Netherlands
Ward, H. (1995) 'Rational choice theory', in Marsh, D. and Stoker, G. (eds) *Theory and Methods in Political Science*, Macmillan, Basingstoke
Williamson, O. E. (2000) 'The new institutional economics: Taking stock, looking ahead', *Journal of Economic Literature*, vol 38, pp595–613

Section IV
GOVERNANCE AND SUSTAINABILITY: CONSENSUS AND CONFLICT

Chapter 8

Local Governance of Public Services: The Role of Partnerships in Sustainable Waste Management

Rachel Slater

Introduction

The planning and delivery of UK public services is changing. A desire to make services more responsive and appropriate to individual and local needs is driving government reforms (Blair, 2004). The centralized, top-down, 'one size fits all' approach is being criticized and bottom-up reform enabled by the centre is seen as the alternative (Blair, 2004). Local governance is a key objective. This involves devolving power and making services more locally accountable, thus forging a modern relationship between the state, citizens and services (Miliband, 2006). Partnership working between public, private and community actors is being offered as a key mechanism. This chapter explores the nature of waste management in this context.

Sustainable waste management is one of the greatest environmental challenges facing the UK (Strategy Unit, 2002). In broad terms it requires a shift away from waste disposal and landfill to minimization, re-use and recycling. The management of household waste has an important part to play. It is a key public service and often the subject of much public interest; this is particularly the case with respect to the location of processing or treatment facilities, because of associated environmental and health issues. A highly visible, front-line service, waste and recycling collections are among the few public services that households receive automatically. Although council tax revenue is spent on many services, the public often perceive waste management to be the main one.

This chapter draws on case-study research that explored the role of partnerships between local authorities and the companies or organizations that provide waste and recycling collection services and run the treatment facilities (service providers). In particular this research focused on the implications of partnership working for policy development and delivery of more sustainable waste and resource management. The chapter explores different types of partnership, including partnerships between authorities responsible for waste disposal and those that deal with waste collection, and partnerships between local authorities and private waste companies and/or organizations in the community waste sector (CWS).

Local governance implies devolution of power to the local level and dispersal of power away from local government. Through partnerships and wider stakeholder participation, local governance might lead to more sustainable processes and technologies. Using two empirical case studies, this chapter assesses what is happening in practice. It shows that membership of partnerships focusing on waste strategy is limited to local authorities, whereas membership is expanded to include non-state actors in the area of service provision. It also shows that waste partnerships can have their own life cycle with different dynamics, motivations and objectives at different stages. These influence the organizational arrangement of partnerships, and their processes and outcomes.

Context and background

Partnerships as modes of local governance

Governance and local communities

Over recent decades the provision of public services to local communities has been associated with centralized policies and top-down decision making, with central government having the balance of power over local government. With the 'modernization' agenda of the current Labour government, however, there is a shift of emphasis from government to governance (Newman, 2001). This includes moves to devolve power to local government and this is justified using ideas of freedom and flexibility. According to Rhodes (1997), this shift has lead to a 'hollowing-out' of the state, with a loss of functions downwards to special purpose bodies and outwards to agencies, as well as upwards to the European Union (EU).

Government is associated with making and enforcing decisions through centralized control and hierarchical structures. Governance, on the other hand, is associated with networks, less centralized power and non-governmental actors becoming involved in public policy. According to Stoker (1998), the objectives of governance and government are the same but different processes are involved. Under governance the role of the state shifts from control to coordination, and new mechanisms are used to guide a plurality of network actors. The boundary between public and private becomes blurred (Stoker, 1998;

Richards and Smith, 2002; Bache and Flinders, 2004). At the local level, this implies power devolved to communities, with public authorities playing a coordinating and enabling role.

In analysing the shift from government to governance at the local level, Sullivan (2001) discusses community government, local governance and citizen governance. In community government, elected local authorities are central and their elected status underpins their legitimacy and the delivery of local services. Local governance involves local authorities establishing the framework for delivery whilst working with local organizations and communities. In this model all stakeholders are seen as equal. Citizen governance privileges communities and citizens and hence focuses on the very local level. This chapter argues that in the area of waste management, although characteristics from other models are starting to emerge, the community government model still dominates.

Partnerships and governance

There is a strong consensus amongst local authorities that partnership working is increasing and inevitable (Wilkinson and Craig, 2002). There are a number of reasons for this. Partnerships are seen as a way of renewing the role of civil society and promoting social inclusion. By re-engaging, partnerships might also help to develop and deliver services that address the needs of the local community. The collaborative nature of partnerships as a type of network is seen as a way of overcoming the problems of inefficiency associated with bureaucratic hierarchies, and the problems of inequality and exclusion arsing from competitive markets (Giddens, 2000).

From a theoretical perspective, hierarchies, markets and networks can be understood as alternative paradigms linked to particular ideologies and eras (Hartley, 2005). However, because they demonstrate characteristics of all three modes of governance, this view has limited analytical value for partnerships in practice. A promising approach is Lowndes and Skelcher's (1998, p314) argument that 'partnership as an organisational structure is analytically distinct from network as a mode of governance'. This argument suggests that partnerships might have a life cycle that encompasses hierarchical, market and network arrangements, which are important at different moments.

On a similar theme, Hartley (2005) argues that governance through hierarchies, markets and networks may be paradigms linked to different ideologies, but in practice 'they co-exist as layered realities for politicians and managers, with particular circumstances or contexts calling forth behaviours and decisions related to one or the other conception of governance and service delivery' (Hartley, 2005, p29). Lowndes and Skelcher (1998) conclude that partnerships might involve hierarchical and market relationships but they have a particular affinity with network governance. This may be true but overall we can say that the failure to distinguish between modes of social coordination and organizational structures like partnerships has constrained theory and research.

Clarke and Glendinning (2002) develop this argument further and suggest that rather than focusing on modes of governance the challenge is to understand partnerships as contingent and potentially contradictory sites of power. They highlight apparent contradictions such as the promotion of partnerships whilst strengthening the power of central government. Mandating partnership working does not fit easily with concepts like 'self-regulating', 'evolving' and 'co-steering', which are associated with networks and partnerships as a mode of governance. In addition, greater social inclusion and improved democracy through local governance sit uncomfortably with central direction and control.

The motivation for partnerships

Understanding the motivations or driving forces behind partnerships is important because they influence their nature, including the type and number of partners, processes employed and agreed objectives. Drawing on the partnership literature, we can briefly consider the motivations of legitimacy and accountability, and synergy and efficiency (adapted from Lowndes and Sullivan, 2004).

In a context of renewed government concern about participation and inclusion, it has been argued that local governance involving a diverse range of social actors is more legitimate and accountable. The development of partnerships can therefore be seen as a response to concerns about the lack of accountability of local public spending bodies (House of Commons, 1999, para. 64). However, critics argue that partnerships do not necessarily improve participation. Often they involve non-elected bodies and self-selected representatives and they can fail to inform and engage the public. Such partnerships can replicate the problems of accountability and exclusion (Lowndes and Skelcher, 1998; Bennington, 2001).

In principal, partnership working offers a number of synergy and efficiency benefits. A framework introduced by Mackintosh (1992) and developed by Hastings (1996) (see Table 8.1), identifies these and is useful for exploring related motivations. Whilst partnerships that rely on resource synergy may deliver economic efficiencies and added value, they risk excluding or marginalizing potential partners who are not able to contribute similar resources. An approach based on policy synergy, however, can bring about a more equal and influential role for partners who are financially marginalized but able to contribute different and valuable perspectives.

Considering this framework in the context of local governance, a partnership based on policy synergy seems more likely to deliver local governance through the inclusion of a wider range of partners. It might also deliver more innovative and locally appropriate services. In contrast, partnerships that focus on resource synergy might restrain local governance and the potential for innovative and locally appropriate services by excluding financially marginalized stakeholders and focusing on the perspectives of dominant partners. The case studies in the following section show how these different motivations shape partnerships and influence technology choices in the waste sector.

Table 8.1 *Concepts of synergy, transformation and budgets in the partnership process*

Concept	Process	Outcome
Resource synergy	Cooperation and coordination over spending of resources	Added value from resources spent: increased effectiveness or efficiency
Policy synergy	Joint approach developed through combining the different perspectives of each partner	New perspectives/innovative solutions. Original difference in culture and objectives between partners maintained
Uni-directional transformation	Partner/s who struggle to modify or change another partner in their own image, and do not see the need for them to change (teaching not learning)	Partners change their organizational culture or objectives to become similar to those of another partner. The partnership takes on the style of the transforming partnership
Mutual transformation	Reciprocal challenges for change (pre-existing culture and objectives), partners seek to teach and learn	All partners change to some extent. New sets of operational styles are developed. Differences between partners are reduced
Budget juggling	Partners negotiate to shift financial commitment, or extract additional funds from other partners	Financial risk is shared / shifted. May marginalize the partners not financially dominant
Budget enlargement	Partners secure additional funding from a third party	Conditions and outcomes may be imposed by third party that are against the interests of one or more of the partners

Source: Adapted from Hastings (1996)

The waste issue

In this chapter I focus on municipal waste, a term used to describe wastes that come under the control of local authorities. The vast majority of this is from households. Municipal waste accounts for a small proportion of all waste, but it presents particular challenges as it tends to be more heterogeneous and subject to greater regulatory control compared to other types. From a governance perspective, the management of municipal waste is an important and interesting case because it brings together a wider array of actors, including from all levels of government, local communities, householders and commercial service providers.

The UK has a long and established history of sending waste to landfills. This has traditionally been the cheapest option. Recycling and composting are increasing, and regulation and fewer landfill sites are pushing up costs, but landfill continues to dominate – 72 per cent of municipal waste collected in 2003/04 (Department of the Environment, Food and Rural Affairs (DEFRA), 2005). Landfill will decline in the future, however, as European and national legislation requires a shift to waste minimization, re-use, recycling and composting. The EU Landfill Directive (99/31) is one of the most significant pieces of recent legislation. It sets out measures intended to improve the management of landfills and to restrict the types of wastes accepted (see Slater and Frederickson, 2001).

One of the most challenging measures for the UK is the progressive reduction of the amount of biodegradable municipal waste that can be sent to landfill. Failure to meet the target carries a penalty of £500,000 per day. To implement this reduction the UK government launched the landfill allowance trading scheme in 2005, the first trading scheme to involve waste. Landfill allowances have been allocated to individual authorities who can meet targets by banking, borrowing or trading. Failure to comply with their allowances will result in local authorities receiving prohibitive fines for every additional tonne landfilled.

Waste services were delivered in-house by local authorities until the Local Government Act of 1988 opened up the service to the private sector. It also introduced compulsory competitive tendering, with service allocation based on cost. This was superseded in 2000 by 'best value', which required consideration to be given to quality and value factors, although cost continues to be a dominant factor when contracts are awarded. In Wales, Scotland and Northern Ireland local authorities are unitary with responsibility for both the collection and disposal functions. England has some unitary authorities but in other (two-tier) cases waste collection and waste disposal authorities are separate.

Over recent years central government has linked partnership working and sustainable waste management. They are driving the agenda using guidance, regulations and funding. The two-tier structure of many English local authorities has been criticized for fragmenting collection and treatment/disposal. Calls for greater cohesion (Strategy Unit, 2002) have been translated through the Waste and Emissions Trading (WET) Act (2003), which includes a statutory requirement for waste collection and waste disposal authorities to produce a joint waste strategy. Many county and district authorities are now working in partnership to deliver this. In the two-tier authorities, the landfill allowance trading schemes applies to the disposal authority and they will be responsible for any fines incurred.

Partnerships are also being galvanized through funding structures. DEFRA's Waste Minimisation and Recycling Fund, for example, had a strong partnership element, and in 2003 it awarded £62.5 million to 14 different local authority partnerships. In addition, public services are increasingly delivered through partnerships between local authorities and the private sector, using the Private Finance Initiative (PFI). In the case of waste management, this involves the public sector agreeing outcome-based contracts focused on proven technologies. The private sector designs, builds, finances and operates the assets over a fixed period for annual payments.

In parallel with the push for public–private partnerships, local authorities are also being encouraged to work in partnership with the CWS. Authorities have a statutory obligation to produce a Community Strategy setting out how local decision making will 'engage and involve local communities … and be based on a proper assessment of needs and the availability of resources' (Department for Environment, Transport and the Regions (DETR), 2000, p3). One of the key objectives of the strategy is to coordinate the actions of local authorities and of the public, private, community and voluntary organizations that operate locally, and to foster and shape the activity of these organizations so that they meet community needs. In the area of waste, guidance encourages working with the CWS to deliver re-use, recycling and composting (DETR, 2001).

Waste management partnerships in practice

Although guidance, regulation and funding promote partnership working in waste services, there is little published research on such partnerships in practice. The following section focuses on two case studies but it is informed by wider research that examined partnership working in the sector. The cases illustrate contrasting models of partnership working with different notions of sustainable technologies. One represents a 'single authority' approach, integrating the two-tier collection and disposal structure, and relying on one main contractor for service delivery. The other illustrates a 'multi-resource' approach, which seeks to harness a range of specialist and local providers. After outlining the cases I examine the different motivations underpinning the partnership models.

Somerset Waste Partnership

Somerset is a rural county in the south-west of England. It has wealthy communities and small pockets of deprivation. The population is just under 500,000 and there are 214,000 households. Unemployment is below the national average (1.9 per cent in Somerset, 3.2 per cent national average) and so is the population of black and minority communities (0.5 per cent in Somerset, 5.5 per cent national average) (Office of National Statistics (ONS), 2001; Audit Commission, 2002). Tourism is an important industry, and in some areas population doubles in the summer. The Somerset Waste Partnership (SWP) is between the two tiers of the local authority responsible for waste collection, treatment and disposal across the county (five district councils responsible for collections and the county council responsible for treatment and disposal).

Over the last decade SWP has evolved from an informal network into a semi-formal partnership. Partners have agreed to develop it further to establish a single Somerset Waste Board in the future. This will have executive responsibility for all waste collection, disposal and recycling services across Somerset. The first working form of the partnership was a Joint Advisory Committee established in 1992. This involved council officers and members sharing knowledge, experience and good practice. At this stage SWP was somewhat like a network (McCabe et al, 1997) or community of practice (Wenger, 2002).

In 1997 SWP signed a Memorandum of Understanding to work together in developing and implementing a Household Waste Management Strategy. In 2000 SWP was the first in England to undertake a Joint Best Value Review. According to the Audit Commission (2002), the process of the review benefited and cemented partnership working by creating ownership of the findings. It also moved the partnership from a talking shop to effective partnership working. It is hoped that the single Somerset Waste Board will formalize partnership working and deliver integration of services. This is likely to result in more standardized collection services across the county.

SWP has adopted a source-separation strategy as the principal means of improving recycling and composting performance (separation takes place before collection). Households are required to keep various recyclables separate from remaining general ('residual') waste. The collector then puts the mixed recyclables through a further stage of separation on the collection vehicle at the kerbside. SWP's source separation targets a large number of dry recyclable materials (paper, glass, plastics, cans and textiles), food waste and garden waste. This approach is combined with reduced collection of residual waste, from weekly to fortnightly, thus providing an incentive for households to participate.

Three of the five collection districts have adopted the weekly collection of dry recyclables and food waste, with a charged fortnightly collection for garden waste, and a fortnightly collection of residual waste. Although established in some areas in Europe, this is the first time a system including separate food-waste collection from low-rise housing has been introduced on a large scale in the UK. Although it will take some time for the scheme to be fully implemented, SWP claims that early indications show an increase in recycling rates to over 50 per cent.

Understanding the interaction between recycling and residual waste is important in this case. For instance, some treatment facilities (such as energy from waste plants) require large quantities of residual waste to operate effectively. The risk is that this will discourage the development of alternatives such as recycling and composting. SWP understands this and stresses the importance of appropriate residual facilities to prevent technology 'lock in' and to give them flexibility in adapting to legislation and policy developments.

Hackney Waste Partnership

Hackney is an inner-city borough in north-east London. The population of 210,000 lives in 90,500 households. It is one of the most ethnically diverse and socially deprived areas in England; unemployment is over 6 per cent, and 56 per cent of the population is from black or minority ethnic communities. Street crime is six times the national average and burglary and vehicle crime is double the national average (Audit Commission, 2004). Over half the housing stock is high-rise purpose-built multi-occupancy and around one-quarter is non-purpose-built multi-occupancy. Neither of these suits traditional kerbside recycling services.

During the 1990s and early 2000s Hackney had one of the lowest recycling rates in the country (around 1 to 2 per cent). Following significant service improvements Hackney now records a rate of 12 per cent and aims to achieve 18 per cent by 2005/06. It has achieved this increase largely through a source separation and collection strategy. Hackney's residual waste collection and street cleansing are carried out by its own in-house Direct Service Organization. The collection of municipal material for recycling and composting, however, is carried out by two community waste sector organizations, Ealing Community Transport (ECT) and East London Community Recycling Partnership (ELCRP).

ECT provides a number of public services and it is the largest not-for-profit integrated waste management company in the UK. They provide weekly multi-material kerbside recycling services to low-rise properties across the borough and a fortnightly garden-waste collection service. Where the kerbside service is unworkable, such as in high-rise estates, they provide a near-entry collection system for dry recyclables. This comprises a number of containers where residents can deposit recyclables. ECT is also trialling a separate food-waste collection service for low-rise properties.

ELCRP is a small community sector organisation specializing in door-to-door services on estates, including collection of recyclables and compostables. It is managed and run largely by people from the community. They successfully undertook a 'closed loop' pilot project of estates-based door-to-door collection and composting of separated food waste, and in partnership with the council are rolling this out across a number of other estates in the borough. The services provided by ELCRP include a couple of 'firsts' in the UK: the first estates-based (high-rise) door-to-door collection of food waste; and the first fully enclosed and controlled (i.e. in-vessel) community-based composting process to be approved under the Animal By-Products Regulations.

ELCRP also works with ECT to collect estates-based dry recyclables door-to-door for deposit in near-entry systems for collection by ECT.

Analysis

In exploring these two cases it is important to bear in mind key differences. SWP brings together collection and disposal authorities whereas the Hackney Waste Partnership (HWP) links the collection authority and service providers. Also, population and environmental conditions are different in each case. This section presents an analysis focusing on two themes: the different motivations for partnership working using the concepts of resource synergy and policy synergy; and the links between partnerships, local sovereignty and local service delivery.

Motivations and partnerships

Partnerships for resource synergy

Resource synergy was a strong driver in both cases. Delivering resource efficiencies was frequently cited as the primary motivation for partnership working by the full range of actors. For local authority partnerships, efficiencies are understood to be deliverable through: integration of collection, treatment and disposal; increased standardization of collection systems; management, administrative and operational efficiencies; economies of scale and/or limiting rising costs; avoidance of duplication through sharing expertise, best practice, research and data, and communication strategies.

In two-tier authority structures the different priorities of collection and disposal can lead to tensions. For SWP, greater cohesion and delivery of a more efficient service are primary motivations. Officers within the partnership spoke of a shift in focus to saving money for the council-taxpayer in Somerset, rather than focusing on savings for individual districts or the county. Greater standardization of services facilitates contract integration, and this is a driving force behind SWP plans to establish a partnership waste board. This board would procure standard services across the whole county.

SWP believes that such developments will deliver administrative and management benefits. Duplication in procurement, for example, will be reduced with decisions being taken by the board rather than districts. There will also be operational efficiencies through economies of scale and the removal of artificial administrative boundaries and rationalizing of service depots. Somerset County Council also believes that the waste board will offer a more defined career path and better opportunities than the present structure. In moving towards a single waste board, SWP is effectively emphasizing the centralization of services.

Such vertical integration, however, places local sovereignty, participation and innovation at risk. Generally speaking, for example, most recycling collection schemes develop within autonomous local districts and there can be a huge variety of types across a county. SWP acknowledges the tension between centralization and local knowledge, engagement and accountability. According to one senior SWP officer:

> ...*[with]integration there's a danger of becoming an anonymous body, and I think that's a real concern that we need to make sure we address. There are clearly economies that we can attain for the benefit of all the councils and we can probably end up with a more co-ordinated high performing service, but if they are inaccessible for the customer they have failed.* (6 May 2005)

SWP also acknowledges that standardized services across the county may not be timely or appropriate for all districts. What may be required is a service that allows for differences between districts but if districts want variations they may incur greater costs.

For HWP, delivering efficiency gains was also an important factor; cost-effectiveness of services is a statutory obligation. Beyond their local partnerships with service providers, the collection authority is working with neighbouring authorities to improve efficiency. This includes specific initiatives to share resources, such as a green waste collection service and an awareness raising programme. However, unlike SWP, HWP stressed the importance of 'added social value' from the locally embedded schemes, which can help address social problems and improve local environments. According to one HWP officer:

> *Obviously percentage targets are the most important factor but here the other factors are always important. Trying to improve the quality of life for those who live in areas that are deprived and recycling facilities help in that which is precisely why we have adopted the ways that we have of getting local groups involved.*
> (11 January 2005)

Partnerships for policy synergy

Policy synergy was important in both partnerships but SWP seemed to emphasize it less than resource efficiencies. This can be illustrated by exploring innovation as an alternative to efficiency. Bringing together different perspectives and sharing experiences can foster innovative approaches. Drawing on experience from other authorities, and the private and community waste sectors, SWP initially developed a range of alternative models and projections for collection systems over the long term. The districts were divided over their favoured model. Mendip favoured separate food-waste collections whilst South Somerset and Taunton Deane favoured combining garden and food waste. Initially it was thought that SWP would adopt both. In the end, however, due to a number of factors, including Mendip's positive experience from the separate food-waste trials, both South Somerset and Taunton Deane chose the separate food-waste system. According to a senior waste officer in Taunton Deane:

> *Initially it wasn't the way I would have chosen to have gone, but I guess when you deal with innovation you don't know the answers … it's difficult to really know what the reaction to this will be until we actually do it, but I am guided by Mendip and South Somerset who have done it before.* (5 May 2005)

Other authority partners within SWP also had a positive regard for partnership working in developing new approaches, but were fearful that a move to a single waste partnership board may constrain that capacity. According to a senior officer at Sedgemoor District Council:

> *Partnerships are a good way of approaching innovation because it gives you more confidence, more heads are better than one, there are opportunities for more debating, to develop ideas and do more trials. If we become a formal partnership working together in one place there won't be partners on this sort of level [district authorities]… and it may mean losing some of the innovative stuff…*
> (5 May 2005)

In bringing together different perspectives SWP relied predominantly on core partners, namely the waste disposal authority and waste collection authorities. In contrast, HWP brings together the waste collection authority and service providers like ECT and ELCRP. These bring different types of knowledge and experience to the partnership. Hackney Council is keen to engage with the CWS and to use niche service providers to address the area's diversity. Given their mixed housing stock and ethnically diverse population, the council recognize that a homogenous system is not viable and policy synergy underpins the idea of developing multiple systems for collection. In the words of one officer:

> *We have got high rise and low rise and different communities ... you can't have a one size fits all approach, it means you need specialists for different areas. For instance East London Community Recycling Partnership are specialists in high-rise and Ealing Community Transport more low-rise, so between them we can cover both aspects... They have so many ideas ... it's not just the council saying this is what you have got to do, it's us saying well what do you think?* (11 January 2005)

Both ECT and ELCRP take a proactive problem-solving approach. They are keen to be flexible to meet the council's objectives. Both supported the council's view on the need to incorporate their experience and expertise in developing services. According to ECT:

> *Working in partnership with Hackney Council means we have common aims and we bring our respective resources and skills to bear to achieve those aims. The primary aim is to hit the statutory recycling target and to provide a level of service that the Council wants residents to get, so the quality is important. We share those aims. Now we don't always share the same ideas about how to achieve them so that will come up for discussion and we will work that through. We talk about what things might work, and they will say 'you guys have a lot of experience in this field, what do you think we should do?'* (22 February 2005)

Partnerships as a business strategy

In both SWP and HWP, key service providers see partnership as an important business strategy. Cleanaway Ltd is a large private waste management company. They collect residual and garden waste for four of the five districts in the SWP. ECT is a large social-enterprise providing kerbside recycling services for both SWP and HWP. Although contracts are involved, both organizations stressed differences in partnership working compared with traditional client–contractor relationships. Authorities are increasingly negotiating with industry, and service providers help to define key performance indicators.

In providing services in partnership with authorities, service providers need to share the aims of the authority, particularly statutory targets and a quality service to the householder. They increasingly need a flexible, problem-solving approach that requires a more consensual-based mindset, in contrast to a contract-led approach, which was often termed by case-study participants as confrontational or adversarial. Nevertheless, service providers for both SWP and HWP acknowledge that partnership working is a business strategy:

> *It's about growing the business, doing a good job and getting a good reputation and being seen as the choice partner for the future.* (ECT, 22 February 2005)

> *We are happy to work in partnership in any way with any authority … it's a very competitive business and we are there to try and cement long-term relationships.* (Cleanaway, 7 June 2005)

Partnership, sovereignty and serving local communities

Having considered motivations and organizational structures, this section looks at the relationship between different structures and local sovereignty and service delivery. Waste and recycling is a highly visible, front-line public service delivered to households. Local knowledge and expertise are important in designing schemes and communication strategies between the collection authority and households are necessary, especially with respect to separation and participation. Normalizing recycling provides scope for increasing awareness of waste and wider environmental and citizenship issues. Both Somerset and Hackney acknowledged the importance of accountability and responsiveness, but how they address these issues is influenced by partnership structures.

Increasingly, two-tier waste disposal and collection authorities are adopting a model similar to the SWP plan: greater centralization and standardization of services delivered through a single waste authority. Such changes imply more distance from communities. According to districts, SWP centralization is likely to result in a loss of sovereignty for individual waste collection authorities. Without careful implementation to maintain local links this could reduce responsiveness and accountability locally. It might also be more difficult for district council members to access officer expertise, and this could limit the capacity for policy synergy. According to one senior officer:

> *One of the things that our members are concerned about is that they will lose people of my level of expertise. So when they go to the board they won't have that expertise to inform them, they won't have the skills and knowledge to challenge what's being put to them, and I think that is really important.* (5 May 2005)

In contrast, the council involved in HWP believe that a larger number of smaller contracts allow them to respond to local conditions (they acknowledge that there might be greater management and administrative costs). Poor performance in some service areas in the past has led to public mistrust of the council and they think that community-based recycling might go some way to addressing this. With this in mind ELCRP is particularly interesting. It is a small-scale organization, committed to being embedded in the communities it serves and to bringing them social and environmental benefits. Residents are engaged in the planning and implementation process via tenants' and residents' associations, and they seek to recruit locally.

This scheme has led to a number of benefits that were not anticipated at the outset. Collecting separated food waste door-to-door has removed food waste from the residual waste collection, which uses chutes and communal containment. This has reduced blockages of chutes, and vermin. In addition, collection teams work in uniformed pairs and feedback suggests they have reduced the fear of crime on the estate. According to ELCRP, embedding the service in the local community encourages participation and they claim take-up rates as high as 80+ per cent in some of the high-rise blocks. Hackney Council recognizes the social benefits and 'added value' delivered by such schemes, although it is difficult to quantify and cost such 'soft' benefits.

Discussion and conclusions

There is a spectrum of partnerships in municipal waste management from informal to formal. The evidence suggests that in some cases, such as SWP, there is a life cycle that involves progress across this spectrum. Informal beginnings help to build relationships and trust and these facilitate more formal commitments. In addition, this research supports the argument that partnerships in practice include aspects of hierarchies, markets and networks (Lowndes and Skelcher, 1998; Hartley, 2005). During the procurement of services, for example, the market can be invoked in tendering and contracts, but afterwards the public authority and service providers can work collaboratively.

Partnerships to bring different parts of the state together, such as SWP, can be both strategic and operational. Waste partnerships that include non-state actors, however, tend to focus on service implementation rather than strategy (e.g. HWP). This supports Pearson (2001) and Taylor (2001), who found that public service strategy continues to be primarily driven by local government, and partnership working is constrained to the delivery of specific initiatives. In addition, although partnership working between two-tier authorities aims to integrate collection and disposal, a hierarchy can remain because the disposal authority has power to stipulate the material type and collection format.

The dominant motivation for partnership in the case of SWP is efficiency. Greater cohesion between two-tier authorities is seen as being able to deliver resource synergy benefits. Authorities are increasingly looking to integrated contracts with service providers to realize these. Such contracts are often large scale, long-term and with one service provider. Thus they can favour larger and well-established incumbent organizations. There is a risk that such contracts will lock public authorities into particular technologies and processes and, in so doing, stifle innovation.

Developments along these lines appear to accompany the tendency to centralize service provision, for example the creation of a single centralized waste management board. This is also, however, a response to greater hierarchical control from central government. Although proponents of single waste authorities claim they are still based on partnerships, efficiencies associated with streamlining decision making need to be balanced against loss of sovereignty at the local level and related benefits. Centralization appears to conflict with localism by distancing decision making and service delivery further from communities.

Although HWP is also motivated by efficiency, it does not believe a standardized collection approach is suitable, and it has adopted a multiple service provider model. In this way it hopes to link diverse specialisms with mixed communities and settings. The multiple-service provider approach encourages innovation. It also creates space to 'embed' certain initiatives and technologies within the communities they serve. The close proximity of provider and user facilitates engagement and service feedback. As well as contributing to waste targets, it is these initiatives that often deliver additional social and environmental benefits. The public authority acknowledges that this approach may require greater management and administrative resources.

Integrated contracts that marginalize small and specialist organizations risk losing the innovative potential of the CWS more broadly. ELCRP argues that its community base increases participation in its schemes. This is supported by evidence from other CWS schemes (Luckin and Sharp, 2004). Engagement with residents also facilitates understanding of the needs of user and service provider. In many ways HWP demonstrates localism in service delivery. That said, although HWP's CWS service providers can make a valuable contribution to policy, they do not necessarily represent the community, making this local rather than citizen governance.

There is some evidence to suggest that successful partnerships develop from small informal projects that give rise to equity, efficiency and trust (Ring and Van den Van, 1994). For established waste partnerships that developed organically, relatively slow evolution through shared experience was an important element in developing consensus and allowing the partnership to become more formal. However, there is an increasing trend for the creation of waste partnerships to be driven externally, either by policy or funding. This raises the question whether 'imposed' partnerships will be able to work successfully without a shared history that has developed understanding and trust.

References

Audit Commission (2002) *Waste Management in Somerset*, Audit Commission, London
Audit Commission (2004) *Waste Service Inspection: London Borough of Hackney*, Audit Commission, London
Bache, I. and Flinders, M. (eds) (2004) *Multi-level Governance*, Oxford University Press, Oxford

Benington, J. (2001) 'Partnerships as networked governance?' in Geddes, M. and
    Benington, J. (eds) *Local Partnerships and Social Exclusion in the European Union:
    New Forms of Local Social Governance?* Routledge, London
Blair, T. (2004) 'The Future for Public Services', The Prime Minister Tony Blair's full
    speech at the Guardian's Public Services Summit, Hertfordshire
    http://society.guardian.co.uk/futureforpublicservices/comment/0,8146,1134531,00.
    html accessed October 2005
Clarke, J. and Glendinning, C. (2002) 'Partnership and the remaking of welfare gover-
    nance', in Glendinning, C., Powell, M. and Rummery, K. (eds) *Partnerships, New
    Labour and the Governance of Welfare*, The Policy Press, Bristol
Department for Environment, Transport and the Regions (2000) *Preparing Community
    Strategies: Government Guidance to Local Authorities*, HMSO, London
Department for Environment, Transport and the Regions (2001) *Guidance on
    Municipal Waste Management Strategies*, HMSO, London
Department of the Environment, Food and Rural Affairs (2005) *Municipal Waste
    Management Survey 2003/04*, DEFRA, London
Giddens, A. (2000) *The Third Way and its Critics*, Polity Press, Cambridge
Hartley, J. (2005) 'Innovation in governance and public services: Past and present',
    Public Money and Management, January, pp27–34
Hastings, A. (1996) 'Unravelling the process of partnership in urban regeneration
    policy', *Urban Studies*, vol 33, no 2, pp253–268
House of Commons (1999) *Quangos*, Select Committee on Public Administration, The
    Stationary Office, London
Lowndes, V. and Skelcher, C. (1998) 'The dynamics of multi-organizational partner-
    ships', *Public Administration*, vol 76, pp313–333
Lowndes, V. and Sullivan, H. (2004) 'Like a horse and carriage or a fish on a bicycle:
    How well do local partnerships and public participation go together?', *Local
    Government Studies*, vol 30, no 1, pp51–73
Luckin, D. and Sharp, L. (2004) 'Remaking local governance through community
    participation? The case of the community waste sector', *Urban Studies*, vol 41, no 8,
    pp1485–1505
Mackintosh, M. (1992) 'Partnership: Issues of policy and negotiation', *Local Economy*,
    vol 7, pp210–224
McCabe, A., Lowndes, V. and Skelcher, C. (1997) *Partnerships and Networks: An
    Evaluation and Development Manual*, Joseph Rowntree Foundation/YPS, York
Miliband, D. (2006) 'Putting people in control', speech by Rt. Hon. David Miliband,
    Minister for Communities and Local Government, delivered at the National Council
    of Voluntary Organisations (NCVO) annual conference, 21 February,
    www.labour.org.uk accessed February 2006
Newman, J. (2001) *Modernising Governance: New Labour, Policy and Society*, Sage
    Publications, London
Office of National Statistics (2001) Census 2001, Office of National Statistics, London
Pearson, S. (2001) 'Local government, anti-poverty strategies and partnership working',
    in Balloch, S. and Taylor, M. (eds) *Partnership Working: Policy and Practice*, The
    Policy Press, Bristol
Rhodes, R. A. W. (1997) *Understanding Governance*, Open University Press,
    Buckingham
Richards, D. and Smith, M. J. (2002) *Governance and Public Policy in the UK*, Oxford
    University Press, Oxford
Ring, P. and Van den Van, A. (1994) 'Developmental processes of co-operative inter-

organisational relationships', *Academy of Management Review*, vol 19, pp90–118

Slater, R. and Frederickson, J. (2001) 'Composting municipal waste in the UK: Some lessons from Europe', *Resources Conservation and Recycling*, vol 32, pp359–374

Stoker, G. (1998) 'Governance as theory; five propositions', *International Social Science Journal*, vol 50, pp17–28

Strategy Unit (2002) *Waste Not, Want Not; A Strategy for Tackling the Waste Problem in England*, Strategy Unit, London

Sullivan, H. (2001) 'Modernisation, democratisation and community governance', *Local Government Studies*, vol 27, no 3, pp1–24

Taylor, M. (2001) 'Partnership: Insiders and outsiders', in Harris, M. and Rochester, C. (eds) *Voluntary Organisations and Social Policy in Britain: Perspectives on Change and Choice*, Palgrave, New York

Wenger, E. (2002) *Cultivating Communities of Practice: A Guide to Managing Knowledge*, Harvard Business School, Boston

Wilkinson, M. and Craig, G. (2002) *New Roles for Old: Local Authority Members and Partnership Working*, Joseph Rowntree Foundation, York

Chapter 9

Wind Power, Governance and Networks

Dave Toke

Introduction

This chapter discusses the influence of governance systems on wind power policy and implementation outcomes. Studying how wind power policy outcomes occur, in particular the volume and rate of deployment of wind power, is important for two reasons. First, so that we can engage in analysis of an area of great public interest and, second, so that we are in a better position to assess how policies can best be shaped to achieve desirable outcomes in this policy field.

Various factors influence wind power planning outcomes, including the financial procurement regime, population density, landscape value, the degree and nature of grass-roots energy initiatives and the planning framework (Toke, 2005a). We cannot directly influence population density, or even the general population's attitude to landscape value, by manipulating governance structures dealing with wind power. However, it may be possible to develop these governance structures to fit around these influences, for instance by deploying wind power in ways that may be more acceptable to the local population. Local people have been identified as the chief influence on planning outcomes in places like the UK where population density is high and where landscape issues loom large (Toke, 2005b).

Discussion of wind power governance structures has so far been mainly limited to a discussion of the relative merits and de-merits of so-called fixed price regimes for funding wind power (REFIT systems) and so-called market-based systems such as the UK's Renewables Obligation (RO). This debate is important because conventional political wisdom poses a relationship between different types of financial procurement regime and wind power outcomes. In particular, market-based systems are said to be cost-effective but are thought to favour the electricity industry establishment, whereas fixed-price 'feed-in' tariffs are said to favour more grass-roots initiatives at the cost of giving some people windfall profits (Lauber, 2004; Toke, 2005c; Mitchell et al, 2006). However, less attention has been given to the different networks that exist in different countries, and the knowledge systems that underpin these networks. We can describe financial procurement mechanisms and also the planning systems that make up the governance systems. We can compare these arrangements in different country case studies. This, however, is a 'realist' approach since we are assuming that the actors in the different countries have the same notion of reality and the same notions of what is right and wrong and how to develop wind power.

It is important to study the networks and the knowledge systems with which they are associated. This is because these networks and knowledge systems may say a lot about wind power deployment that is not necessarily related to whether the financial procurement system is fixed price or market based. We can study this area by utilizing the distinction between ontology and epistemology.

As an article in a philosophy journal puts it:

> *Ontological concepts are those of object, process, particular, individual, whole, part, property, and quality. Epistemological concepts are those of belief, knowledge and uncertain or wrong knowledge.* (Poli, 2001, p2)

It could also be added, as far as ontology is concerned, that it involves relationships, a point made by Gruber (2005) who says (in the context of a discussion about artificial intelligence) that:

> *an ontology is a description (like a formal specification of a program) of the concepts and relationships that can exist for an agent or a community of agents.* (Gruber, 2005)

The nature of the networks is an ontological issue since it involves the shape and quality of the wind power industry and its relationships. These are the nature of the networks that constitute the wind power industry, the relationships between developers and the rest of the electricity and wind power industry, the relationships to particular localities, and the financial linkages in terms of investment patterns. In different countries, there is, as we shall see, a different 'reality' as far as the structure and relationships of the wind power industry is concerned.

The nature of the knowledge systems associated with the networks is an epistemological issue. The epistemologies are what, in different countries, is thought to be the right or most practical way of developing wind power (e.g.

through corporate or cooperative or local investment), and the way that knowledge about wind power is collected and disseminated.

The UK has what is arguably the largest relatively pure market-based system, and also a rapidly developing wind power sector. We can compare this with the three countries with the highest proportion of electricity from wind power to date, namely Denmark (21 per cent), Germany (5 per cent) and Spain (7 per cent). I also include The Netherlands, since this country has also had a long-standing renewable energy procurement programme.

I shall begin in a conventional way by describing the deployment outcomes (e.g. quantities of wind power capacity, types of schemes) and the nature of the financial procurement systems. In the rest of the chapter I go on to study the non-governmental networks involved, using the concepts associated with ontology and epistemology.

Financial governance

Renewable energy feed-in tariffs have been associated with the bulk of wind power deployment in Europe, as can be seen in Figure 9.1 for Germany, Denmark and Spain. Feed-in tariffs involve paying renewable energy generators guaranteed set prices for each unit of electricity produced.

The UK and, until recently, The Netherlands, have been associated with market-based systems. These involve the creation of 'green electricity certificates', which electricity suppliers have to buy from renewable electricity generators in order to satisfy their targets for renewable electricity supply.

There are some stereotypical notions about the relative performance of feed-in tariffs and market-based systems:

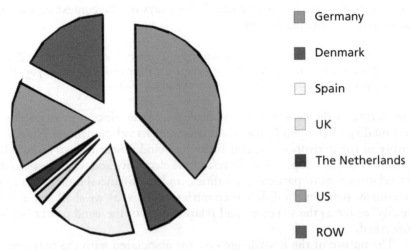

Note: 'ROW' means 'rest of world'.
Source: Wind Power Monthly (January, 2005)

Figure 9.1 *World wind power capacity by nation for 2004*

- Market-based systems are more cost-effective than feed-in tariffs. This opinion is supported by Eurelectric, the peak organization representing the European electricity industry (Eurelectric, 2004).
- Feed-in tariffs are necessarily better for grass-roots ownership. This notion is supported by left-of-centre and anti-nuclear activists (Wind-works, 2004).

However, these are not borne out by the evidence.

First, let us compare the returns per MW (megawatt) from the different systems, the Spanish and German being feed-in tariffs and the UK system being market based. The UK figure is based on an average return likely for typical contracts with electricity suppliers, and the German figure is based on 2004 payments to electricity suppliers in the first year of 5.9p/kwh (pence/kilowatt hour) but reducing this to 5.5p/kwh to take some account of the fact that the payments decline in later years. Even the starting point is being reduced by 2 per cent each year in nominal terms (never mind real terms because the payments are not inflation indexed).

It can be seen from the figures in Table 9.1 that once different capacity factors are taken into account, the UK's market based RO is not necessarily more cost-effective in delivering wind power. Indeed on these figures the British system seems to be the most expensive, and the German system the cheapest, in terms of expected rates of return per MW.

The point about the RO is simply that it is not very competitive. Although there may be a market in incentives, that is green electricity certificates, which the electricity suppliers need to buy in order to demonstrate that they are meeting the targets, this market does not help developers, who need long-term contracts. There is no long-term market in the green electricity certificates. Hence the developers are beholden to the electricity suppliers, who are needed to give them contracts to supply electricity. Even so, the value of the Renewable Obligation Certificates (ROCs) becomes higher the more the RO target is unful-

Table 9.1 *Cost-effectiveness of the UK 'renewable obligation' in delivering wind power*

Country	Tariff in p/KWh	Average capacity factor (%)	Annual return per installed MW (£)
Germany	5.5 (declining)	18	87,000
United Kingdom	5.0 (15-yr contract) 7.0 (annual contract)	28	123,000 172,000
Spain	4.5	28	110,000

Note: German and UK capacity factor figures are based on analysis of operating data for years 2001, 2002, 2003 and 2004. The Spanish capacity factor figure is based on interviews with wind power development representatives of Iberdrola (electricity utility) and EVE (Basque Energy Agency). UK tariff figure is based on interviews with developers about contractual terms with electricity suppliers, and German and Spanish tariff figures are based on rates set by government. (Interview with Gonzalo Saenz de Miera (Iberdrola) 9 December 2004 and Enrique Monasterio and Javier Marques (EVE) 10 December 2004. Also see Toke (2005c)).

filled. In addition, renewable generators can sell their electricity for baseload prices. The oligopolistic electricity suppliers who dominate electricity markets have a vested interest in maintaining the value of their investments (and not seeing the price of ROCs crash), so the targets will remain unfulfilled, thus keeping up the value of the ROCs (Toke, 2005c). Hence, in practice, there are very good terms available for renewable generators from electricity suppliers (in terms of British wind conditions), whether they want long-term guarantees (15-year contracts) or are willing to take short-term contracts in return for much higher payments for renewable electricity.

The 'neo-liberal' stereotype of market solutions delivering cost-effectiveness may be misplaced in this case. However, a 'left-wing' stereotype may also be misplaced, namely the notion that fixed tariffs help farmer and cooperative schemes whilst market-based approaches help the schemes planned by big companies.

We can see this in Figure 9.2 below, which shows proportions of capacity owned by cooperatives, farmers and corporate concerns. In fact, in Germany most of the financing of even the 'corporate' sector is raised through popular share offers. In the 'corporate' cases, however, the shareholders are high income earners who do not necessarily live anywhere near the schemes, but who can benefit by offsetting high marginal tax rates against their investments in wind power. In Denmark the cooperatives largely pioneered the early deployment of wind power, although in later years of expansion it was farmer ownership that predominated.

However, whilst it may be the case that decentralized wind power coexists with feed-in tariffs in Germany and Denmark, this is not the case in Spain, where practically no wind power is owned by local people. Moreover, in the Netherlands, a big farmer-owned sector and some cooperatives were built up in a market-based system that was changed only in 2005.

It does seem from this discussion that the nature of the financial procurement system may not be the biggest factor influencing the patterns of ownership of the wind power industry. This, of course, assumes that incentives offered to wind power developers are good enough to offer the possibility of widespread economic viability for wind power schemes.

Even within the UK it seems plausible that the relative lack of farmer-owned and cooperative-owned wind power schemes is related to cultural differences with Germany and Denmark. This includes the lack of a militant anti-nuclear movement. In any event there have been very few initiatives in the UK to create locally owned wind power schemes.

On the other hand, it is even plausible to argue that the RO actually offers more financial possibilities for cooperative schemes compared to conventional ones. This is because cooperatives, such as the ones organized by Baywind Co-operative and Energy4All, can dispense with the long-term contracts with electricity suppliers that allow these electricity suppliers to take a lot of the value of the ROCs. They can reclaim more or less their full value, so earning around £70 per MWh (assuming the RO is two-thirds fulfilled) compared to only £50 to £55 per MWh if they agree to a 15-year contract.

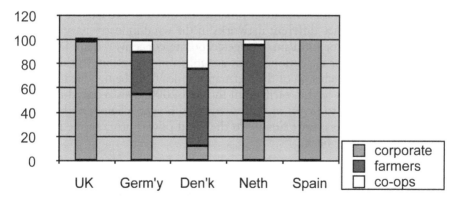

Source: Data collated from interviews with representatives of wind industry associations in the different states

Figure 9.2 *Patterns of ownership of wind power*

Indeed, at the time of writing, a farmer in Oxfordshire is in the process of setting up a community wind farm using precisely these terms. Adam Twine, of Watchmill, Oxfordshire, has won planning consent for a 6.5MW project, which will be financed by a cooperative share offer aimed principally at the local population. The share offer is being organized by Energy4All – an offshoot of the Baywind Energy Co-operative, which runs the UK's first commercial scale wind power cooperative in Cumbria, north-west England. There could be a lot more like him. The slowness to develop locally owned wind power in the UK seems to be connected with a shortage of numbers of determined individuals rather than a lack of financial possibilities.

There is also a farmer-owned project at Moel Maelogen in Conwy, Wales. This began with a 3.9MW project, but in November 2004 this gained planning permission for an extension to around 15MW. This is the sort of size adopted by conventional developers, yet it is being developed by a cooperative of three farmers who have acted as their own developers. The financial advantage for the farmers is that they receive the profits in respect of their share holdings, as opposed merely to the 2 per cent royalty that accrues to farmers who merely rent their land to corporate developers. The point here is that these farmers are succeeding in developing wind power themselves and have secured the necessary contracts and bank loan to do this. The fact that there is a paucity of others following suit seems to be because there is a lack of suitably motivated volunteers, not because the RO prevents them from doing so.

It should also be noted that any supposed preference for 'larger' schemes under market-based arrangements is also very dubious. Again, the Spanish wind power scene is dominated by large schemes. On the other hand, in Germany, there are some quite large farmer-owned wind farms and even large cooperatives (interview, Hans Detlef Feddersen, 2 September 2004). In Denmark, farmer-owned schemes have been much smaller, since each farmer has been limited, by law, to owning just one machine. We can see here that there is evidence that the different financial linkages involved in the feed-in tariffs do not necessarily produce different networks in the wind industry itself since the incentive structures for local/small/large/corporate concerns remain largely the same. The only major exception, albeit a significant exception, to this pattern may have been the exclusion of the German utilities from being able to develop wind farms using the feed-in tariff until the year 2000. This reduced the incentives for the utilities to invest in their own wind power schemes and may also have made the utilities more hostile to the wind power programme than they might otherwise have been.

Governance and planning

The UK is marked out by having the most conflictual system of wind power planning. This does not just reflect opposition to wind power, for planning consent for wind power is not necessarily easier to obtain in The Netherlands than in the UK. In The Netherlands, the large bulk of decisions appear to take place before the schemes are formally proposed. In the UK, however, the large majority of cases will be decided through formal application and voting by local councillors on development and control committees. It may appear that the UK planning system presents more problems for developers than other systems, but this appearance is deceptive. If anything, many of the rules actually favour wind power developers in the UK (compared to other countries) since developers who are refused planning consent at a local authority levels can appeal, often successfully, to government inspectors. Indeed this facility was strengthened by the revised planning guidance note on renewable energy (PPG22) that came into effect in November 2004.

Spain is distinguishable from other European states in that its planning is centred on the regions, and some of the regional governments take a strong proactive stance in planning wind farm development. The local municipalities are involved in the process, but they rarely stop projects going ahead. Although there are sometimes campaigns organized by local wildlife conservation groups to protect particular hills, there is no organized landscape protection body as such in Spain. This may explain the relatively greater ease with which wind power schemes gain planning consent in Spain compared to say, the UK, rather than the nature of the planning framework itself. However, the differences between planning outcomes and ownership patterns in other western European cases are not explained purely by differences in attitude to landscape value. Hence, we are posed a question. How can we explain such differences?

In the UK, Denmark, Germany and The Netherlands (in contrast to Spain), public authorities take a passive stance in that they merely react to proposals when they arise. Regional targets are indicative rather than prescriptive. Nevertheless, in Germany and Denmark laws enacted in the 1990s have placed responsibilities on local authorities for identifying areas within their localities where wind power developments should be placed.

It does not seem from this evidence that particular governmental planning structures are associated with either relatively strong or weak deployment of wind power capacity. It also seems to be the case from the earlier discussion that there is no clear link between the type of financial governance and the networks of ownership and the type of relationships that help constitute the wind industry. Hence we need to investigate the nature of the networks themselves and the understandings that surround them if we are to understand the shape of the wind power industries in different countries.

Different ontologies of networks

The organization of the wind industries in Germany and Denmark can be contrasted with the dominant networks in the UK and Spain. In Germany and Denmark the relationship between, on the one hand, the individual investor and/or owner and, on the other hand, the wind farm itself, has been an important part of the network making up the wind industry (Toke and Elliot, 2000). By contrast, local/individual investor/owners are of marginal or no importance in the UK and Spain.

The Danish and German wind industries have relied heavily on local networks of agents of wind generator manufacturers, low-cost local consultants who have often doubled as political enthusiasts, farmer-owners and local organizers of cooperatives. The farmers and cooperatives have very often been the developers themselves, and have negotiated their relationships with local authorities, banks and wind generator manufacturers. The role of 'developers' in this model is limited largely to final construction of the projects after the details have been tied up by the local actors. In Denmark the large bulk of the onshore wind power capacity has been organized in this way, with only a small proportion of the onshore developments being organized by the electricity utilities. The intensity of this 'localist' ontology was built up on the basis of the Danish grass roots 'bottom upwards' development of wind power technology itself. This developed almost as a rural enterprise, mixing a unique blend of agricultural and engineering technology (Karnoe, 1990).

On the other hand, in Germany, half the market has been organized by corporate developers. However, these are not like the corporate entities in states such as the UK and Spain since the investment comes from individual high income earners through public share offers. The high income earners have been able to use Germany's tax laws, which enable the high German marginal tax rates for high income earners (over 50 per cent) to offset taxes against investments in wind power. However, as the level of the feed-in tariff has fallen these companies' offers have been perceived as much less attractive, and the financial position of these companies has been weakened by recent low wind-yield years. Moreover, it is expected that changes will be made in regulations, so reducing the scope for tax concessions. Given these changes, it is not surprising that rates of deployment of German wind power are declining.

In Germany the utilities were (until 2000) denied access to the feed-in tariff, which has deterred them from developing wind power and encouraged them to construct wind power as competing for market share with their own investments in conventional generation. This situation has been associated with utilities opposing the feed-in tariff. Interestingly, while companies like E.ON and RWE have opposed subsidies to wind power in Germany, they have at least tolerated the British RO. E.ON and RWE together control around a third of the UK electricity supply market. In the case of the UK the electricity oligopolies have more control over the wind power investments and more ability to make money out of them than is the case in Germany. In Denmark individual and cooperative development of wind power has stopped (apart from repowering and offshore programmes) following the cut-off of subsidies at the end of 2001. This followed from a combination of events. As in Germany, Danish utilities were critical of the costs of supporting the wind power programme, and also, since November 2001, Denmark has for the first time in many decades been governed by a solely right-wing coalition that excludes even centre parties. In Denmark wind power has been most favoured by the centre and left-wing parties.

The developing offshore wind power industry in Denmark and Germany is more corporate-oriented. However, even here there has been a substantial cooperative input. Half of the equity of Denmark's first offshore installation (Middlegunden) is owned by a cooperative, and what is projected to be the second German offshore project, a very large scheme at 240MW, will be owned entirely by a cooperative (Budentiek, 2005).

By contrast, in Spain, and mostly in the UK, the notion of developers is synonymous with large electricity companies, or developers that are backed by large electricity or engineering concerns. No farmer-owned or cooperative-owned wind farms exist in Spain, and very few locally owned projects exist in the UK. Indeed, developers are implicitly accepted as being necessary for the planning and financing of schemes. Wind power is a highly professionalized type of activity in Spain and the UK, and there is a close relationship between developers, merchant banks and venture capitalist outfits. The big difference in networks between the UK and Spain is the significance, in the UK, of anti-wind power networks. These exist at local and national levels. Indeed, it is ironic that there are also strong local wind power networks in Denmark and Germany, but these are mostly pro-wind power networks consisting of activists and local owners/investors, whereas in the UK practically the only voluntary local activists are opposed to wind power. In the UK local anti-wind power networks are serviced by an organization known popularly as the Country Guardians. In Spain there is no national anti-wind power organization.

Wind power developments tend, on average, to be much less controversial in Spain than in the UK. There are differences in local wind power networks, in that in the UK anti-wind power networks are much more common than in Spain. A minority of wind power developments in Spain do become items of dispute on account of objections from local nature conservation groups (although not on landscape grounds). However, such difficulties tend to be resolved by additional sums of money being earmarked for local purposes (interview, Alfonso Cano, 9 December 2004).

However, in the case of the wind power industry itself, the ontology of the wind power industry in the UK is much closer to that existing in Spain, rather than Germany and Denmark. In the UK most wind power is owned by corporate-backed developers. These corporate players are sometimes theoretically independent, but most are at least funded by one of the five or six big electricity suppliers. They are non-local developers and their networks are non-local in nature. Usually the only significant network link with the locality is that they give royalties to the farmer whose land is needed for the wind farm. Some developers also offer income streams to the local parish council. There is usually no local ownership, the schemes are inspired and piloted through the planning process by the outside developer, not local people.

This has important implications for planning outcomes. As Loring (2004) suggests, the existence of active local networks supporting wind power proposals boosts their chances of gaining planning consent. The point about local ownership of wind power in its effects on the planning systems is that if a scheme is locally inspired then the local proponents can utilize their social networks to increase the chances of gaining planning consent compared to schemes organized by outside developers with few local contacts. In Spain it does not matter so much that wind power is dominated by outside developers because there is much less concern for landscape impact in Spain compared to the UK, and also the population density is much lower in Spain. If population density is lower then there are likely to be fewer local people to object to wind farm planning applications.

It should also be pointed out that there is, in practice, little concrete evidence for the popular view that somehow small wind farms are more acceptable per se in planning terms than large wind farms. In a statistical analysis of 51 wind farm planning cases Toke (2005b) found that there was no association between the size of a scheme and its chances of being given planning consent. Danish experience does indeed suggest that the small farmer-owned and cooperative wind power schemes proved to be much more acceptable in planning terms than larger schemes proposed by the utilities. As one report issued by the Danish government puts it:

> *The local environmental disadvantages of wind power can lead to a lack of public acceptance of wind farms. Local ownership of wind turbines (local farmers, co-operatives or companies) can ensure local acceptance of projects.* (Andersen, 1998, p7)

Hence we can see that the tendency for smaller schemes to be accepted by the planning system can be explained by different patterns of ownership, rather than size itself. It happens that the cooperatives and the farmer-owned schemes in Denmark were small. Indeed, under Danish law each farmer is permitted to own only one wind turbine. By contrast the schemes proposed by the utilities were much larger, and generally had much more difficulty in gaining planning approval. However, it is the local ownership that gave them the edge in the planning system, as discussed earlier, not their size.

Different epistemologies of networks

When I talk about epistemologies in this context I mean those epistemologies associated with the wind power networks themselves. This is to be distinguished from the type of 'discourse coalition' talked about by Hajer (1995) or other types of interest group alliance concerned with mobilizing pressure on policy issues. Of course, many involved in the networks do engage in policy pressure work, but this is a different matter to the beliefs and modes of knowledge accumulation concerned with the business of the wind power industry in particular countries. It is this latter notion of which I speak.

In Denmark people earning large profits from wind power was thought to be very wrong – and, indeed, each owner could have only one machine. Only the utilities were allowed to own more than one machine. In Germany it was thought wrong for the electricity utilities to gain the benefit of the feed-in tariff for wind power. On the other hand the electricity utilities were strongly opposed to the feed-in tariff. In Denmark there has been a strong cooperative tradition since the quasi-religious cooperative movement promoted by Gruntveg in the 19th century. This has provided a cultural justification for cooperative wind power. This was buttressed by the bottom-up path of development of Danish wind power to which I referred earlier. This grass-roots tradition has entrenched the notion that energy schemes can and should be organized on decentralized lines. Indeed, a large proportion of fossil fuel generation is conducted through decentralized gas-fired combined heat and power schemes that were started by local cooperatives.

As the 1990s wore on, the bulk of wind power schemes were organized by farmers. Farmer confidence in the ability to make a lot of money grew, and they, rather than the cooperatives, tended to dominate the market. However, it is important to note that the basis of wind power deployment remained local in nature, as were the networks of agents and consultants who serviced this development. These local networks were legitimized and provided with a big stream of activists by an active anti-nuclear movement in Denmark, including the OVE (Organisation for Renewable Energy), which was closely associated with the anti-nuclear movement.

Although there is not quite the same intensity of cooperative tradition in Germany, there were other political trends that generated a powerful pressure for locally organized wind power developments. The citizens' initiative movement, which grew up in Germany in the 1970s and 1980s, provided the political basis for the emergence of the German Green Party in the 1980s. This movement also became associated with a very militant (indeed still militant) anti-nuclear movement. As in the case of Denmark, this provided a stream of activists interested in organizing local energy initiatives. This movement also legitimized a general trend towards supporting alternative energy activities, the influence of which spread throughout society and included more traditionally conservative sectors such as farmers.

In addition, in Denmark and Germany, finding and evaluating sites has itself been a low-cost exercise. Charges for site and project evaluation and assistance in bringing projects to development are low compared to the UK and Spain. Local networks of wind generator agents and consultants provide these low-cost services, including achieving access to financial support from local banks. There has been limited use of wind monitoring compared to countries like Spain and the UK. The frequent existence of flat topography has helped this low-cost way of discovering knowledge about wind speeds. Another aspect of differing ways of finding and generating knowledge is the general disposition to share data among operators and developers. However, this disposition of cooperation rather than competition is the hallmark of the cooperative, (or at least not-as-corporate) approach that is much in evidence in Denmark, Germany and The Netherlands (which also has a tradition of local energy activism). Such cooperation is avoided in the corporate-dominated wind industries in Spain and the UK.

These epistemologies are interpreted differently in Spain and the UK. The dominant piece of knowledge is that wind power is the business of big companies, and that local people can play little or no role in ownership of wind power developments. This culture is especially strong in Spain, where it is unheard of for farmers or cooperatives to engage in wind power development. On the other hand, it is a very strong view in Britain and Spain that wind power represents a very profitable exercise for institutional investors and generally people with money to invest. Consultancy services are remote from the locality of the site and expensive in nature. Indeed the whole of the industry in Spain and the UK is highly professionalized and the need to buy-in expensive consultancy advice is emphasized as the price that needs to be paid for site and project evaluation and also for project financing. Knowledge about wind speeds is always gained through very extensive wind speed monitoring. People are wary of sharing information, and a disposition towards competition between developers is dominant.

Certainly, the environmentalist movement was relatively weak in Spain in the 1970s and 1980s, and provided very little basis for decentralized initiatives. On the other hand, the trend towards rural depopulation has militated against a widespread feeling that wind power is encroaching on a valuable landscape asset. By contrast, in other European countries much of the countryside has been suburbanized, or at least assumed a considerable amenity value because of the desire by middle class people to live in the countryside rather than the city. The environmentalist movement has been much stronger in the UK, yet the anti-nuclear movement was relatively restrained compared to some continental counterparts, and much of the strength of British environmentalism resides in landscape and wildlife protection – which is sometimes not wind power's strongest suit.

Conclusion

It would seem that there is no clear relationship between financial governance structures or planning systems and, in particular, the nature of the networks and epistemologies that dominate in different wind power cases. Indeed, it may be that there is a case for arguing that the influence is more the other way around. That is, a localist tradition is likely to restrict the financial incentives open to major electricity companies to deploy wind power, as happened in Germany.

However, by tracing the ontological and epistemological natures of the different wind power regimes in the different countries that have been discussed we can see some possible relationships between epistemologies and the ontologies of the non-government networks themselves. Local pro-wind power networks are strong in Denmark and Germany, in Spain they are not needed because of a lack of opposition to wind power (on landscape impact grounds at least), and in the UK the local wind power networks are most usually concerned with opposing the technology. However, Spain and the UK have in common both a lack of local pro-wind power networks and the domination of the wind energy industry by a network of corporate developers and centrally organized professionalized infrastructure. In Germany and Denmark, and to a great extent in The Netherlands, this wind power industrial infrastructure is more localized. Belief systems concerning the 'truth' about wind power mirror these different configurations. In Spain, for example, wind power is something that big companies, not local people, organize, and this is also broadly the case in the UK. In Denmark, and to a great extent in Germany, this knowledge is different in that local ownership and organization of wind power is thought to be not only practical, but also preferable in the eyes of many parts of the wind industry. Methods of collecting data necessary for implementation of wind power schemes are also different, with German and Danish local developers relying on less expensive locally based sources of expertise.

References

Andersen, P. D. (1998) 'Wind power in Denmark', Ministry of Energy and Environment, Copenhagen

Budentiek (2005) www.butendiek.de/ accessed 10 March 2005

Eurelectric Working Group Renewables & Distributed Generation (2004) *A Quantitative Assessment of Direct Support Schemes for Renewables* (1st Edition), Eurelectric, Brussels

Gruber, T. (2005) www-ksl.stanford.edu/kst/what-is-an-ontology.html, accessed 25 November 2005, where the author cites his own work in *Knowledge Acquisition*, vol 5, no 2, pp199–220, 1993

Hajer, M. (1995) *The Politics of Environmental Discourse*, Oxford University Press, Oxford

Karnoe, P. (1990) 'Technological innovation and industrial organisation in the Danish wind industry', *Entrepreneurship and Regional Development*, vol 2, no 2, pp105–123

Lauber, V. (2004) 'REFIT and RPS: Options for a harmonised community framework', *Energy Policy*, vol 32, pp1405–1414

Loring, A. (2004) 'Wind development in England, Wales and Denmark – The role of community participation and network stability in project acceptance and planning success', D Phil thesis, University of Sussex

Mitchell, C., Bauknecht, D. and Connor, P. M. (2006) 'Effectiveness through risk reduction: A comparison of the renewable obligation in England and Wales and the feed-in system in Germany', *Energy Policy*, vol 34, no 3, pp297–305

Poli, R. (2001) 'Foreword', *Axiomathes*, vol 12, pp1–5

Toke, D. (2005a) 'Comparing wind power planning outcomes in different countries', Paper to the 11th International Sustainable Development Research Conference, 6–8 June, Helsinki

Toke, D (2005b) 'Explaining wind power planning outcomes, some findings from a study in England and Wales', *Energy Policy*, vol 33, no 12, pp1527–1539

Toke, D (2005c) 'Are green electricity certificates the way forward for renewable energy? An evaluation of the UK's Renewables Obligation in the context of international comparisons', *Environment and Planning C*, vol 23, no 3, pp361–375

Toke, D. and Elliott, D. (2000) 'A fresh start for wind power?', *International Journal of Ambient Energy* vol 21, no 2, pp67–76

Wind-works (2004) www.wind-works.org/ accessed 25 August 2004

Chapter 10

Multi-Level Governance and Energy Policy: Renewable Energy in Scotland

Mark Winskel

Introduction

Themes and Issues

Recent policy studies research has introduced a number of concepts to analyse the widely observed trend toward the fragmentation of national government powers. Among other themes (see Joseph Murphy's introductory chapter for a fuller account), contributions here have included the 'hollowing out of the state' (Rhodes, 1999), the shift from 'government to governance' (Pierre and Peters, 2000), and the emergence of 'multi-level governance' (Bache and Flinders, 2004a; Lyall and Tait, 2004, 2005). The latter is particularly relevant for the concern here with the impact of devolution on policy making.

As Bache and Flinders (2004b) point out, multi-level governance (MLG) attempts to capture both 'horizontal' and 'vertical' dimensions of the dispersal of state powers. Horizontally, this refers to distributed responsibilities between national government departments, statutory bodies and other non-government groups.[1] Vertically, this spans international, national, regional and local policy makers. Bache and Flinders go on to note that the term has particular resonance in contemporary UK politics following the devolving of powers to executives and parliaments in Scotland, Wales and Northern Ireland at the end of the 1990s, and that this process of quasi-federalism marked a significant departure from the highly centralized Westminster model. At the same time, UK devolution is part of a wider domestic and international pattern toward the dispersal of national state powers. Domestically, for example, regional development authorities in the UK have recently assumed greater powers for energy policy implementation, while international policy agreements, such as European Union (EU) directives, exert an increasingly powerful influence on domestic energy policy.

Following the recommendation of Bache and Flinders (2004b), this chapter considers the working out of MLG in a particular setting: recent developments in UK energy policy. More specifically, the focus here is on policy contributions and initiatives aimed at promoting renewable energy innovation, which are part of a wider remaking of policy in response to climate change. As will be discussed, this case reflects pervasive issues in contemporary politics: the adaptation of established industrial systems to become more environmentally sustainable, and the alignment of economic and environmental policy agendas in attempting this change.[2]

Alongside MLG, a second analytical theme here is innovation studies accounts of the relationship between technological change and sustainable development, and especially the innovation systems framework (Edquist, 1997; Edquist and McKelvey, 2000; Carlsson et al, 2002). The innovation systems framework offers an integrated way of looking at emergence and spread of new technologies, and the role of policy in enabling (or inhibiting) change. Among other insights, innovation systems research draws attention to the distinctive phases of technological development (such as research and development (R&D), demonstration and pre-commercial stages), and the importance of interaction and feedback between different parts of the system, such as technology developers, users, financiers and regulators. These insights imply the need for appropriate policy interventions at different development stages, for promoting networking across the system, and for coherence of policy support between stages and over time (Foxon et al, 2005).

Recent innovation studies research has recognized the particular challenges involved in building sustainable innovation systems (Elzen et al, 2004; Weber and Hemmelskamp, 2005). Sustainable technologies are typically 'disruptive' to established systems, and so require particular policy interventions to encourage their development, such as the creation of temporary protected spaces – referred to as 'strategic niche management' (SNM) (Kemp et al, 1998). Disruptive innovation within niches tends to be carried out by small outsider firms, rather than larger established groups (Bergek and Jacobsson, 2002; Garud and Karnøe, 2003). (As Sauter and Watson explore in their contribution to this collection, however, this disruptiveness should not be taken for granted, as it depends on the specific forms and contexts of deployment.)

Innovation studies has also recognized a recent trend toward the regionalization of innovation systems – an increased influence for regional factors in innovation success, alongside national and international forces (Cooke et al, 2000; Cooke et al, 2004). Clearly, this is related to political devolution. In the present case, for example, devolution encouraged a heightened focus on specifically Scottish innovation systems. At the same time, this also reflects greater recognition of the role of local and informal relationships and dynamics in technological change – an influence often referred to as 'social capital' (Saxenian,

1994; Lundvall et al, 2002; Cooke 2004). As will be argued below, innovation systems-based insights on technological change – stressing the role of networking, policy integration and social capital – fed into the UK energy policy review process. Given the greater experience in renewable energy innovation outside the UK, these references often drew on international experiences. This added a dimension of international policy transfer to the national-regional MLG mix (Mytelka and Smith, 2002).

Energy systems present particular characteristics for policy and governance. Rather than being easily responsive to policy and regulatory interventions, they reflect long-term historical forces and crisis events, and tend to inertia and lock-in rather than novelty or change (Unruh, 2000). As is discussed below, the policy changes associated with devolution were played out on a UK energy system with an embedded orientation to 'financial capital' – concentrated commercial interests, and an emphasis on market competition. However, devolution also coincided with a number of significant ongoing changes in the UK energy system, including a growing import dependency on oil and gas supplies as North Sea reserves were depleted, the prospect of a shortfall in generation capacity as ageing nuclear power plants were retired, and domestic and international pressures for stronger climate change mitigation policies.

The chapter proceeds by outlining the historical context for the emergence of MLG in the UK energy system. The interaction between devolution and the recent policy review is then considered in more detail by looking at specific contributions, debates and initiatives in UK and Scottish policy arenas. The final section reflects on the case in the context of the wider themes outlined above.

Political and technological heritage

Long before political devolution (a process which started only after the election of a reform-minded Labour government in 1997) the UK energy system was transformed under successive Conservative governments in the 1980s and 1990s. The privatization of the UK electricity supply industry (ESI) at the end of the 1980s was a notably disruptive process. ESI privatization took place shortly after gas industry privatization, and, in response to criticism of the privatized monopoly created by the former, the government imposed significant restructuring on the ESI, including the break-up of the monopoly generator company (Roberts et al, 1991).[3]

Liberalization ended the 'technocratic corporatism' that had governed the ESI since its reorganization around nuclear power in the 1950s (Winskel, 2002a). After privatization, the UK energy system – although still steered by the UK Department of Industry (DTI) and a powerful new regulatory body, the Office of Gas and Electricity Markets (Ofgem)[4] – was shaped by multiple commercial interests. Other than continued protection for nuclear power (always a special case for energy policy), technology choice in the 1990s, ESI was driven primarily by market forces – liberalization meant that only those technologies able to secure international loans and guarantees were deployed on significant scale. This was embodied by the 'dash for gas', a huge programme of investment in combined cycle gas turbines, a technology that had been over-looked in the nationalized ESI (Winskel 2002b; Watson, 2004). The dash for gas further eroded established authority in the industry, and remains a powerful symbol of its opening-up to international capital and engineering.

Liberalization also resulted in the running-down of most of the UK's energy research, development and demonstration programmes (MacKerron, 1994). While these had been dominated by nuclear power, this rationalization also affected clean coal and renewables R&D, as well as the loss of much of the industry's testing and research support infrastructure. Rather than technologi-cal innovation, the main intellectual and strategic effort was now focused on 'commoditizing' electricity – constructing and exploiting a competitive market in power generation, trading and supply. A series of policy and regulatory inter-ventions were made in this cause during the 1990s (Helm, 2003).

A limited set of more technology-specific interventions were incorporated within this 'economic liberalism' policy regime. The main support mechanism for renewable energy in the first decade after privatization was the Non-Fossil Fuel Obligation (NFFO). Although devised primarily to subsidize nuclear power, NFFO also required power supply companies to contract for a small amount of renewable generation.[5] The obligation was fulfilled by renewables projects, selected under a competitive bidding process, which were offered tech-nology-specific supply contracts. While deployed renewable generation capacity in the 1990s remained insignificant under NFFO, the scheme at least enabled the limited public funds on offer to be distributed across a range of different technologies (Mitchell and Connor, 2004).

After the fragmentation of the ESI at privatization, the 1990s saw a signifi-cant degree of horizontal and vertical reintegration, typically involving international power companies buying-up domestic generators and suppliers. By the late 1990s, the UK energy system had been transformed by a decade-long shaping by international capital and engineering under the economic liberalism policy regime. While these changes reflected a global trend to energy sector liberalization (Jacquier-Roux and Bourgeois, 2002), the UK case went much further than most in the scope of its reforms – and the degree of their consequences.

Reform before the Review

In the late 1990s, at the same time as it began the process of political devolu-tion, the newly elected Labour government undertook reform of the regulatory framework of the ESI established at privatization. This involved two main changes: a new set of rules for wholesale power trading between generators and suppliers, and a new support mechanism for renewable energy. While both carried significant implications for overall energy policy, the changes were devised and implemented ahead of the wider policy review in the early 2000s. In carrying out the reforms, the government worked within the economic liber-alism policy regime established by its Conservative predecessors, and which was closely associated with the industry regulator, Ofgem. This meant a continued focus on market competition, and the use of predominantly technology-blind market interventions.[6]

In an effort to promote greater market transparency in wholesale power trading, a set of New Electricity Trading Arrangements (NETA) were introduced to regulate deals between generators and suppliers.[7] At the same time, a new Renewables Obligation (RO) was devised to replace the NFFO scheme. Under the RO, supplier companies are obliged to contract for a designated proportion of their supply from renewable sources. The RO targets increase annually in line with government targets for renewable generation, and suppliers demonstrate compliance by presenting Renewables Obligation Certificates (ROCs) to Ofgem. Rather than contracting directly from renewable generators, suppliers may satisfy their obligation by buying certificates on the ROC trading market.

Both NETA and RO reforms were largely successful on their own terms – NETA was associated with a significant drop in wholesale power prices in the early 2000s, and the RO led to much greater deployment of renewable energy than under NFFO. At the same time, both introduced additional market risks that tended to strengthen the position of large integrated power companies, while weakening independent project developers (Carbon Trust, 2003b). According to Helm (2003, p311), NETA encouraged the emergence of a 'vertically integrated oligopoly' in the ESI. The RO, by concentrating state support for renewables on the cheapest technologies (in practice, onshore wind power biomass co-firing and landfill gas), offers no direct incentive for the development of less commercially mature renewables (Mitchell and Connor, 2004). As such, the reforms represented an extension of 1990s economic liberalism into the early 2000s.

Devolution and policy review

Introduction

The devolution settlement of the 1998 Scotland Act involved the sharing of powers between UK and Scottish executives across a range of policy areas (Lyall, 2004). This was exemplified by the arrangements for energy policy: although overall energy policy and regulation remained a reserved power for the UK DTI and Ofgem, responsibilities for the promotion of renewable energy and energy efficiency were devolved to the new Scottish Executive. While a narrow reading of these arrangements may have offered little scope for devolved policy making, in practice, the Scottish Executive and Parliament interpreted their powers widely enough to encourage the development of a distinctive policy arena in energy. As this section considers, the UK-wide policy review of the early 2000s developed an unexpected momentum in Scotland, characterized by a strong interest among Scottish policy actors in promoting local industry building in renewable energy technologies, especially marine energy (wave and tidal stream power).[8]

Renewable energy has a long history of marginalization in the UK energy system, under both technocratic corporatism and economic liberalism policy regimes. The absence of any powerful champions for renewables in the nationalized ESI meant that their development was left to organizations for which they were secondary (and disruptive) concerns (Russell, 1993). Reflecting this, the dominant policy response to the 1970s energy crisis was retrenchment around existing technologies and interests, especially nuclear power and the domestic coal industry. Given this position, renewable energy interests were essentially unrepresented in the institutional remaking of the ESI at privatization – a process which was dominated by the Conservative government's determination to secure the future of nuclear power (Eikeland, 1998; Winskel, 2002a).[9] As described above, in the decade after privatization, energy policy reflected and enacted a view of electricity as a commodity good, competing on price.

Nevertheless, renewable energy has a significant history at the edges of the UK energy system. Renewable technologies attracted some policy and financial support in the 1970s, and although this proved to be a limited and temporary effort, it can be seen, retrospectively, as building an important base for the re-emergence of interest and activity in the 2000s. This is exemplified by marine energy. As part of wider interest in renewables in the wake of the 1970s energy crisis, the UK Department of Energy established a Wave Energy Programme to identify a device capable of rapid economic upscaling. Given the embryonic stage of wave power technology at the time, this was unrealistically ambitious, and the programme was scaled-down in the early 1980s under escalating cost estimates and organizational and political hostility (Thorpe, 1992, 1999; Ross, 1995, 2002). Under the market liberalism of the 1990s, marine energy attracted no significant policy interest or research support – a pattern repeated internationally among the handful of countries that had experimented with the technology in the 1970s and early 1980s. Nevertheless, the programme left a significant legacy of interests and skills among a small number of university-based researchers.

By the early 2000s, the UK energy system faced growing tensions between economic and environmental policy agendas. While these tensions had been resolved within the economic liberalism policy regime of the 1990s, the environmental benefits of the dash for gas (as coal-fired plants were replaced by gas-fired plants) were now largely played out. The UK energy system looked increasingly ill-equipped to meet national and international policy targets for reduced carbon emissions.

Under shifting policy drivers, renewable energy began a gradual revival – a process initially unrelated to devolution. In its report on *Energy – The Changing Climate*, the Royal Commission on Environmental Pollution (RCEP) called for a long-term remaking of the UK energy system, to enable a 60 per cent reduction in carbon dioxide emissions by 2050 (RCEP, 2000). At the same time, a number of reports encouraged a revival of interest in marine energy, including a positive review of the technology's potential from a UK foresight panel (Office of Science and Technology (OST), 1999), and a detailed inquiry on marine energy carried out by the House of Commons Science and Technology Committee (HCSTC, 2001). The Committee's report expressed regret at the lack of support for marine energy in the past, and called for a long-term policy commitment to attract private investors; the potential social and economic returns, it concluded, were huge:

> *the UK could ... create a new multi-billion pound domestic and export industry, employing thousands of people. The UK has the resource, the technology and the skills base; we have a unique opportunity to seize the lead and develop a world-class industry. We can no longer afford to neglect the potential of wave and tidal energy.* (HCSTC, 2001, pvi)

In the early 2000s, the UK government initiated a wide-ranging energy policy review – the first such exercise to be carried out since the 1970s. While the review centred on a 2003 white paper, it included numerous parliamentary inquiries, expert reports and wider contributions to the debate. A series of specific policy initiatives were also made in the course of the review. The next two sections consider, in turn, the review process within UK and Scottish policy arenas, with a focus on those contributions and initiatives most closely related to renewables innovation and marine energy.

UK policy arena

For many contributors to the policy review, emerging tensions in the UK energy system highlighted the need to reinvigorate public funding of energy research, especially for renewable energy technologies. Major investigations carried out by the Royal Commission and the Cabinet Office ahead of the DTI white paper both recommended expanded support for renewables, including marine technology (RCEP, 2000; Performance and Innovation Unit (PIU), 2002). The white paper itself (DTI, 2003) marked a repositioning of renewable energy from the policy margins to centre stage. For the first time, a UK government established specific targets for renewable generation.[10] The white paper identified marine energy research as a priority area, where enhanced support had the potential to lead to a 'step change' breakthrough, contributing significantly to carbon emission reductions.

Recognizing this potential, a series of UK-wide policy initiatives aimed at accelerating marine renewables innovation were introduced in the course of the review. As well as expanded capital grant support for device R&D under the DTI's Technology Programme, a number of dedicated research programmes were established. These included the Carbon Trust's Marine Energy Challenge, which partnered together small-firm wave power device developers with established engineering firms, and the Engineering and Physical Science Research Council's SuperGen Marine consortium of academics and industrialists, brought together to collaborate on a series of generic R&D themes. A number of UK and Scottish public funding agencies sponsored the setting-up of the European Marine Energy Centre (EMEC) in northern Scotland, with the aim of creating a focal point for device testing, and internationally accepted standards and accreditation procedures.

A number of contributors to the policy review argued that while these initiatives were encouraging, stronger interventions and institutional reforms were needed for the acceleration of marine energy innovation, and delivery of the wider policy targets for renewables. These views were reflected, for example, in UK parliamentary inquiries carried out in the course of the review. A report by the House of Commons Environmental Audit Committee (HCEAC) argued that overall spending on renewables in the UK remained inadequate – compared to Denmark or Germany, the UK had 'reaped the reward of its parsimony' (HCEAC, 2002, p23). The committee criticized a lack of policy coherence, with specific initiatives often being made in isolation by one of many different bodies involved. The committee suggested a Sustainable Energy Policy Agency be established to improve policy coordination. For marine energy, it argued that a structured support programme be devised to enable gradual learning, cost reductions and market growth, aimed at the commercial-scale deployment of the technology by 2020. In another report, the House of Commons Science and Technology Select Committee (HCSTC) was also critical of what it saw as inadequately resourced and poorly focused renewable energy R&D, and the fragmentation of activity across multiple groups (HCSTC, 2003). The committee called for the setting-up of a Renewable Energy Authority, with strong ministerial direction, to oversee delivery of the white paper policy targets; without such reform, it concluded, there was no prospect of achieving the targets.

A number of wider contributions to the review highlighted the industrial development potential presented by marine energy – and pointed to specific policy changes needed to realize the opportunity. The Carbon Trust suggested that UK firms had the chance to dominate marine energy device design, manufacture, installation and operation (Carbon Trust, 2003a). Mott MacDonald noted the 'very significant national opportunity' presented by marine energy – with wave power offering the biggest job creation potential per unit output of all renewables – but warned that without stronger policy intervention, development of the technology could migrate to more supportive policy environments abroad (DTI, 2004). Climate Change Capital (CCC) stated that securing domestic industrial growth in marine energy required the setting-up of a technology-specific premium tariff for marine generation (so called 'feed-in' support), to be set at a level equivalent to a recently introduced Portuguese scheme (British Wind Energy Association (BWEA)/CCC, 2004).

After setting out the broad redirection of energy policy in its white paper, the DTI commissioned a series of more detailed research exercises as part of a Renewables Innovation Review (RIR). These included a detailed analysis of the UK innovation system for different renewables technologies. This found that marine energy development was being driven by a handful of small firms, with only limited links to suppliers and universities, and significant competition and intellectual property (IP) barriers to further networking (Imperial College Centre for Energy Policy and Technology (ICEPT)/E4tech Consulting, 2003). The report added that more policy support was needed to bridge a post-R&D funding gap. Another contribution contrasted the piecemeal innovation system for renewables in the UK with more integrated approaches elsewhere, and also suggested that a technology-specific feed-in tariff was needed to bridge the funding gap (ICEPT (Foxon et al), 2003). In its conclusions to the RIR, the DTI acknowledged the long-term potential of marine energy, but made clear that it remained unpersuaded by the case for dedicated feed-in support (DTI/Carbon Trust, 2004).

Wider contributions to the review identified systematic barriers to marine energy development in the UK. A survey of investor attitudes found that immature technologies such as wave and tidal stream struggled to attract interest from the most powerful commercial organizations in the industry, including the utility companies, oil and gas majors and independent financiers (Carbon Trust, 2003b). Marine energy was seen by some investors as a high-risk technology with a mixed track record of prototype device performance (House of Lords Science and Technology Committee (HLSTC), 2004). Potential investors also expressed concern about the inconsistent track record of UK policy interventions in the energy sector – other European countries were seen as presenting less 'political risk' (Carbon Trust, 2003b). At the same time, utility and investment groups cautioned against any efforts to replicate more interventionist overseas support policies for renewables, such as feed-in tariffs (HLSTC, 2004). From this perspective, Danish and German renewable systems, although they had led to local economic development and sizeable industrial exports, had been built at huge public expense – and so didn't represent appropriate role models for the UK.

Several contributors identified the RO as a particular barrier to renewable energy industry building. The HCEAC noted the difficulties the RO presented for innovation in anything other than the most commercially developed technologies (HCEAC, 2002). The HCSTC called for the RO's replacement by a carbon tax, able to distinguish between technologies at different stages of development (HCSTC, 2003). In evidence to a House of Lords inquiry, a leading wave energy device developer called for policy learning from the Danish wind power case, where long-term feed-in support had encouraged gradual upscaling, production optimization and supply chain building (HLSTC, 2004, Q439, p460). In response, the UK energy minister pointed out that the RO had been deliberately devised as an 'explicitly market-led mechanism' to favour the most commercial renewables, and that more targeted technology-specific support, such as that provided by NFFO, was considered inconsistent with market liberalization (HLSTC, 2004, Q363).

Nevertheless, a range of contributors continued to press the case for more targeted support for marine energy, particularly at the post-R&D stage. In early 2005, after a period of further consultation, the DTI announced the setting up of a marine energy demonstration scheme, which would offer dedicated feed-in support to a small number of selected wave and tidal stream devices (DTI, 2005a). While welcoming the scheme as a significant step forwards, potential device developers noted the scheme's limitations, especially its capping of the total amount and time span of revenue support awarded to any one developer. Renewables proponents and others continued to make the case for more generous and longer-term support.

Scottish policy arena

The energy policy review of the early 2000s developed a distinctive flavour in the devolved policy arena. This reflected the widely held perception of a particular Scottish opportunity in renewable energy industry building, especially marine energy – a perception that sprung from an abundant marine energy resource, an established heavy and offshore engineering skills base, and a long-standing interest in marine energy among a handful of Scottish universities and device developers. These interests sought to exert influence in the new Scottish policy arena – and at the same time they themselves became a focus of attention for the devolved executive, parliament and other policy actors.

An early indicator of this interest was the awarding of supply contracts to three marine energy prototype devices under the Scottish version of the NFFO scheme in the late 1990s, shortly before its replacement by the RO (HCSTC, 2001). At the outset of the review process in the early 2000s, a number of consultants' reports highlighted the industrial development potential of marine energy in Scotland. In a detailed assessment of different renewables technologies commissioned by the Scottish executive, Garrad Hassan identified a window of opportunity for Scotland to become a 'world-leading industrial base' for marine energy (Scottish Executive/Garrad Hassan, 2001). Future Energy Solutions (FES) suggested that marine energy could act as a diversification pathway for the Scottish shipbuilding industry, provided that technology-specific feed-in support was introduced to stimulate domestic market growth, technology transfer and cost reductions (FES, 2002).

In parallel with the publication of the DTI's energy policy white paper, the Scottish Executive issued a policy statement laying out ambitious plans for exploiting Scotland's renewable energy resources, including the setting of Scottish targets for renewable generation that went well beyond the UK targets (Scottish Executive, 2003).[11] At the same time, the Executive announced specific institutional reforms to help meet the targets. It established an expert advisory group, the Forum for Renewable Energy Development in Scotland (FREDS), to monitor delivery of the policy targets, and funded the setting-up of an Intermediary Technology Institute for Energy (ITI Energy) to sponsor innovation across the energy sector. During this period Scottish universities developed significant roles in UK-wide marine energy research networks, including the UK Centre for Marine Renewable Energy, a network of four organizations (three Scottish-based, including the EMEC marine energy test centre described above) aimed at offering marine device developers an integrated research, development, testing and certification infrastructure.

Before publishing its policy statement, the Scottish Executive had invited contributions from across the new Scottish policy arena. The consultation exercise revealed a significant body of criticism of existing UK energy policy and calls for greater support of renewables. For example, the industry-sponsored Scottish Renewables Forum (SRF) argued that UK renewables support lacked a coherent system to pass projects between different development stages toward commercialization (SRF, 2003). SRF called for a policy focus on indigenous business development, in the style of energy policy making elsewhere in Europe. SRF also suggested specific additional financial support for marine energy, through the issuing of 'top-up' Renewable Obligations Certificates (ROCs). In a later statement, after publication of the DTI white paper, SRF criticized what it saw as the UK government's self-fulfilling policy cautiousness, as lack of ambition for marine energy starved the technology of resources (SRF, 2004). It also identified an emerging danger of fractured regional support for renewables in the UK.

Following the executive's policy statement, the Scottish Parliament Enterprise and Culture Committee (SPECC) carried out a detailed inquiry on renewable energy in Scotland (SPECC, 2004). The committee's report stated that Scotland had an opportunity to 'become to wave and tidal power what Denmark is to wind power' (SPECC, 2004, p47). However, the building of a strong domestic market – which had been critical in Danish and German wind power success – was being frustrated by the technology-blind RO, and the committee argued that reform of the mechanism was essential to incentivize non-wind renewables. In their evidence to the committee, however, the two Scottish utility companies, Scottish Power (SP) and Scottish and Southern Energy (SSE), cautioned against any such reform, and warned of the destabilizing impact of such changes on the ROC trading market. SP argued that capital grants were the appropriate support mechanism for non-wind technologies (SPECC, 2004, c433). SSE stated that RO modifications to offer more technology-specific support played 'the game of trying to pick the winners' (SPECC, 2004, c438). The committee concluded, nevertheless, that recent policy initiatives to promote marine innovation, though significant, were inadequate – as well as RO reform, greater resourcing of the EMEC test centre was needed to give it equivalent stature to the Danish wind power test centre (SPECC, 2004, c653). A subsequent report from the Scottish Executive's FREDS expert group also called for greater support of EMEC, better integration of marine energy research initiatives, and a stronger policy lead from the Executive and DTI (Scottish Executive/FREDS, 2004).

By early 2005, a statutory review of RO was underway. The review process revealed, for the first time, a clear difference of policy intent for marine energy between the DTI and Scottish Executive. At the outset, the DTI declared that the RO was working well, and added that any proposed changes would be assessed against their impact on investor confidence (DTI, 2005b). In a parallel document, the executive highlighted additional 'Scottish-specific' issues, including RO reform, to support the development of non-wind renewables (Scottish Executive, 2005a). After a period of preliminary consultation, the executive declared its intention to award additional ROCs to marine energy (Scottish Executive, 2005b). The statement was immediately criticized by a utility company as damaging for investor confidence (*Scotsman*, 2005), and the DTI subsequently restated its position that additional support for non-wind renewables should be provided outside the RO (DTI, 2005c). The Executive responded that while investor confidence was vital, existing levels of support were insufficient to match its ambitions for wave and tidal energy, and went on to confirm its intention to offer additional ROCs to marine energy (albeit now after the statutory review had been completed, and following an analysis of the impact of multiple ROCs on marine innovation and the wider market; Scottish Executive, 2005c). Marine developers welcomed the Executive's initiative as an essential step for encouraging industry take-off and bridging the post-R&D funding gap (SRF, 2005).

Conclusions

Multi-Level Governance of the UK energy system has emerged (and continues to emerge) in an exploratory and unpredictable manner, conditioned by underlying long-term trends and more immediate circumstances and opportunities. At the start of the devolution process in the late 1990s, the UK energy system reflected a decade-long influence of economic liberalism, manifested in concentrated ownership, financing and stakeholding, and a policy orientation to short-term market efficiency and technology-blind intervention. Within this, emerging environmental policy imperatives ran secondary – even in the early 2000s, regulatory reforms continued to prioritize economic liberalism. The emergence of MLG was in part a reaction to this institutional and policy heritage.

The early 2000s saw increased tensions between environmental and economic imperatives in energy policy, and more insistent challenges to market liberalism. The subsequent launch of a major UK-wide policy review meant that the Scottish policy arena faced a relatively fluid and contested energy politics. This turbulence presented a 'window of opportunity' for fledgling policy actors in the devolved arena to test their (unclearly defined) set of powers. Broadly similar evidence, arguments and interests were represented in policy review contributions in UK and Scottish arenas, and the review provoked a revival of interest in renewable energy across the UK. While both UK and Scottish policy executives saw this revival as opening up opportunities for industry building, this was an especially powerful driver in Scotland. The Scottish Executive's setting of highly ambitious targets for renewable generation suggested a rather different set of policy priorities, and marine energy – a technology with a notable Scottish heritage and potential – was a particular focus of interest and action in the devolved arena.

Many contributors to the review drew on the experiences of countries with longer-standing support for renewable energy development and deployment. As Smith (2004) noted, efforts to transfer policies from abroad are deeply intertwined with domestic politics, and the drawing of international lessons in the review were strongly shaped by local interests. For example, the Danish wind power experience – an especially powerful reference case in Scotland – was seen as both a good and bad exemplar by renewables advocates on the one hand, and incumbent utility and financial groups on the other. While many of the references to overseas experience went no further than superficial analogies, a number of contributions were informed by more considered IS comparisons.

These highlighted the significant role, in renewables industry building, of technology-specific support (especially feed-in tariffs) and social capital (such as inter-organizational research networks and testing centres). By doing so, these contributions challenged the established market liberalism policy regime, and this challenge was made particularly strongly in Scotland. At the same time, the presence of powerful voices of resistance to importing renewables policies within both UK and Scottish policy arenas highlighted the barriers to transfer between different institutional settings.

The review process highlighted a number of policy tensions and contradictions in the UK energy system. For example, although a number of policy initiatives in the course of the review sought to encourage small developer firms (those most likely to initiate renewables innovation), they were introduced into a wider system that was reinforcing the position of large established firms. At the same time, repeated calls for policy and institutional reforms in response to emerging system barriers (such as the post-R&D funding gap) were met with utility and financier insistence on the stability and predictability of policy frameworks. Scottish policy actors showed a greater willingness to confront objections to change than those in the UK, and the Executive's proposed reform of the main renewables support mechanism to 'match its ambitions' for marine energy was a notable departure from established UK policy. These tensions and divergences can be seen as a battle between different styles of innovation system – based on either financial or social capital (Cooke et al, 2000).

Many contributors to the review also demanded a more coherent and integrated system of policy and institutional support for renewable energy innovation (and indeed, the review coincided with increased UK-wide regulatory integration). However, devolution opened up a new arena for policy experimentation, and a divergence away from the established policy regime associated with the DTI and Ofgem. Given the wider trend toward MLG, this suggests that policy integration may be something of a chimera, and some degree of diversity may be inevitable, and perhaps even useful (Murphy and Chataway, 2005; Tait and Lyall, 2005). From this viewpoint, the rather unexpected emergence of a distinctive Scottish energy policy arena may be seen as an incubation space for a transition from a dominant policy regime increasingly ill-suited to contemporary challenges. MLG presents an opportunity to bypass lock-in, and develop more sustainable innovation systems.

Acknowledgement

This chapter is based on research carried out under the UK Economic and Social Research Council's Sustainable Technologies Programme. The author wishes to thank STP colleagues and others for their comments. He assumes full responsibility for the views expressed here.

Notes

1   While the concern here is the UK and Scottish energy policy arenas – the vertical axis of MLG – the sustainable development policy agenda also cuts across embedded horizontal demarcations in government, and has tended to be marginalized. Policy structures have traditionally reflected and reinforced producer interests in the energy system (Hertin and Berkhout, 2005).

2   From an 'ecologically modern' perspective (Spaargaren and Mol, 1992) this can be addressed by technological innovation, while retaining a commitment to economic growth. For others, such as many within the alternative technology movement, the sustainability challenge requires a much more fundamental reassessment of socio-economic trends and aspirations (see Smith in this volume).

3   This applies only in England and Wales. The two Scottish public electricity boards were privatized as unrestructured vertically integrated companies (now known as Scottish Power and Scottish and Southern Energy).

4   Before its incorporation within Ofgem, the ESI's regulatory body was known as the Office of Electricity Regulation (Offer).

5   The NFFO equivalent mechanism in Scotland was known as the Scottish Renewables Obligation (SRO). Reference to NFFO here also includes the SRO.

6   While the continuity of policy regimes between different administrations reflected particular local circumstances, it can also be seen as an example of the durability of 'policy framings'. Once established, basic assumptions about policy problems and solutions tend to endure and resist reformulation; Unruh (2000) referred to the 'lock-in' of policy systems.

7   The NETA reforms applied only to England and Wales. Trading between the generator and supplier arms of the two Scottish power companies continued to take place through less formal 'regulated arrangements'. More transparent NETA-type arrangements were introduced by Ofgem in 2005 under the British Electricity Trading and Transmission Arrangements (BETTA), which created a unified British-wide market for power trading. In response to Ofgem's desire to establish 'cost-reflective' rules for generation and transmission, BETTA imposes higher charges on more remote projects – with potentially significant effects on the economics of renewable energy in northern Scotland (Ofgem, 2005; SRF, 2005).

8   For an introduction to marine energy devices, see IEA-OES (Bond, R.), 2003; Duckers, 2004.

9   Elsewhere in Europe, more established renewable interests sought to secure enhanced support prior to liberalization (Jørgensen and Strunge, 2002; Jacobsson et al, 2004).

10   Rising from 3 per cent in 2003, to 10 per cent in 2010, and an 'aspirational' 20 per cent by 2020 (DTI, 2003).

11   Renewable generation in Scotland was targeted to rise from 11 per cent in 2003, to 18 per cent by 2010, towards an 'aspirational' target of 40 per cent by 2020. Scotland has a relatively high installed renewables capacity, mainly from hydropower plant; it also has a high wind and marine resource base.

References

Bache, I. and Flinders, M. (eds) (2004a) *Multi-Level Governance*, Oxford University Press, Oxford

Bache, I. and Flinders, M. (2004b) 'Themes and issues in multi-level governance', in Bache, I. and Flinders, M. (eds) *Multi-level Governance*, Oxford University Press, Oxford, pp1–11

Bergek, A. and Jacobsson, S. (2002) 'The emergence of a growth industry: A comparative analysis of the German, Dutch and Swedish wind turbine industries', in Metcalfe, S. and Canter, U. (eds) *Change, Transformation and Development: Schumpeterian Perspectives*, Physica/Springer, Heidelberg

British Wind Energy Association/Climate Change Capital (2004) *Into the Blue: Financing the Future of the Emerging Wave & Tidal Power Sector*, BWEA, London

Carbon Trust (2003a) *Building Options for UK Renewable Energy*, London, Carbon Trust

Carbon Trust (2003b) *Investor Perspectives on Renewable Power in the UK*, Carbon Trust, London

Carlsson, B., Jacobsson, S., Holmen, M. and Rickne, A. (2002) 'Innovation systems: Analytical and methodological issues', *Research Policy*, vol 31, no 2, pp233–245

Cooke, P. (2004) 'Regional innovation systems – an evolutionary approach', in Cooke, P., Heidenreich, M. and Braczyk, H-J. (eds) *Regional Innovation Systems: The Role of Governance in a Globalised World*, Routledge, London

Cooke, P., Boekholt, P. and Todtling, F. (2000) *The Governance of Innovation in Europe: Regional Perspectives on Global Competitiveness*, Pinter, London

Cooke, P., Heidenreich, M. and Braczyk, H-J. (eds) (2004) *Regional Innovation Systems: The Role of Governance in a Globalised World*, Routledge, London

Department of Trade and Industry (2003) *Our Energy Future: Creating a Low Carbon Economy*, The Stationery Office, London

Department of Trade and Industry (2004) *Renewable Supply Chain Gap Analysis: Summary Report*, DTI, London

Department of Trade and Industry (2005a) *Marine Renewables: Wave and Tidal Stream Energy Demonstration Scheme*, DTI, London

Department of Trade and Industry (2005b) *2005-6 Review of the Renewables Obligation: Preliminary Consultation Document*, DTI, London

Department of Trade and Industry (2005c) *Review of the RO: Statutory Consultation Document*, DTI, London

DTI/Carbon Trust (2004) *Conclusions of the Renewables Innovation Review*, DTI/Carbon Trust, London

Duckers, L. (2004) 'Wave energy', in Boyle, G. (ed) *Renewable Energy: Power for a Sustainable Future*, Oxford University Press, Oxford, pp298–340

Edquist, C. (ed) (1997) *Systems of Innovation: Technologies, Institutions and Organizations*, Pinter, London

Edquist, C. and McKelvey, M. (eds) (2000) *Systems of Innovation: Growth, Competitiveness and Employment*, Edward Elgar, Cheltenham

Eikeland, P. O. (1998) 'Electricity market liberalisation and environmental performance: Norway and the UK', *Energy Policy*, vol 26, no 12, pp917–927

Elzen, B., Geels, F. W. and Green, K. (eds) (2004) *System Innovation and the Transition to Sustainability: Theory, Evidence and Policy*, Edward Elgar, Cheltenham

Foxon, T., Pearson, P., Makuch, Z. and Mata, M. (2005) *Transforming Policy Processes to Promote Sustainable Innovation: Some Guiding Principles: A Report for Policy Makers*, ESRC Sustainable Technologies Programme/Imperial College, London

Future Energy Solutions (2002) *Opportunities for Marine Energy in Scotland: A Report for the Scottish Executive*, FES, Harwell

Garud, R. and Karnøe, P. (2003) 'Bricolage versus breakthrough: Distributed and embedded agency in technology entrepreneurship', *Research Policy*, vol 32, no 2, pp277–300

Helm, D. (2003) *Energy, the State and the Market: British Energy Policy since 1979*, Oxford University Press, Oxford

Hertin, J. and Berkhout, F. (2005) 'Environmental policy integration for sustainable technologies: Rationale and practical experiences at EU level', in Lyall, C. and Tait, J. (eds) *New Modes of Governance: Developing an Integrated Policy Approach to Science, Technology, Risk and the Environment*, Ashgate, Aldershot, pp139–157

House of Commons Environmental Audit Committee (2002) *A Sustainable Energy Strategy? Renewables and the PIU Review*, HC 582-I, 2001–02

House of Commons Science and Technology Committee (2001) *Wave and Tidal Energy*, HC 291, 2000–01

House of Commons Science and Technology Committee (2003) *Towards a Non-Carbon Fuel Economy: Research, Development and Demonstration*, HC 55, 2002–03

House of Lords Science and Technology Committee (2004) *The Practicalities of Developing Renewable Energy*, HL 126-I, 2003–04

Imperial College Centre for Energy Policy and Technology (Foxon, T., Gross, R. and Anderson, D.) (2003) *Innovation in Long Term Renewables Options in the UK: Overcoming Barriers and 'Systems Failures'*, ICEPT, London

Imperial College Centre for Energy Policy and Technology/E4tech Consulting (2003) *The UK Innovation Systems for New and Renewable Energy Technologies: A Report to the DTI Renewable Energy Development and Deployment Team*, London, ICEPT/E4tech Consulting

International Energy Agency – Ocean Energy Systems (Boud, R.) (2003) *Wave and Marine Current Energy*, IEA, Paris

Jacobsson, S., Andersson, B. A. and Bångens, L. (2004) 'Transforming the energy system: The evolution of the German technological system for solar cells', *Technology Analysis and Strategic Management*, vol 16, pp3–30

Jacquier-Roux, V. and Bourgeois, B. (2002) 'New networks of technological creation in energy industries: Reassessment of the roles of equipment suppliers and operators', *Technology Analysis and Strategic Management*, vol 14, no 4, pp399–417

Jørgensen, U. and Strunge, I. (2002) 'Restructuring the power arena in Denmark: Shaping markets, technology and environmental priorities', in Sørensen, K. H. and Williams, R. (eds) *Shaping Technology, Guiding Policy: Concepts, Spaces and Tools*, Edward Elgar, Cheltenham, pp197–222

Kemp, R., Schot, J. and Hoogma, R. (1998) 'Regime shifts through processes of niche formation: The approach of strategic niche management', *Technology Analysis and Strategic Management*, vol 10, no 2, pp175–195

Lundvall, B-A., Johnson, B., Andersen, E. S. and Dalum, B. (2002) 'National systems of production, innovation and competence building', *Research Policy*, vol 31, no 2, pp213–23

Lyall, C. (2004) *Concurrent Power: The Role of Policy Networks in Multi-Level Governance of Science and Innovation in Scotland*, Edinburgh University PhD Thesis, Edinburgh

Lyall, C. and Tait, J. (2004) 'Foresight in a multi-level governance structure: Policy integration and communication', *Science and Public Policy*, vol 31, no 1, pp27–37

Lyall, C. and Tait, J. (eds) (2005) *New Modes of Governance: Developing an Integrated Policy Approach to Science, Technology, Risk and the Environment*, Ashgate, Aldershot

MacKerron, G. (1994) 'Innovation in energy supply: The case of electricity', in Dodgson, M. and Rothwell, R. (eds) *Handbook of Industrial Innovation*, Edward Elgar, Cheltenham

Mitchell, C. and Connor, P. (2004) 'Renewable energy policy in the UK 1990–2003', *Energy Policy*, vol 32, no 17, pp1935–1947

Murphy, J. and Chataway, J. (2005) 'The challenges of policy integration from an international perspective: The case of GMOs', in Lyall, C. and Tait, J. (eds) *New Modes of Governance: Developing an Integrated Policy Approach to Science, Technology, Risk and the Environment*, Ashgate, Aldershot, pp159–176

Mytelka, L. K. and Smith, K. (2002) 'Policy learning and innovation theory: An interactive and co-evolving process', *Research Policy* vol 31, no 8–9, pp1467–1479

Office of Gas and Electricity Markets (2005) *Ofgem Approves New Charges for High-Voltage Network*, press release R/12, 25 February, Ofgem, London

Office of Science and Technology (1999) *Marine Foresight Panel Report: Energies from the Sea – Towards 2020*, HMSO, London

Performance and Innovation Unit (2002) *The Energy Review*, Cabinet Office, London

Pierre, J. and Peters, B. G. (2000) *Governance, Politics and the State*, Macmillan, Basingstoke

Rhodes, R. A. W. (1999) 'Foreword: Governance and networks', in Stoker, G. (ed) *The New Management of British Local Governance*, Macmillan, Basingstoke

Roberts, J., Elliot, D. and Houghton, T. (1991) *Privatising Electricity: The Politics of Power*, Bellhaven Press, London

Ross, D. (1995) *Power from the Waves*, Oxford University Press, Oxford

Ross, D. (2002) 'Scuppering the waves: How they tried to repel clean energy', *Science and Public Policy*, vol 29, no 1, pp25–36

Royal Commission on Environmental Pollution (2000) *Energy – the Changing Climate*, The Stationery Office, London

Russell, S. (1993) 'Writing energy history: Explaining the neglect of CHP/DH in Britain', *British Journal of the History of Science*, vol 26, pp33–54

Saxenian, A. (1994) *Regional Advantage: Culture and Competition in Silicon Valley and Route 128*, Harvard University Press, Cambridge, MA

Scotsman (The) (2005) 'Centrica attack', 10 September, p50

Scottish Executive/Garrad Hassan (2001) *Scotland's Renewable Resource 2001*, Scottish Executive, Edinburgh

Scottish Executive (2003) *Securing a Renewable Future: Scotland's Renewable Energy*, The Stationery Office, Edinburgh

Scottish Executive/Forum for Renewable Energy Development in Scotland (2004) *Harnessing Scotland's Marine Energy Potential: Marine Energy Group (MEG) Report 2004*, Scottish Executive, Edinburgh

Scottish Executive (2005a) *2005-06 Review of the Renewables Obligation: Preliminary Consultation*, Scottish Executive, Edinburgh

Scottish Executive (2005b) 'Scottish Executive announce they will amend the RO to give additional ROCs to wave and tidal output', press release 7 September 2005, Scottish Executive, Edinburgh

Scottish Executive (2005c) *Renewables Obligation (Scotland) Review 2005/6 Statutory Consultation*, Scottish Executive, Edinburgh

Scottish Parliament Enterprise and Culture Committee (2004) *Renewable Energy in Scotland*, SP Paper 194

Scottish Renewables Forum (2003) *2020 Vision: Building Scotland's Renewable Future*, SRF, Glasgow

Scottish Renewables Forum (2004) *Marine Energy: Supporting True Innovation*, SRF, Glasgow

Scottish Renewables Forum (2005) *Harvesting the Sea: Scottish Renewables Marine Energy Seminar*, 8 December 2005, Edinburgh

Smith, A. (2004), 'Policy transfer in the development of UK climate policy', *Policy and Politics*, vol 32, no 1, pp79–93

Spaargaren, G. and Mol, A. (1992) 'Sociology, environment and modernity: Ecological modernization as a theory of social change', *Society and Natural Resources*, vol 5, no 4, pp323–344

Tait, J. and Lyall, C. (2005) 'A new mode of governance for science, technology, risk and the environment?', in Lyall, C. and Tait, J. (eds) *New Modes of Governance: Developing an Integrated Policy Approach to Science, Technology, Risk and the Environment*, Ashgate, Aldershot, pp177–188

Thorpe, T.W. (1992) *A Review of Wave Energy*, Energy Technology Support Unit, Report R72, ETSU, Harwell

Thorpe, T. W. (1999) *A Brief Review of Wave Energy*, Energy Technology Support Unit, Report R120, ETSU, Harwell

Unruh, G. C. (2000) 'Understanding carbon lock-in', *Energy Policy*, vol 28, no 12, pp817–830

Watson, J. (2004) 'Selection environments, flexibility and the success of the gas turbine', *Research Policy*, vol 33, no 8, pp1065–1080

Weber, M. and Hemmelskamp, J. (eds) (2005) *Towards Environmental Innovation Systems*, Springer, Berlin

Winskel, M. (2002a) 'Autonomy's end: Nuclear power and the privatization of the British electricity supply industry', *Social Studies of Science*, vol 32, no 3, pp439–467

Winskel, M. (2002b) 'When systems are overthrown: The "dash for gas" in the British electricity supply industry', *Social Studies of Science*, vol 32, no 4, pp565–599

Section V
CONCLUSION

Chapter 11

Governing Technology For Sustainability

Joseph Murphy

Introduction

Sustainable development is a formidable challenge for the 21st century. The concept implies a balance between environmental protection and economic development that is unlikely to be reached until society is reorganized along different lines. The list of environmental problems that we currently face includes climate change, biodiversity loss, collapsing fish stocks and persistent organic pollutants. It is likely that more problems like these will emerge in the future. Famine and poverty, and health challenges such as malaria and HIV-AIDs, are amongst the most pressing development problems. Economic growth and higher standards of living are part of the solution but many developing countries are being left behind as others get richer.

In the years ahead it seems likely that environmental protection and economic development will collide even more forcefully than they are doing today, and this may lead us to revisit 'limits to growth' arguments of the 1970s (Meadows et al, 1972). The newly industrialized countries, including China and India, are growing rapidly, and their populations are increasingly urban. Through complex processes they are beginning to adopt western consumer lifestyles. These two countries have a combined population of 2.365 billion, compared to 760 million in the US and EU, and the ecological implications of their development trajectories are staggering. They can, however, argue that they have a right to enjoy the high standards of living found elsewhere.

In this book we have made a contribution to the ongoing debate over sustainable development by focusing on the richest countries – particularly the UK and

Europe. Two assumptions have underpinned the discussion: that production-consumption systems in the richest countries must be reorganized in profound ways to address ecological problems and to create ecological space for poorer countries; and that the challenge for the richest countries is also a social one because sustainable development implies progress on such things as reinvigorating citizenship and participation in decision making, equitable distribution of wealth, and social and environmental justice. In the first section of this chapter I argue that these ecological and social challenges and opportunities are linked.

Earlier sections focused on people, technology and governance. The contributors to this collection share the view that technology has an important role to play in the transition to sustainability but they have argued that it cannot be separated from people and governance. I develop this argument further in the second part of this chapter where I argue that there is a sustainability nexus that links people, technology and governance. In the third part I argue that this nexus should become the focus for interdisciplinary research and policy. Throughout this chapter I refer to earlier ones to highlight specific points and to draw out the contributions they have made.

What is a sustainable development?

The concept of sustainable development began to attract attention in the late 1980s (World Commission on Environment and Development (WCED), 1987, p43), and meetings of the UN in 1992 and 2002 added further momentum to academic, policy and public debates. The success of the concept, at least in part, can be explained by its vagueness, and the way it is linked to a wide range of policy agendas. In the 1990s, for example, 'sustainable production', 'sustainable business' and 'sustainable waste management' began to be discussed. More recently 'sustainable consumption', 'sustainable cities' and 'sustainable communities' have attracted attention. Despite its flexibility, however, it has analytical and practical value because it helps us to link ecological-material and social-cultural problems and opportunities.

Ecological and material concerns

The undermining of ecosystems is a core issue for sustainable development. As Chapter 1 showed, however, this process is understood in different ways. Most authors worry about the integrity of ecosystems over the long term and many draw attention to society's relentless consumption of resources and production of wastes. A good example is research in the industrial ecology tradition (e.g. Socolow et al, 1997). Other scholars, however, focus on the ecological implications of unpredictable technological risks. Such risks can threaten ecology and human health in insidious or explosive ways. They can also reveal how little we know about ecological processes; for an example, see Murphy et al (2006) on the environmental risks of genetically modified *Bt* maize.

Climate change is perhaps the most obvious and important ecological problem explored in this book. By focusing on energy production and consumption, Chapters 3, 6, 9 and 10 in particular engaged with the climate change debate. In Chapter 10, for example, Mark Winskel examined innovation in marine energy technology in Scotland – wave and tidal flow devices. Because of its Atlantic coastline, Scotland has a large marine energy resource, and knowledge and skills in marine technology are valuable legacies of the North Sea oil industry. Not surprisingly, some policy makers have linked these and identified marine energy technology as a source of future economic growth, in addition to the contribution it might make to addressing climate change.

The ecological perspective on sustainable development can be extended by adding a material dimension. Buttel (2000, p22) argues that materialism focuses our attention on 'the material substratum of human life'. Materialism, therefore, is more anthropocentric than ecology. It is important in this discussion because many of our most vital needs are material ones, for example, food, water and shelter (Jackson, 1996). Technologies play a central role in helping us to cater for these needs because they transform the material world in relation to the production and reproduction of our lives. Materialism, therefore, is the social scientific equivalent of the ecological perspective (which is scientific in origin), and the concept of sustainable development benefits from both.

Various contributions to this collection have examined material aspects of sustainable development. Rachel Slater (Chapter 8), for example, discussed the very material problem of waste management. In Chapter 3 Robin Roy and his colleagues made a valuable contribution by exploring the adoption and use of low and zero carbon products and systems – for example, compact fluorescent lamps (CFLs), condensing boilers, solar water heaters, micro wind turbines and domestic photovoltaic (PV) systems. These technologies are associated with basic material concerns like heating and washing. In this case, however, the material perspective was extended to explore how people interact with material objects in addition to the role they play in sustaining their lives.

Sustainable development requires us to think about the relationship between ecological and material imperatives over the long term. Chapter 5 by Adrian Smith is useful here because it explored this relationship through housing. Smith's chapter focused on eco-homes, including examples built by the alternative technology (AT) movement, and more recent developments like BedZED (Beddington Zero Emission Development). A large number of ecological concerns are implicit in such developments. The use of water conservation technologies, for example, is an effort to address hydrological problems. The homes discussed, however, are also places where people reproduce their lives materially and these are linked. Active water management, for example, is more likely if people understand hydrological problems in relation to the material reproduction of their lives.

Social and cultural commitments

In addition to ecological-material concerns, the concept of sustainable development raises profound social and cultural questions. As discussed in Chapter 1, for example, sustainable consumption research critically examines increasing levels of consumption in the richest countries (Murphy and Cohen, 2001; Princen et al, 2002). Consumption is usually defended using ideas of freedom and rights, or as a source of welfare and happiness, but in the richest countries such arguments are being challenged. A second example comes from the environmental justice debate. Scholars have argued that before any society can be called developed it must also be just (Agyeman et al, 2002). Justice, therefore, becomes an aspect of sustainable development. This argument can apply to distribution of wealth and risks, within and between countries, and perhaps across generations.

Various contributions have unpacked social and cultural issues like these. In Chapters 4 and 10, for example, Patrick Devine-Wright and Mark Winskel discussed the energy supply system in the UK. Devine-Wright argued that increasing participation in decision making is an integral part of sustainable development. He also pointed out, however, that in relation to the energy system people are understood as poorly equipped to participate. In practice they are cast as disinterested consumers of energy produced elsewhere. Drawing on Winskel's chapter we can see that the framing of people along these lines has been a feature of the UK energy supply system for many decades. The introduction of market forces in the 1980s and 1990s led to existing hierarchical and technocratic decision-making structures being replaced but a limited view of public participation remained.

A related example of social and cultural commitments is local or devolved versus centralized and hierarchical models of development. In Chapter 9, for example, Dave Toke discussed the deployment of wind power across Europe. One of the interesting aspects of his discussion is the contrast between the 'localist', 'grass-roots' and 'bottom-up' development and deployment of wind power in Demark and the more centralized approach in places like Spain and the UK. In Chapter 6 Raphael Sauter and Jim Watson argued that micro-generation technology will decentralize the electricity infrastructure because power will be generated in peoples' homes. They also argued, however, that there are different and competing models of deployment. The technologies might be owned and controlled by utility companies or local cooperatives, for example. These examples show how sustainable development raises questions about how society is or should be organized.

The concept of sustainable development, then, is an opportunity to engage with underpinning social-cultural assumptions and commitments. This takes us well beyond the relatively narrow focus on ecological-material issues. It is important to take this challenge seriously because the imperative of sustainable development can be used to further embed social and cultural commitments and tendencies that are unsustainable from this perspective. It might be argued, for example, that we must consume our way to a sustainable society by buying more and more 'green' products, thus entrenching existing consumption-related problems. Similarly, the imperative of sustainable development might be used to justify centralized technocratic decision making, which erodes democracy and undermines participation and active engagement by people as knowledgeable and concerned citizens.

Linking ecological-material and social-cultural aspects

Building on these observations, the imperative of sustainable development appears to involve solving the problems and answering the questions that emerge at each level – ecological-material and social-cultural – as if they are separate. In practice, however, the challenge is more subtle and difficult. Beyond problems at each level, sustainable development draws attention to a dysfunctional relationship between the ecological-material and social-cultural levels. This means that many social-cultural commitments we have made are implicated in ecological-material problems, and addressing them will involve recasting the social-cultural level along different lines.

All of the contributions to this book link ecological-material and social-cultural concerns, drawing attention to tensions in the relationship. In Chapter 2, for example, Seonaidh MacDonald and her colleagues focused on consumption. The research targeted people who want to make their consumption more sustainable because they are concerned about its environmental and social implications. The authors highlight the numerous difficulties that they face. One of the most perplexing is how to reconcile different ecological-material challenges, such as water consumption versus energy efficiency, and how to express ecological and social concerns simultaneously. The sustainable development debate places a great deal of emphasis on consumers but this contribution draws attention to the profound difficulties they face in practice.

Tim Foxon and Rachel Slater provide two further examples of how the ecological-material and social-cultural levels of sustainable development are linked. In Chapter 7 Foxon discussed the Dutch government's interest in the transition management approach to sustainable development. The theory and practice of transition management engages with the link between environmentally unsustainable practices and related social and cultural conditions. This leads to a better understanding of what a transition to sustainability might involve. In Chapter 8 Rachel Slater contrasts two approaches to waste management at the local level. One of these, managed by the Somerset Waste Partnership (SWP), divorces ecological-material from social-cultural concerns. The other, managed by Hackney Waste Partnership (HWP), links them by taking a more local and participatory approach. As a result these partnerships operationalize different models of sustainable waste management.

The discussion in this section has shown that sustainable development is a valuable and challenging concept. It draws attention to ecological-material and social-cultural dimensions of society and the fact that these are linked and constantly shaping each other. The challenge of sustainable development involves replacing a dysfunctional relationship between these levels with a harmonious and perhaps positive one. This process will involve rethinking the relationship between people, technology and governance. In fact, understanding and recasting the people-technology-governance nexus might be two of the most important challenges associated with sustainable development.

Sustainability and the people-technology-governance nexus

I have argued that technology mediates the relationship between environment and society because it transforms the world in relation to the production and reproduction of our lives. For this reason technology is a central concern for sustainability. It does not, however, operate in a vacuum. People use technology and both are changed as a result. Technology is also governed in complex ways. People, technology and governance, therefore, are bound together in a web of relations. In this section I establish a baseline understanding of each one and how they link with the imperative of sustainability.

People and sustainability: Appreciating multiple identities

The people who populate the sustainable development debate in the richest countries tend to be consumers. If they buy the right products they are understood to be knowledgeable, otherwise they are understood as lacking the information they need. It is relatively easy to account for this translation of people into consumers and the way they are understood. It reflects, amongst other things, the fact that we have basic physiological needs that we satisfy by consuming, the recasting of the richest countries as consumer societies, and the dominance of the market and related forms of knowledge (e.g. neoclassical economics).

In Chapter 2 Seonaidh MacDonald and her colleagues engaged directly with the stereotypical view of the consumer and showed that in practice things are much more complex. For example:

> ... the same consumers who regularly seek out information about working conditions for the production of the food and clothing products that they buy are apt to ignore the production processes, distribution networks and retailers of their white good purchases.

This observation is interesting because it undermines the idea that consumers have a relatively stable set of preferences that they express in all purchases. This is just one of many examples of consumption in practice diverging from prevailing models.

In addition to being consumers, of course, people have many other identities. In fact, even in a consumer society, other identities are at least as important and perhaps more so. People are also activists with causes, members of communities, citizens of countries, sufferers of injustice and carriers of knowledge, to name just a few of their multiple identities. In different ways all of these are important for sustainable development and for this reason we must reach beyond the consumer perspective. As I argued in Chapter 1, one of the main risks associated with the sustainable consumption debate is that it reinforces the view that people are only consumers, even as it tries to give a more sophisticated account.

In Chapter 3 Robin Roy and his colleagues focused on people as users of sustainable technologies. This is a subtle but important shift because it draws attention to technology that is not designed with people in mind. This can lead to products being purchased and installed, only to be used at less than optimum levels or rejected entirely. When this happens the dominant model of the consumer suggests that he/she purchased the wrong product, probably because of a price or information problem, or the product was the right one but his/her behaviour is wrong. Such arguments imply certain policies, for example price manipulation, subsidies and education. As Roy et al point out, however, a more important problem might be that the technology does not take sufficient account of people and this implies that a more people-centred and participatory approach to design is required.

This discussion suggests that one of the key challenges for sustainable development is to acknowledge and engage with the multiple identities of people and to avoid radical and distorting simplifications. In Chapter 4 Patrick Devine-Wright made the following point in relation to the energy system:

> ... *the centralized energy system is embedded within, and has helped produce, a social representation of the 'energy public' that is overwhelmingly characterized by deficits: of interest, knowledge, rationality and environmental and social responsibility. Moreover, it is argued that this is a self-fulfilling prophesy – the more the representation is assumed to be common sense by decision makers, the more it is likely to lead to 'out of sight, out of mind' energy policies, institutions and technologies that foster its continuity, creating a context with limited scope for public engagement with the energy system.*

In this passage Devine-Wright draws attention to the actual work that is done by partial or inaccurate representations of people in policy debates.

Technology and sustainability: Contextualized accounts

Scholars in technology studies and innovation studies define technology in overlapping ways. Researchers in both traditions agree, for example, that a technology includes the artefact itself and the things that surround it that make it useful, such as knowledge and social practices. In Chapter 1, drawing on the technology studies tradition, I quoted Bijker (1995) who argues that technology includes the artefact itself and related activities, knowledge and traditions. In innovation studies, and following Chris Freeman, Kemp (1997, p7) has observed that technology '... is frequently used to encompass both the knowledge itself and the tangible embodiment of that knowledge'. Both of these traditions, therefore, give contextualized accounts of technology.

Such contextualized accounts are important for a discussion of technology and sustainability because technology is regularly discussed in decontextualized ways. Perhaps most importantly, contextualized accounts undermine the idea of plug-in 'technological solutions' to environmental and social problems – technologies that will deliver sustainability without changing the context or being changed by it. The possibility of such technological solutions is an attractive one because it implies that technologies are interchangeable and that more sustainable (and profitable) ones can be inserted in ways that are predictable and uncontroversial. This perspective also suggests that politically difficult challenges like changes in lifestyle and behaviour can be bypassed.

Adrian Smith explored the relationship between technology and context in Chapter 5. He focused on eco-housing and the transfer of technologies from the alternative technology (AT) context into mainstream house building. Smith argued that technology includes the artefact and its context and history, and that this has implications for the transfer of more sustainable technologies between settings. He showed that the AT socio-technical context is very different to mainstream volume house-building. It involves a large number of unique beliefs and practices and it is important not to forget the circumstances that led to the creation of a particular artefact. As Smith says:

> ... *socio-technical lessons relate not only to the narrow technical and economic aspects of green housing, such as water systems, but also to the kinds of social practices and meanings upon which those technologies are predicated, such as active management of water use.*

This analysis focuses attention on the search for technologies that are flexible enough to be transferred between contexts and ways of facilitating this transfer, such as 'intermediary developments' like BedZED.

In Chapter 6 Raphael Sauter and Jim Watson discussed micro-generation technology in a contextualized way. In this case the context is provided by the existing energy system, which these authors understand as a large technical system (LTS). LTSs include technologies, institutions, regulations and actors and they resist radical change. This chapter examined how micro-generation technology will disrupt the existing LTS of energy generation and supply, depending on how it is deployed. The authors argue that the technology will change the existing system, particularly by localizing energy production, but the extent of its impacts on the existing context – incremental or radical and disruptive – will depend on the model of adoption, including arrangements for ownership, financing, operation and technological integration.

In Chapter 7 Tim Foxon argued explicitly for a contextualized view of technology and innovation, particularly as a basis on which to build policies that aim to encourage innovation for sustainability. His systems perspective leads him to argue that unsustainable development should be viewed as a 'systems failure', and not, as is often the case, as a failure of technology or the market. This argument acknowledges the complex processes and relationships that surround technology. The innovation policies that are consistent with it are different from those that emerge from conventional policy analysis, even if the objective, such as the promotion of more sustainable technologies, is the same. In part this is explained by the fact that policy makers must understand themselves as an endogenous part of the system and not as an exogenous influence on it.

Governance and sustainability: Consensus and conflict

As discussed in Chapter 1, governance has been defined as 'policy making through complex networks' (Bache and Flinders, 2004b, p4). In disciplines like political science and policy studies, the concept has emerged as a way of understanding the contemporary relationship between state and society and policy-making processes, particularly as an alternative to hierarchy and markets. In these debates 'hierarchy' describes the state making policy in relative isolation, based on its authority to do so, whereas 'the market' refers to policy being made by the forces of supply and demand. Governance, in contrast, involves a wide range of policy actors, making and implementing policy together.

Rachel Slater makes a valuable contribution to this debate in Chapter 8 by questioning the extent to which politics has actually been recast along these lines. Her analysis of 'partnerships' in sustainable waste management at the local level reveals a wide range of actors working together in conventional *and* novel ways. Partnerships might be based on contracts, for example, and in this way the market is invoked. They might also be driven to achieve targets that are handed down to them, and in this way a more centralized and authoritative model of the state-society relationship is involved. These are important observations, which warn us against embracing the idea of a wholesale shift to governance in relation to sustainability.

As I discussed in Chapter 1, many parts of the governance analysis intersect with the challenge of sustainability. Some scholars, for example, draw attention to the role that new problems and controversies, such as climate change and genetically modified crops, have played in bringing about the rise of governance. As Hajer and Wagenaar (2003, p3) note: 'It is probably no coincidence that these [governance] practices are more developed in 'new' spheres of politics such as the environment and the 'life politics' of food and technology.' Problems and controversies such as these have reinvigorated civil society groups and created new opportunities for them. At the same time they have raised doubts about the state's authority and its ability to solve problems and make progress towards sustainability.

Observations like this take us to the distinction between functional and critical accounts of governance (Murphy and Levidow, 2006). Functional accounts suggest that governance involves cooperation to deal with problems that policy makers are unable to solve on their own. From this perspective governments allow power to move vertically and horizontally away from them because doing so is more likely to lead to solutions. A critical perspective, however, suggests that governance is a way of managing conflicts such as those associated with (un)sustainable development. Many problems, with climate change being the most obvious, create legitimacy problems for the state as it fails to address them. Participation in policy design and implementation, therefore, helps to manage conflict by drawing some critics into a relationship with government and others.

Contributions to this collection have explored functional and critical accounts of governance. These have often been explored together. In Chapter 9, for example, Dave Toke analysed governance networks associated with wind power in five European countries. He drew attention to the different ways that wind power is understood and the implications that this has for conflict or consensus around deployment of the technology. There is, for example, much more controversy around wind power in the UK than there is in Denmark. In the former it is synonymous with corporations, investment companies and centralized utilities, whereas in the latter it is associated with locally owned and managed installations. Inevitably, therefore, governance involves conflicts around the meaning of the new technology and efforts to manage these.

In Chapter 10 Mark Winskel examined innovation in marine energy technology against the backdrop of reforms in the electricity sector and government authority in the UK. He observed that liberalization of the electricity sector in the 1980s and 1990s led to a pluralizing of authority. It also overthrew the technocratic corporatism synonymous with the industry since its reorganization around nuclear power in the 1950s. More recently, various developments have led to the transfer of power away from central government to higher and lower political levels: the devolution agenda, developments within the EU and at the international level in relation to the Kyoto Protocol. For marine energy technology innovators in Scotland, this has created a highly complex governance context with new problems and opportunities.

Drawing on existing research I have discussed the multiple identities of people, contextual accounts of technology and the tension between consensus and conflict views of governance. These themes were distilled from the literature I discussed in Chapter 1 and the contributions of the other authors in Chapters 2 to 10. Although they were discussed in turn, it is also clear that people, technology and governance are linked in ways that have important implications for sustainability. Governance, for example, can involve framing technology and people so that certain policies appear logical and necessary. People, on the other hand, can challenge and resist governance processes and technologies in unpredictable ways. This directs our attention to the people-technology-governance nexus.

Sustainability: Understanding the people-technology-governance nexus

People, technology and governance are often treated separately in relation to sustainable development. Behaviour, for example, is understood as something that must change but little thought is given to how it is shaped by technology. When this link is made, few researchers or policy makers think carefully about how to govern changes in both of these simultaneously. One explanation for this impasse is the interdisciplinary nature of the people-technology-governance nexus. In this section I illustrate how this barrier might be overcome by linking analytical resources from different disciplines.

Metagovernance, transition management and social representations

In Chapter 1, and earlier in this chapter, I argued that the shift from government to governance involves power moving horizontally and vertically away from central governments. As this happens, non-state actors, and lower and higher levels of government, become more important in policy design and implementation. Such multi-actor and multi-level governance, however, leaves central governments in a difficult position. They lose power and authority but retain the responsibility for achieving specific objectives. Indeed, to a significant extent, their legitimacy depends on them doing so. If the governance analysis is accepted, sustainable development is a profound challenge; governments are expected to make progress on related issues, but they have less power.

Jessop's (1998, 2004) concept of metagovernance might help us to understand how central governments (should) act in such complex multi-actor and multi-level contexts. This involves efforts to manage complexity and interactions, possibly by creating visions and agreeing targets in more deliberative ways, whilst at the same time choosing when implementation should be pursued through market, hierarchical and more participatory or novel mechanisms. In this mode policy implementation involves subtle steering as much as command-and-control. As Walls et al (2005) have argued, rather than simply witnessing a shift from government to governance, we might be witnessing a shift to governance *and* the state's response to this, the governance of governance – metagovernance.

The concept of metagovernance links well with the transition to sustainability debate, which is ongoing in innovation studies. As discussed in various chapters (1, 5 and 7 in particular), transition management involves the wider adoption of new technologies and practices that have emerged in niches (Geels, 2004a, b). The metagovernance concept is useful because it helps us to understand the state's role in promoting the transition from one socio-technical regime to another. Governments should avoid trying to impose specific technologies or transition paths, but through metagovernance mechanisms they might create the conditions under which they are agreed and pursued. In Chapter 7 Tim Foxon discusses an iterative and flexible approach as 'goal-oriented incrementalism'.

The metagovernance of a transition to sustainability will involve recasting socio-technical systems along different lines. This raises questions about the way we understand key elements and roles they play. In Chapter 4 Patrick Devine-Wright drew on the social-psychology tradition to analyse models and assumptions in policy using social representations theory. Social representations, he argues, are powerful shared ways of thinking, which exist in particular social contexts, and which come to be understood as common sense. For example, understanding the public only as consumers, with deficits of interest, knowledge, rationality and environmental and social responsibility, 'suggests that decision making about [energy] system evolution is best left to the experts ... already involved in managing the centralized system at the national level'. It also supports the view that strategies that focus on centralized energy production technologies are preferable.

Such common sense representations or frames, therefore, may appear to be relatively harmless but in practice they have profound implications and channel power. This is a difficult challenge for a transition to sustainability. As Devine-Wright makes clear, underneath representations there can be fundamental conflicts over such things as the form that democracy should take (representative or participatory) and the models of technological change that should be pursued (centralized or decentralized). The metagovernance of a transition to sustainability must, therefore, involve efforts to question and if necessary recast frames and representations, because of the strategic role they play in supporting some policy agendas rather than others. To a large extent it is frames and representations, rather than problems, solutions or technologies, that must be (re)negotiated.

Dave Toke's (Chapter 9) comparative perspective is useful here. He shows that people understand and relate to wind turbines in different ways in different contexts, and this underlines the importance of resisting efforts to simplify or caricature people. They can, for example, be cast as NIMBYs because they use energy but object to energy production facilities. Resistance to wind turbines, however, might relate to ownership and management arrangements and not to their aesthetic aspects, even if this is the way it is caricatured. If the metagovernance of a transition to sustainability does require concerted effort to overcome and resist simplifying representations or framings of people and technology, it seems likely that this will require new institutions designed with this in mind.

Institutional transformations, new social practices and interpretive flexibility

Formal and informal institutions are bound up with (un)sustainable development (see Parto, 2005 on the difference). Commercial R&D institutes, government planning departments and NGO campaign offices, are obvious examples of the former. A large amount of sustainable development research has examined these, often drawing attention to conflicts around technology. From the discussion so far it is clear that governing a transition to sustainability will involve profound transformations of institutions, including the relationships between them, as well as the creation of entirely new ones (see Chapter 1 on ecological modernization and the transformation of institutions).

In Chapter 8 Rachel Slater discussed the governance of waste management at the local level and in doing so drew attention to a wide range of formal institutions, including local government departments, waste management firms, housing associations and residents groups. More specifically she explored the transformation of institutional arrangements through the creation of partnerships – SWP and HWP. Both of these can be described as new formal institutions but there are important differences between them. Interestingly, these partnerships make different assumptions about waste, technology and people, and the relationships between them.

The contributions to this book also draw attention to the importance of informal institutions, including group norms and social practices. In Chapter 1, for example, I discussed Elizabeth Shove's work on group norms related to cleanliness and warmth (Shove 1997, 2004). Shove emphasizes how norms and technology co-shape each other, particularly in domestic settings, and how this happens in relation to social practices like clothes washing and room heating. She also argues that focusing on informal institutions in the domestic setting involves overcoming a bias in policy debates in favour of supply-side analysis.

In this collection Robin Roy and his colleagues (Chapter 3) explored the institutions that surround the adoption, use and, in some cases, rejection of a range of more sustainable technologies. There are numerous examples in this chapter of norms and practices linked to technologies. One of the examples that extend Shove's work on cleanliness is the potential adopter of a solar water heating system who suggests that it offers a 'spiritually pure' experience of bathing unmediated by geopolitics. Transforming formal and informal institutions, then, is profoundly important for sustainability, in part because it is bound up with new ways of understanding and doing.

The concept of interpretive flexibility from technology studies suggests that such changes might be accompanied by changes in the meaning of technology. Interpretive flexibility refers to the way that the same artefact can mean different things to different social groups (Kline and Pinch, 1999, p113). GM crops or nuclear power, for example, might be solutions to environmental problems or serious threats to sustainability. This flexibility is linked to the way that different social groups frame technology and it has implications for its adoption and further development (Bijker, 1992, p98).

As discussed in Chapter 1, researchers in this area have identified a process of closure through which the meaning of a technology becomes stable and widely accepted. The car, for example, became synonymous with freedom and autonomy. When this happens the technology is taken for granted and its contested origin is forgotten. Interestingly, however, the interpretive flexibility of a technology can return under some circumstances. Something that is taken for granted can be recast as problematic. Transformations of formal and informal institutions in relation to sustainability might be accompanied by and facilitated by the return of interpretive flexibility.

In Chapter 2 Seonaidh MacDonald and her colleagues drew attention to the similarity between interpretive flexibility and the cultural studies concept of decoding. She pointed out that both concepts suggest that artefacts are 'read' differently by different social groups. In Chapter 6 Raphael Sauter and Jim Watson recognized the interpretive flexibility of technology and argued against the labelling of micro-generation as 'radical' or 'disruptive' because this might create (or express) unnecessary resistance in the existing energy supply system. Drawing on this discussion we can say that the interpretive flexibility of technology will play an important role in the transformation institutions and that in some cases change is unlikely unless interpretive flexibility returns.

Novel policies, innovation niches and citizenship

In Chapter 10 Mark Winskel confirmed that new institutions often lead to new policies. He showed how devolution allowed renewable energy policy in Scotland to diverge from policy in England and Wales. When this happened a new and unique context was created for marine energy technology innovators. As Winskel points out, in examples like this we see how ideas of governance intersect with the concept of innovation niches as developed in the transition management literature. He refers to these as 'temporary protected spaces' where innovation 'tends to be carried out by small outsider firms, rather than larger established groups'.

In Chapter 5 Adrian Smith also made a link between new institutions, policies and innovation niches in his analysis of the eco-housing. As he argues, eco-housing is a particularly interesting case because the AT enthusiasts of the green building movement did not set out to transfer individual technologies to the mainstream. They wanted to transform society as a whole and their innovations were an expression of a different vision of how it should be organized. In the modern day context of climate change, however, governments and mainstream house builders have become interested in some, but not all, of the technologies developed in this niche. This has led to discussion of policies that might help to transfer/translate between the niche and the mainstream.

There is, then, a close relationship between new institutions and policies, innovation niches and transfer/translation between niche and mainstream. Governance for sustainability will involve efforts to transfer/translate between niche and mainstream but, as Adrian Smith points out, there are at least two possibilities: adapting artefacts, lessons and practices from the niche for the mainstream; or altering the socio-technical context so that it moves closer to the niche. In the context of housing he argues:

> *Considered in this translation light, existing policies, such as building regulations, can be understood differently. They seek to transfer socio-technical practices that have sufficient flexibility to translate easily between contexts. An additional, and more ambitious, governance strategy would seek to try and transform the mainstream socio-technical context itself. It would try and steer that change closer to the values and guiding principles that exists currently in green niches.*

These options have different implications for policy and people. The first strategy invokes people as consumers of technologies that are being translated out of the niche and into the mainstream. The second strategy, however, involves engaging with people more broadly as citizens as well as consumers. In Chapter 4 Patrick Devine-Wright discussed the idea of 'energy citizenship' and in Chapter 8 Rachel Slater discussed 'citizen governance'. In both cases these authors suggest that policy should aim to involve people much more intimately in adopting and managing new technologies for sustainability and that citizenship should extend far beyond formal arrangements such as voting in elections every four or five years. It seems likely that policies that aim to change context must build on such an understanding of the potential role of people.

Conclusion

This book has explored the imperative and opportunity of sustainable development, focusing on people, technology and governance. With the help of the contributing authors I have argued that a transition to sustainability is impossible unless we understand and recast the people-technology-governance nexus. This nexus is a web of relationships, with each element constantly reproducing or reshaping the other two. Governance, for example, leads to strategic decisions about technology, based in part on assumptions about people. At the same time, however, people can resist those assumptions and the way they are used to justify some technologies and not others.

Drawing on the contributions to this book we can distinguish between the governance *of* sustainability and governance *for* sustainability. Because there are different ways of understanding (un)sustainable development, and the roles that people and technology (might) play, the imperative of sustainability is powerful but vulnerable. Perversely, it can be used to justify technologies that are unsustainable or less sustainable than they might be. The governance *of* sustainability, therefore, can be understood as a process of co-opting the sustainability agenda to other policy agendas. Caricatures and simplifications of technology and people play an important role in this process.

Governance *for* sustainability, on the other hand, takes disagreements and differences of opinion over (un)sustainable development as a starting point. Because contemporary environmental and social problems can be understood in different ways, and the meaning of sustainable development is not fixed, deliberation and argument, and institutions that facilitate them, are important. Drawing on this book it is clear that such arguments must engage with more complex and accurate accounts of people and technology and how they are linked. Most importantly, they must reflect on the way that technology and people shape each other, and how this insight implies different policies and policy-making processes.

It is important to note, therefore, that governance *of* sustainability and governance *for* sustainability cast people passively and actively in different ways. The governance *of* sustainability makes people passive in relation to decisions about technology, often by emphasizing the knowledge of technical experts. It also casts people passively in relation to technology they encounter in their daily lives. Governance *for* sustainability, however, encourages people to be active and engaged in decision making about technology, partly because it views them as having useful knowledge, and partly because it anticipates an active relationship with it in the future. The meaning of 'governing technology for sustainability' starts to become clearer when it is explored in this way.

References

Agyeman, J., Bullard, R. and Evans, B. (2002) 'Exploring the nexus: Bringing together sustainability, environmental justice and equity', *Space & Polity*, vol 6, no 1, pp77–90

Bache, I. and Flinders, M. (eds) (2004) *Multi-level Governance*, Oxford University Press, Oxford

Bijker, W. (1992) 'The social construction of fluorescent lighting, or how an artifact was invented in its diffusion stage', in Bijker, W. and Law, J. (eds) *Shaping Technology/Building Society: Studies in Sociotechnical Change*, MIT Press, London, pp75–104

Bijker, W. (1995) 'Sociohistorical Technology Studies', in Jasanoff, S., Markle, G., Petersen, J. and Pinch, T. (eds) *Handbook of Science and Technology Studies*, Sage, London, pp229–256

Buttel, F. (2000) 'Classical theory and contemporary environmental sociology: Some reflections on the antecedents and prospects for reflexive modernization theories in the study of environment and society', in Spaargaren, G., Mol, A. and Buttel, F. (eds) *Environment and Global Modernity*, Sage, London, pp17–39

Geels, F. (2004a) 'From sectoral systems of innovation to socio-technical systems: Insights about dynamics and change from sociology and institutional theory', *Research Policy*, vol 33, pp897–920

Geels, F. (2004b) 'Understanding system innovations: A critical literature review and a conceptual synthesis', in Elzen, B., Geels, F. and Green, K. (eds) *System Innovation and the Transition to Sustainability: Theory, Evidence and Policy*, Edward Elgar, Cheltenham, pp19–47

Hajer, M. and Wagenaar, H. (eds) (2003) *Deliberative Policy Analysis: Understanding Governance in the Network Society*, Cambridge University Press, Cambridge

Jackson, T. (1996) *Material Concerns: Pollution, Profit and Quality of Life*, Routledge, London

Jessop, B. (1998) 'The rise of governance and the risk of failure', *International Social Science Journal*, vol 50, issue 155, pp29–45

Jessop, B. (2004) 'Multi-level governance and multi-level meta-governance', in Bache, I. and Flinders, M. (eds) *Multi-level Governance*, Oxford University Press, Oxford, pp49–74

Kemp, R. (1997) *Environmental Policy and Technical Change: A Comparison of the Technological Impact of Policy Instruments*, Edward Elgar, Cheltenham

Kline, R. and Pinch, T. (1999) 'The social construction of technology', in MacKenzie, D. and Wajcman, J. *The Social Shaping of Technology*, Open University Press, Maidenhead, pp113–115

Meadows, D. H., Meadows, D. I., Randers, J. and Behrens, W. (1972) *The Limits to Growth: A Report for the Club of Rome's Project on the Predicament of Mankind*, New American Library, New York

Murphy, J. and Cohen, M. (eds) (2001) *Exploring Sustainable Consumption: Environmental Policy and the Social Sciences*, Elsevier Science, Oxford

Murphy, J. and Levidow, L. (2006) *Governing the Transatlantic Conflict over Agricultural Biotechnology*, Routledge, London.

Murphy, J., Levidow, L. and Carr, S. (2006) 'Regulatory standards for environmental risks: Understanding the US–EU conflict over GM crops', *Social Studies of Science*, vol 36, no 1, pp133–160

Parto, S. (2005) '" Good governance" and policy analysis: What of institutions?',
MERIT-Infonomics Research Memorandum Series 2005-001, Maastricht Economic
Research Institute on Innovation and Technology

Princen, T., Maniates, M. and Conca, K. (eds) (2002) *Confronting Consumption*, MIT
Press, Cambridge, MA

Shove, E. (1997) 'Revealing the invisible: Sociology, energy and the environment', in
Redclift, M. and Woodgate, G. (eds) *The International Handbook of Environmental
Sociology*, Edward Elgar, Cheltenham, pp261–273

Shove, E. (2004) 'Sustainability, system innovation and the laundry', in Elzen, B., Geels,
F. and Green, K. (eds) *System Innovation and the Transition to Sustainability:
Theory, Evidence and Policy*, Edward Elgar, Cheltenham, pp76–94

Socolow, R., Andrews, C., Berkhout, F. and Thomas, V. (1997) *Industrial Ecology and
Global Change*, Cambridge University Press, Cambridge

Walls, J., O'Riordan, T., Horlick-Jones, T. and Niewöhner, J (2005) 'The meta-governance of risk and new technologies: GM crops and mobile telephones', *Journal of
Risk Research*, vol 8, no 7–8, pp635–661

World Commission on Environment and Development (1987) *Our Common Future
(The Brundtland Report)*, Oxford University Press, Oxford

Index

Note: page numbers in *italics* refer to figures and tables